06/16
25°

This Is Not My Life

This Is Not My Life

A Memoir of Love, Prison, and
Other Complications

DIANE SCHOEMPERLEN

HARPER**AVENUE**

Published by Harper Avenue, an imprint of HarperCollins Publishers Ltd

First edition

HarperCollins books may be purchased for educational, business, or sales
promotional use through our Special Markets Department.

HarperCollins Publishers Ltd
2 Bloor Street East, 20th Floor
Toronto, Ontario, Canada
M4W 1A8

www.harpercollins.ca

Library and Archives Canada Cataloguing in Publication information is
available upon request.

ISBN 978-1-44343-420-1

Printed and bound in the United States
RRD 9 8 7 6 5 4 3 2 1

This book is dedicated to my beloved friend
Joanne Page
1943–2015

Never in a million years did I expect to be part of this story, but then isn't life really what we thought would never happen in a million years?
—Bridget Kinsella, *Visiting Life: Women Doing Time on the Outside*

If memory is a fiction and our identity the result of the stories we tell ourselves, how can we ever know the truth of our own lives?
—Tristine Rainer, *Your Life as Story*

This is not my life. These are not my cobwebs. This is not the darkness I was designed for.
—Colum McCann, *Let the Great World Spin*

AUTHOR'S NOTE

*There's the story, then there's the real story, then there's
the story of how the story came to be told. Then there's what you
leave out of the story. Which is part of the story too.*
—MARGARET ATWOOD, *MADDADDAM*

This is my story, my version of the story, built on my experiences, my observations, my perceptions, and my memories. I like to think I am a reliable narrator, but writing it all down changes things—for better and for worse.

Most of the names I've used are pseudonyms, except those of myself and my son, as well as those of public figures like former Prime Minister Stephen Harper and former Public Safety Minister Vic Toews. Some identifying details and place names have also been changed.

For reasons of both privacy and length, I've had to leave a number of people and events out of these pages. For those who are disappointed not to find themselves here: I'm sorry. For those who are relieved: you're welcome.

PART ONE

January 2006 to September 2007

It is safe to say that never once in my life had I dreamed of being in bed with a convicted killer, let alone one with his teeth in a margarine container in the kitchen, his mother in the next room, and the word HI! tattooed in tiny blue letters on his penis.

Years have passed, almost ten years now since I first met Shane. After all was said and done, my friend Dorothy, shaking her head in disbelief, said, "I still can't believe you thought that story was going to have a happy ending." But I did. For the longest time I did.

Sometimes I can come close to understanding why I stayed with him for almost six years, why I went back to him after everything fell apart, why I fell in love with him in the first place. Other times it's as if it all happened to somebody else, somebody who looked just like me, lived in my house, slept in my bed, wore my clothes, and wrote my books.

And where was I then? Where was I when all of this was going on?

HE WAS A POWERFUL-LOOKING MAN, somewhere in his late fifties, tall and well-built with broad shoulders, muscular arms and slim hips. From a certain angle, he reminded me of Vince Vaughn, one of my favourite actors. He walked with a limp, barely noticeable at first, but growing more pronounced as the hours passed. He was clean-shaven, with perfectly straight white teeth and thick shiny brown hair so dark it looked black, with a small bald spot at the back.

I'd been volunteering at the Saint Vincent de Paul free hot meal program for three months when Shane arrived in early January as our new Friday dishwasher. We all knew where he'd come from, but we didn't know how long he'd been there or what he'd done to end up in prison in the first place. We were curious but not especially concerned. We are used to prisons here. With eight of the eleven federal institutions for men in Ontario located in or near Kingston, including the legendary maximum-security Kingston Penitentiary, our small city is indeed the prison capital of Canada. Our modest population of fewer than two hundred thousand includes a relatively large number of ex-convicts and parolees and their families. Many of the men who came to eat regularly at Vinnie's had done time.

We were already busy with the lunch preparations when Shane came in that morning and didn't have time to pay him any extra attention. Once the director had introduced him around, we put him to work, thankful for another pair of hands, wherever they came from.

He was on an Escorted Temporary Absence, an ETA, not to be confused with what this acronym stands for out here in the free world: Estimated Time of Arrival. In the prison world, an ETA allows an inmate, either alone or in a group, to leave the institution accompanied by one or two correctional officers or by an approved citizen escort. Shane's escort was an elderly nun named Sister Frances. We didn't any of us say what we were thinking: that she didn't fit the picture of what we thought we knew of "escorts," shapely women for hire prancing around in stilettos and skimpy skin-tight skirts. Given the age and frailty of Sister Frances and the fact that Shane had come from Frontenac, a minimum-security prison, we assumed his crime couldn't have been too serious, certainly not anything violent.

On that first day, Shane didn't say much to anyone except Sister Frances. When he did speak, his voice was gravelly and deep. As well as taking care of the dishes, he helped with the preparation of our usual Friday lunch: soup, coleslaw, french fries, and grilled cheese sandwiches, a deceptively simple meatless meal that involved a lot of chopping and dicing and the buttering of at least two hundred slices of bread. He worked quickly and efficiently. He also helped serve the meals, which were delivered one plate at a time to the tables in the dining room. He avoided making direct eye contact with anyone, a tendency I took to mean he was shy. Soon enough I would learn that this matter of not making eye contact was a protective prison habit. He was definitely not shy.

With tattoos on the backs of both hands and one creeping above his collar, he certainly looked the part. After the oven was lit and the kitchen began to heat up, he rolled up his sleeves and there were more on both arms.

I like a tattoo, have liked them since long before they became a mainstream embellishment, no longer the radical or rebellious expression of outlaws and outsiders. Even Shane's crude prison tattoos I didn't find unattractive. Standing next to him at the sink, I could see a small teardrop tattooed just below his left eye. Much as I liked them, I was not then familiar with the language of tattoos. Nor, it seemed, were any of the other volunteers. Nobody mentioned it.

That first day, after we were all done cooking, serving, and cleaning up, Shane, Sister Frances, another volunteer, and I happened to be heading out to the parking lot at the same time. With more than seventy patrons for lunch, it had been a hectic day, and we were all tired. The other volunteer said she could hardly wait to get home and put her feet up, have a beer or two.

In his first show of levity all day, Shane said, "Not me." Then he looked directly at me and said, "You?"

His eyes, now that I could actually see them in his handsome face, were dark and intense. Later I would discover that while the intensity of his eyes never varied, the colour did: usually dark brown, as they were that first day, but sometimes hazel, and other times more green than brown. If only I could have figured out a pattern in those shifting colours, could have used them as a kind of ocular mood ring. But the colour changes, as far as I could ever see, were inconsistent and provided no clues as to what might be going on inside his head.

That day in the parking lot, I laughed and said, "Me neither. I haven't had a drink for almost fourteen years. Today's not the day."

He said, "Good for you. Been clean and sober six years myself."

That was the extent of our first personal conversation. Later he would say this was the day he fell in love with me. I never did believe this, but still, I liked it when he said it.

∞

IT WAS MY FRIEND DOROTHY who got me started volunteering at Vinnie's. I was suffering from yet another broken heart after yet another regrettable relationship gone wrong. In times of emotional distress, my creativity tends to desert me, so I was also suffering from writer's block and had been for months. I'd turned fifty-one that summer and was wondering where my life had gone wrong. Dorothy had been volunteering at Vinnie's for many years, and for several weeks, she'd been trying to get me to join her there. She said it would be good for me, she said I would enjoy it, she said it would lift me out of my misery. I kept resisting, saying I couldn't come because it was from eight-thirty in the morning until two in the afternoon, and that was my prime writing time. Finally Dorothy said, "You're not writing anyway." She was right.

But still I said no. Because any day now I was going to start. Yes, I was. Any day now I was going to have a thought worth writing down. Most mornings I was just sitting in front of my computer trying to put one sentence after another. And failing. Most afternoons I was napping or hanging around in bookstores torturing myself.

On the Wednesday before Thanksgiving, the phone rang early, shortly before nine. Dorothy was calling from Vinnie's. She said they were desperate. They were serving their big Thanksgiving meal that day, and several of the volunteers hadn't shown up. They were likely to have ninety or more people for lunch. Could I please come and help? I said I had no idea how to make lunch for ninety people—how could I possibly be of any help? She asked if I knew how to peel potatoes. I had to admit that yes, I did.

Dorothy said, "We've got fifty pounds here that need peeling. Please come. And bring your potato peeler. Ours is crappy."

So I went, potato peeler in hand.

Dorothy met me at the door and outfitted me with an apron and a baseball cap. She introduced me to the other volunteers (of whom there seemed to be plenty) and also to the fifty pounds of potatoes.

I had the best day. If I'd expected a soup kitchen to be a grim and depressing place, it was anything but. It was lively, rowdy, and rude, vibrant with a raw intensity of life I'd never experienced before. I was hooked.

AT VINNIE'S, I HAD THREE GUIDING PRINCIPLES. Two of them were passed on to me by Dorothy: don't judge and don't assume. The third was of my own making. Shortly after I started volunteering, I heard a radio interview with a photographer whose current project was a series of portraits of the mentally ill. He told the story of one woman who looked puzzled after he'd taken her picture. When he explained again what he was doing, she asked with surprise, "Can you see me?" When he said yes, he definitely could, she said, "That's funny. Most people can't see me."

I imagined this was how our lunch patrons must feel when they were out in the world. Invisible. I made it my mission to show them they were not.

Don't judge.

Don't assume.

Can you see me?

Despite once being advised by another volunteer never to make eye contact with any of them, I held fast to these principles, and they served me well.

I have never felt entirely comfortable within myself, but at Vinnie's, not only was I lifted out of my misery as Dorothy had predicted, but I could forget about myself altogether, possibly for the first time in my life. This came as a great relief.

Working there among the wounded, the damaged, the addicted, the broken, the broke, I would look around and find my spirit swelling with joy. Over and over again, I thought, These are my people. Finally I felt like I belonged. Not because their wounds were worse than mine but because there I didn't have to pretend I wasn't also wounded.

There had always been a curtain between me and other people, the people I called my friends. They had all lived lives so different from mine, lives that seemed clearer, calmer, simpler, more refined. None of them, I thought, had ever made any serious mistakes or bad choices, had ever screwed up their lives, not even once, not even a little bit. With them, I always felt *less than*. I realize now that I have too often fallen into the trap of what Anne Lamott in her book *Bird by Bird: Some Instructions on Writing and Life* calls "that business of comparing my insides to other people's outsides."

I come from the working class in Thunder Bay, a small city of just over 109,000 people located on the western shore of Lake Superior at the head of the Great Lakes—a city that has long prided itself on being "a lunch-bucket town," a city that has more than once had the highest homicide rate in the country. Almost everyone I knew in Kingston came from much higher-class backgrounds. They were what Shane called "uptown" people. He said this in the same sneering, scornful tone my mother used when referring to someone successful and well-off: "Oh, he thinks he's a *big shot*."

I know I had class issues. Perhaps I had a chip on my shoulder. None of my friends had grown up in a rough part of a rough city in a tiny wartime bungalow with mice in the dugout and plastic lawn ornaments in the front yard. Both my parents came from large Manitoba farming families. Neither of them had finished high school. My father worked in a grain elevator; my mother ran a post office outlet in the back of a drugstore. They didn't understand me any better than I understood them. I've often wondered where my early love of books and writing came from. The only books we had in our house were an old edition of *Webster's New World Dictionary* that my father used when doing crossword puzzles and a set of the Funk & Wagnalls Encyclopedia you could buy at Safeway, one volume per week for ninety-nine cents each. I always spent my weekly allowance on books. My mother found this disturbing. She often asked why I couldn't just buy a blouse or a skirt or earrings or something—"like a normal girl."

I never felt that I belonged there, but I didn't feel that I belonged here in Kingston either. Perhaps I'm just a chronic malcontent, always longing for the other place, the other person I could have been, the other life I could have lived. One of my son's elementary school teachers once described him as being like Pluto, always on the edge of the group. I was the same with my friends, an outsider circling on the periphery, never fully part of the group, *any* group.

I was not raised to like myself. I was raised to compare myself to others and find myself wanting. My mother instilled this in me from an early age: why couldn't I be more like my cousin Connie, why couldn't I be more like my friend Holly, why couldn't I be more like Shelley Morton, who lived across the street? I don't remember now what it was about these other girls that my mother wanted me to emulate. I only remember knowing that I was not good enough.

After she died, my father stepped up and continued the family tradition. One evening he called to tell me he'd run into Shelley Morton at the drugstore, and she said she remembered how I'd been so smart in school when we were kids, how she'd always envied and admired me. On the phone my father snorted and said, "You sure had her fooled!" When I once made the mistake of telling him I was nervous about an upcoming television interview, he said, "No wonder. What have *you* got to tell anybody about?" I come from Alice Munro territory, not geographically, but in the psychological sense—deeply entrenched in the treacherous province of "Who do you think you are?" One year when my father was here for Christmas, and I was all dressed up in a new outfit to meet friends downtown for dinner, he looked me over and sneered, "Who are you supposed to be?" Indeed.

Only once in my life do I remember him telling me he was proud of me. In 1999 I was given the Lakehead University Alumni Honour

Award and went back to Thunder Bay to receive it at spring convocation. My mother had died twelve years earlier; my father was suffering from Alzheimer's by then and living in a nursing home. My aunt Clara brought him to the ceremony. Afterwards he said he was proud of me. Ten minutes later he didn't know who I was. I don't remember my mother ever saying she was proud of me. I don't remember either of them ever telling me they loved me.

In Kingston I envied my friends their unwavering certainty about where they belonged in the world, their self-confidence, their money, their perfect immaculate houses. I envied them their travels too, even though I don't like travelling. Quite justifiably one of the seven deadly sins, envy is something nobody ever wants to admit to. As poisonous as cyanide and as corrosive as battery acid, a large helping of envy is inevitably served up with savoury side dishes of self-pity, resentment, guilt, and shame.

I know this was my problem, not my friends'. I wanted to be just like them and knew I never could be. I'd spent years hiding parts of myself, trying to pass as one of them, trying to convince them and myself that I belonged. It was exhausting and self-destructive. It made me dislike myself even more.

BEFORE I MET SHANE, the only encounter I'd ever had with an actual prisoner had taken place almost twenty years earlier. My son, Alex, was four years old. He was having digestive problems, with recurrent bouts of severe cramping and constipation. It wasn't until he was seven that we finally received a diagnosis, thanks to the work of a diligent pediatric allergist who determined that he had an intolerance to milk protein, easily remedied by dietary changes. But in the years before that, his pain was sometimes so intense that we ended up in Emergency. This was one of those times.

I'd kept him home from daycare, and when the pain hadn't subsided by mid-morning, we went downtown to Hotel Dieu, the smaller of the two hospitals in the city. As usual, the waiting room was almost full, and we had no idea how long it would be before we could see a doctor.

We settled in, Alex on my knee crying quietly and me trying to comfort and distract him with the children's books buried in the pile of newspapers and old magazines. I knew he was starting to feel better when he got down off my knee and went over to the toy box in the corner. We'd been there often enough that he knew exactly what he was looking for. He pulled out the blue plastic truck that had become his favourite hospital toy.

As he pushed the truck around on the floor with appropriate zooming noises, the automatic doors at the rear opened. Most people came in through the front door, so everyone in the room looked up. Two uniformed guards entered with a prisoner between them in handcuffs and leg irons. The guards were both middle-aged men, and the prisoner looked to be about my age, mid-thirties, with a swath of white gauze wrapped around his head, blood seeping through it in the middle of his forehead. They were all three chatting amiably as the prisoner was checked in. I was sitting near enough that I could hear bits of what they were saying, both to the triage nurse—"He walked into a steel beam"—and to the prisoner himself, good-naturedly—"That'll teach you not to watch where you're going." Then they led him to a chair close to mine and helped him sit down.

The guards stood near him, one beside and one behind, while everyone else first stared and then looked studiously down at their own unshackled feet. Soon the others turned back to their magazines or their seatmates, although most were also sneaking surreptitious glances at the prisoner from the corners of their eyes.

Only Alex continued to stare, still on his knees playing with the truck, inching ever closer to him. The guards were watchful but not alarmed. Alex zoomed the truck to a stop near the prisoner's feet.

"Hey, mister," said my usually shy son. "Wanna play with this truck?"

Now everyone, including the guards and the prisoner, was staring at me. I nodded and smiled. The guards nodded in return, and the prisoner smiled back.

"Sure, little buddy," he said. "That's one nice truck you got there."

"It's my favourite," Alex declared, sending the truck straight towards the prisoner's feet. "I've got three more trucks at home and a big yellow digger too. I'm gonna be a worker man when I grow up."

Still shackled, the prisoner leaned forward and nudged the truck back to him with one foot. "That's a good idea," he said. "You'll have lots of fun."

They continued passing the blue truck back and forth between them, both making *vroom-vroom* noises and grinning. Then our last name was called, and I stood up, reaching for Alex's hand. He came willingly enough, leaving the truck at the prisoner's feet.

"Bye-bye, mister," he said, waving as we headed towards the nurse holding open the door to the examining rooms. "Hope you feel better soon."

"You too, little buddy," said the prisoner, managing an awkward wave with both his cuffed hands. "You too."

He looked at me then and said, "Thanks, lady. That's one great kid you got there."

"Thanks," I said. "I think so too."

As we walked back to the car afterwards, Alex was obviously feeling much better, and I was immensely relieved. I felt compelled to say something about the prisoner in the waiting room. I explained about prison as best I could, keeping it appropriately vague, I hoped, for a sensitive four-year-old. I expected him to ask what the man might have done to end up in such a place, but he didn't.

He said, "I hope his head is okay now."

I had to ask. "What made you want to play with him?"

"Everybody was looking at him funny," Alex said with indignation.

I had to agree that yes, they were.

"I thought he needed a friend."

I had to agree with that too.

∞

As the winter months wore on, I did what I could to battle the despair I'd fallen into over the end of my previous relationship. I still wasn't anywhere near being able to write, but slowly, slowly, I began to climb out of the abyss. For no particular reason, I started knitting scarves, one after another, dozens and dozens of them. I was always running out to buy more wool. I spent every evening knitting until my hands were numb—and also, I hoped, the parts of my heart and my head that were broken. I was now going to Vinnie's three days a week, sometimes four if they were short-handed. I took the scarves with me, handed them out to the other volunteers and all the lunch patrons. Shane wore his proudly.

When not knitting scarves, I was cleaning out my closets and culling my bookshelves, bringing boxes of stuff to the Vinnie's warehouse every week. Situated in a separate building behind the kitchen, it housed not only a food pantry but also many racks of donated clothing, small household items, towels, bedding, and several bookshelves that I was now keeping well stocked for the patrons. Several of the regulars were especially fond of poetry and literary fiction. Before and after lunch, the warehouse was full of happy shoppers who could take whatever they wanted for free.

Arriving each Friday morning with Sister Frances, Shane was usually the only man there for the first three hours until another volunteer named Fred came in to dish up the soup and help serve the meal. Shane already knew Fred from the convent of the Sisters of Providence of Saint Vincent de Paul, where he and several other inmates were taken to attend mass every Sunday morning. He was more comfortable now, no longer alarmed by the bunch of us women singing and dancing around the crowded little kitchen to the classic rock always playing on the radio on top of the fridge. He got used to our joking and teasing, and was soon dishing out his share with the soup, salad, and sandwiches. He especially appreciated the sign on the fridge door that said, SARCASM SERVED HERE. Quick-witted, intelligent, and flirtatious, with an outrageous and facetious sense of humour, he could always make me laugh.

He usually wore a pair of black track pants, and when he bent down to load or unload the dishwasher, he displayed a classic case of "plumber's pants." I was elected by the other volunteers to tell him he was giving a show not only to those of us in the kitchen but also to the whole dining room. I was mortified, but they insisted. "He likes you, he likes you!" they cried. So the next morning when we went outside together for a "breath of fresh air"—as we all called it when going outside to smoke—I told him. Now *he* was mortified. He soon found another pair of pants. Later he would say this was when he knew I loved him too.

———

ALEX ALSO VOLUNTEERED at Vinnie's several times. Now twenty-one, he'd been working for two or three years as a cook at a popular downtown restaurant famed for its prime rib. He might have been unimpressed by our low-budget high-quantity meals, but he was too polite to say so. Except for Dorothy, whom he'd known almost all his life, he was shy with the other volunteers, most of them women my age or older. He and Shane, however, quickly became friends. Shane told him often that he was a lucky guy to have a mother like me. What could Alex do but agree? Shane said if he'd had a mother like me, he never would have ended up in prison.

With the arrival of spring, the scarves were put away and the sandals came out. On the first warm days, all the other female volunteers began showing up with their toenails painted. One Friday, even Sister Frances came in with her little old nun toes glowing neon pink. That day after lunch, I went to the drugstore and headed straight for the nail polish aisle. How was it that at almost fifty-two years of age, I had never once in my life painted my toenails? The next morning, I arrived at Vinnie's with my toes sporting a vibrant red called Strawberry Electric, and everyone applauded.

LATE IN THE SPRING, Shane told us he had a parole hearing coming up in the summer. He was hoping to be granted day parole and moved to a halfway house in Ottawa. He wondered if anyone would be willing to write a letter of support to the Parole Board on his behalf. He handed around some copies of official Correctional Service of Canada (CSC) paperwork. This was when we finally learned why he'd ended up in prison in the first place and that he'd been there for almost thirty years. Now we understood that in the language of tattoos, the teardrop below his left eye meant he had killed someone. Now we knew he was serving a life sentence for second-degree murder. Whatever initial alarm we might have felt about this was tempered by the fact that it had happened so long ago and that he had become an essential and popular part of the kitchen crew. We saw him as a person who had paid his debt to society and deserved a second chance.

I knew so little about the Canadian justice system that I wasn't even sure about the difference between first- and second-degree murder. Shane explained it to me in the simplest terms. Only a murder conviction automatically results in a life sentence. Then it's a matter of degree. First-degree murder means you planned to kill him, you intended to kill him, and you did. Second-degree murder means you didn't plan ahead of time to kill him, but you intended to kill him, and you did. Manslaughter means you didn't plan to kill him, you didn't intend to kill him, but you did. In each case, someone ends up dead and someone else ends up in prison.

In the argot of the inmates, Shane was doing "a life bit on a murder beef," the word *bit* meaning the sentence and *beef* meaning the crime. Like Canada itself, prison has two official languages, that of the inmates and that of CSC.

The language of the carceral world, like all language anywhere, is always changing. In Canada, prisons are no longer officially called "prisons." Only two or three are still called "penitentiaries." The rest are now "institutions"—not to be confused with all those other institutions with which most people are familiar: financial, educational, religious, and mental institutions, not to mention the institutions of marriage and democracy. The people who work in these penal institutions are now called "correctional officers," not "guards." Shane usually called them "the coppers" or, on a bad day, "the pigs." He always called himself, and liked to be called, a "convict." Not for him the new softer sanitized terms "inmate" or "offender." To him these were just mealy-mouthed euphemisms akin to saying someone has "passed away" instead of just plain died.

I soon learned more about the intricacies of the prison world from Shane's LifeLine worker, Stuart, who sometimes came to Vinnie's to see him. Founded in 1991, LifeLine was a national organization funded by CSC and run by the St. Leonard's Society to provide specialized support for inmates serving life sentences. There were about two dozen LifeLine workers, all of them lifers themselves, having been on parole successfully for many years since their own murder convictions and now working with thousands of other lifers across Canada.

Another lifer from Frontenac, a wiry whippet of a man named Lenny, came to Vinnie's once too, accompanied by another LifeLine worker, Evan. Lenny and Shane were close friends, had been doing time together for decades. Shane said Lenny was definitely "institutionalized," but he was not and never would be. I had only a vague idea of what this word meant, but Shane's insistence on who was and who wasn't reminded me of my father once insisting that his doctor had told him he would never get Alzheimer's even though three of his five siblings already had. He was in the early stages of the disease himself by then, although we didn't know—or at least hadn't acknowledged—it yet.

If Alzheimer's is, as it's sometimes called, the old-timers' disease, institutionalization, I thought, must be the long-term prisoners' disease. In retrospect, I realize that I should have taken the time right from the beginning to understand what it actually meant.

Lenny had been thinking he might like to volunteer at Vinnie's too, but after one shift he said it was too hectic for him and he didn't like people all that much anyway. He ended up volunteering at the Humane Society instead.

I had now met four murderers in a matter of months—Shane, Stuart, Lenny, and Evan—four more than I had ever expected to meet in my entire life.

THE HOT MEAL PROGRAM AT VINNIE'S would be closing for the summer, reopening in September, the day after Labour Day. The other volunteers were looking forward to a two-month vacation, but I was dreading it, afraid that without the place and the people to keep me occupied and anchored, I would slide back into the black hole of depression. Only the warehouse was open during July and August, just on Tuesday mornings. I decided I'd volunteer there for the summer, sorting the donations, hanging the clothes, stocking the food pantry, doing whatever needed to be done. One morning a week, I hoped, might be enough to keep me sane.

Our last lunch was served on Friday, June 30. The Friday before, I'd given Shane a signed copy of my novel about the Virgin Mary, *Our Lady of the Lost and Found*. He'd often talked about how much he liked to read and also about his weekly ETAs to Sunday mass at the convent. Because I knew nothing about prison then, it didn't occur to me that he might not be allowed to take the book back in with him. But somehow he managed it, and by the following Friday, he'd read the whole book and was eager to talk to me about it.

After lunch was served, Shane and I went outside to smoke before Sister Frances took him back to the prison. We talked about the book (he loved it, and his comments were intelligent and astute) and also about his impending surgery in July (this would be the second replacement of his right knee). Then he asked if we could keep in touch over the summer, if he could write me a letter.

I said, "Sure, why not?" and gave him my address.

Why not, indeed?

It was only after I got home that I wondered if this was a good idea.

The following Friday I received a letter in the morning mail. Two handwritten pages in which Shane made it clear that he was hoping for a romance, that I was, in fact, the woman of his dreams. I stewed about his letter all weekend. On Monday morning, when I was still trying to figure out what to do about it, the mailman brought me another one. A single page this time, in which Shane took back everything he'd said in the first letter.

At the warehouse the next morning, I was energized with relief, an even more potent pick-me-up than straight caffeine. I emptied and sorted four bags of clothing, unpacked and shelved three cases of Kraft Dinner and another two of tomato soup, and filled the freezer with the weekly donation of muffins and pies from Costco. Then I went outside for a breath of fresh air. A red car was just pulling into the parking lot. More donations, I assumed. Two men got out of the car. One was Stuart from LifeLine, and the other was Shane.

I didn't know how he'd engineered it, but there he was, grinning. Stuart went into the warehouse, and Shane and I stood shuffling our feet in the gravel like teenagers. I offered him a cigarette and lit myself another one.

He said, "You got my letters."

I said, "Yes, I did," then launched into the dreaded "Let's just be friends" speech. I prattled on about how I wasn't looking for a relationship, was still getting over the last fiasco, just wanted to get back to writing and leave romance alone. I was looking more at his feet than his face, trying to tell them gently that I wasn't interested.

He said, "You're right. I don't know what I was thinking. I'm sorry. Yes, let's be friends."

When Stuart reappeared, Shane shook my hand and followed him to the car. Then they drove away.

RETURNING TO THE KITCHEN AT VINNIE'S after Labour Day, I was worried that things might be awkward with Shane. If he was there at all, that is. If his summer parole hearing had been successful, he would already have been moved to Ottawa, and I would never have seen him again. I hadn't heard anything more from him over the summer. I'd thought about sending him a card to say I hoped his knee surgery had gone well, but I didn't. I had continued going to Vinnie's on Tuesdays. The rest of the time, for fear of jinxing myself, I tried not to pay too much attention to the fact that my writer's block seemed to be lifting and I was writing a short story—a story about, among other things, a misguided relationship and a writer who cannot write. The story kept getting longer and longer. My friend Lily said, "You're writing a novel!" I insisted I was not. But she was right, and by the end of the summer I was working on the second draft.

In September, Shane was indeed back at Vinnie's and, much to my relief, he was not uncomfortable at all. This made it easy for me too. We caught up on the events of the summer. He didn't seem unduly upset about the negative outcome of his hearing, saying he'd just have to try again next year. His surgery had gone well, but without proper physiotherapy afterwards, he was still in pain and limping. He was supposed to be using a cane but seldom did, because he said it made him feel like a decrepit old man.

He was coming to Vinnie's three days a week now. We slipped back easily into working together, joking, teasing, flirting a bit, and occasionally breaking into song. We were right back to irritating each other too, him messing up the towel under the dish rack right after I'd straightened it, and me saying, "You are the most annoying man I've ever met!" and straightening it again. He pretended never to be able to remember what I'd called him. "What did you call me?" he often asked. "The most what?" Just so I would say it again.

Was this when I began to fall in love with him?

By the end of September, it was clear that Sister Frances wouldn't be able to continue as his escort. The requirement that she must keep him in "sight and sound" meant she had to stay at Vinnie's for the entire five hours, and this was too much for her. Shane asked all the volunteers if anyone was willing to take over as his escort. Three of us said yes: me, a woman named Laura who knew Shane from the convent before he began working at Vinnie's, and Russell, the regular driver of the Vinnie's van. First we each required a criminal background check known as a CPIC, the acronym for Canadian Police Information Centre. Russell was deemed unacceptable because he had a minor criminal record from forty years ago. Laura and I would go together to Frontenac one afternoon for the volunteer training session. This would be the first time in my life I would enter a prison. More than anything, I was curious.

I'd been living in Kingston for twenty years then but had no more knowledge of prison than the next person. Although prison is indeed part of our society, we tend not to think of it that way. Hidden behind stone walls and founded on secrecy, it is a parallel universe to which we are forbidden access and which we're just as happy to think has nothing to do with us. Like most city residents, I had driven past these institutions thousands of times without paying them much attention. They were so much a part of the city that I took their presence for granted. If I did give them more than a passing thought, it was only when I happened to be driving down King Street past Kingston Penitentiary and was struck yet again by the incongruity of its location in one of the most attractive, desirable, and expensive residential areas of the city, on the shore of Lake Ontario beside a three-hundred-dock marina filled with pretty sailboats. Or when I found myself waiting at a red light on Bath Road right beside Collins Bay Institution and had time to observe the majestic castle-like architecture and soaring red spires that had earned it the local nickname "Disneyland."

Behind Collins Bay and not distinguishable as a separate prison from the street, Frontenac Institution was a much smaller facility consisting of unremarkable two-storey brick and stucco buildings and several barns. Opened in 1962 and intended to house 132 inmates, it was originally the Collins Bay Farm Annex. With the prison farm still in operation, minimum-security Frontenac was what I came to think of as "a walk-away prison," usually referred to by both inmates and staff as "camp." It had no perimeter fence, no stone walls, no coils of razor wire, no looming guard tower except for the one at the back corner of medium-security Collins Bay that overlooked Frontenac as well.

Once or twice a year, an inmate does walk away from one of the minimum-security prisons in Kingston, and the resulting news articles always refer, sometimes in graphic detail, to the crime of which he was convicted. Many members of the public are outraged to discover that murderers, rapists, and other violent criminals are housed in "minimum security." The term seems to suggest that the men held there must have committed lesser crimes, that they are just petty thieves, non-violent burglars, computer hackers, and other white-collar criminals. I thought that too before I met Shane. In fact, very few long-term inmates, even those serving life sentences, will spend the entirety of their time in maximum security.

The Canadian prison system operates on the principle of graduated release, with federal institutions being designated at three basic security levels: maximum, medium, and minimum. Inmates are housed at each level according to the risk they pose to staff, other inmates, and the public. An inmate in maximum can be moved to medium if he's done the required programming and generally behaved well. From medium he can then be moved to minimum, again if he has fulfilled his requirements and behaved himself. Having earned his way to a lower security level, he must continue to stay out of trouble in order to remain there. Inmates who successfully make their way through the security levels are said to be "cascading down through the system" as they work towards the ultimate goal of release back into society.

People are also confused about what a life sentence actually means. A person convicted of first-degree murder in Canada receives a life sentence with no chance of parole for twenty-five years. In a second-degree murder conviction, the parole eligibility date is usually set at fifteen years. When the media reports on these cases, members of the public are often outraged and aghast. "He'll be out in twenty-five years!" they cry. "With good behaviour, he'll be out before that!" Part of this confusion arises because, generally speaking, we are more familiar with the American justice system than our own. In Canada, there is no such thing as getting out early on a murder charge for good behaviour or for any other reason. The practice of statutory release by which an inmate may be freed after serving two-thirds of his sentence is never applicable in a murder conviction.

A life sentence with no chance of parole for twenty-five or fifteen years does not mean the offender will be released automatically at the end of that period. There is nothing automatic about it. What it means is that at that time, the Parole Board of Canada is required by law to give him a hearing. It does not mean they have to or will grant him parole. It means they have to read his case files, question him, listen to him, and make their considered decision.

In Canada a life sentence really does mean life. Although not many murderers will spend their entire lives in prison, those who are eventually released on full parole will be forever under the supervision of the Correctional Service of Canada, must abide by all conditions imposed upon them by the Parole Board, and must report regularly to the

Parole Office for the rest of their lives. They will never be entirely free. As stated on the Parole Board website, offenders serving life sentences "can only successfully complete full parole by dying."

ON THE DAY OF OUR VOLUNTEER TRAINING, Laura and I were met in the parking lot by the session leader, who took us to the main building to sign in at the front desk. Already I could see that prison, at least at the minimum-security level, wasn't at all what I had expected. It did not feel menacing or dangerous. It was not grim and dark like a dungeon. It was not quiet. Why had I imagined it would be quiet? In fact, it was a busy bustling place, with inmates, officers, and other staff members all heading to wherever they were supposed to be, some laughing and calling out to each other as they passed. Laura and I were then taken back outside and across to the programs building. A large food truck was backing up to the loading dock of an adjacent building, with half a dozen men waiting to unload it. A pair of inmates in shorts and running shoes were jogging around the building. Three briefcase-carrying men in suits were coming up the road. These, I would understand later, were members of the Parole Board there to conduct a hearing.

Laura and I spent the afternoon learning what would be required of us as citizen escorts. There were pamphlets to be read and forms to be filled out. Having watched Sister Frances in this role for all those months, I had no doubt that I could do it too. Our numbers were added to Shane's telephone list. The session leader explained that an inmate was allowed to make calls to a list of approved numbers, land lines only, cell phones not permitted. His calls would be collect, at the cost of seventy-five cents each. Laura and I had our pictures taken for our official escort IDs, and then we were done. Once the paperwork was completed at their end, our escorting duties would begin.

LATER THAT WEEK, I made my second trip to Frontenac for an entirely different reason. In the summer, Shane and Lenny had rescued an orphaned kitten from the prison farm and were allowed to keep him in their unit. They knew this was a temporary arrangement, and they'd now been told they'd have to find him a home, or he would be euthanized. There were more than enough feral cats on the prison grounds. Shane already knew me well enough to know that it wouldn't take much persuasion for me to agree to give their kitten a home.

When I drove up to the main door that Friday afternoon, Shane, Lenny, and a guard were waiting on the steps. Nestled in Shane's large hands was a small grey tabby with a white bib and big ears. I lifted the cat carrier out of the car and straightened the blanket in the bottom. Shane held the kitten to his face and rubbed his cheek on its fur. Lenny did the same. Then Shane slipped the kitten into the carrier and shut the door. The kitten began to yowl as I put him in the back seat and got back in the car. Lenny and Shane stood there, waving and teary-eyed, the guard grinning beside them, as I drove away.

Shane called twice that evening and twice more over the weekend to see how the kitten was doing. Knowing they wouldn't be able to keep him forever, Shane and Lenny had never named him. I decided to call him Sammy, something of a short form for "San Quentin." My old cat Max sniffed him a couple of times, let him eat out of his dish and pee in his litter box without complaint, and then proceeded to ignore him. My little dog Nelly was overjoyed to have a new playmate, one much friskier than old Max, and Sammy had already figured out that if he got up on the back of the couch, she couldn't reach him. All was well.

As Shane's escort, when I picked him up at Frontenac in the morning, I had to go in and sign for him at the front desk, called the "horseshoe" because of its shape. When I brought him back after lunch, I had to go in to the horseshoe again, sign him back over to them, and write a brief report on how things had gone while he was in my care.

Together in the car, we talked about all manner of things, especially books. Being an avid and intelligent reader, Shane credited books and all writers in general with having helped him do his time for all these years. He said one of his happiest memories was of the time he and his second wife, Brandy, were reading together in the same room, not talking, just reading, and he'd never felt so peaceful in his entire life. This took place during a PFV, a Private Family Visit, what used to be called "a conjugal visit," during which an inmate and his family and loved ones can stay overnight in a trailer designed for this purpose on the prison grounds.

Over time he told me many other things about Brandy too: how he met her when she came to visit her brother in the same prison, and they soon got married inside when he was forty-five; how, two years later, shortly before his parole eligibility date, he had escaped because he thought she was screwing around on him, and, sure enough, he found her in bed with the landlord. But it was the image of the two of them reading together that most stayed with me, an essential part, I think now, of what hooked me in the first place. Why did this simple recollection make my heart sing? Perhaps because the peaceful picture he drew encapsulated my idea of the perfect relationship. Maybe this is all I really want: someone I can read with, not talking, not touching, not interacting, just reading separately but still together. Perhaps this is my idea of perfection. Maybe what I want most is someone with whom I can share a companionable literary silence.

When not talking about books, we talked about ourselves, trading bits and pieces of our lives back and forth the way all people do when getting to know each other. The twenty-minute drive between the prison and Vinnie's didn't give us nearly enough time to talk, and within a week, he was calling me in the evening too, so we could continue the conversation. An inmate could not receive calls, but there was no limit to the number he could make. For the seventy-five-cent cost of each call, we could talk for an hour, and then, after a three-minute warning on his end that I couldn't hear, the call was automatically terminated and the line went dead. He could, however, call me right back and talk for another hour for another seventy-five cents. We both tended to be rather loquacious once we got going. Our conversations were meandering, convoluted, labyrinthine, an intricately braided laying bare of ourselves. At Vinnie's we were still teasing and flirting and joking around, but alone in the car or on the phone, we could be serious. In this first rush of telling him about myself, I felt there was nothing I had to hide from him, nothing I needed to be embarrassed about or ashamed of, nothing about me that he would judge and find wanting.

For each significant event from my life that I offered him—graduating from university in Thunder Bay in 1976 and going to The Banff Centre to study writing; moving to Canmore that fall; publishing my first book in 1984; giving birth to Alex in 1985; moving to Kingston the following year and buying my house the year after that; publishing more books in 1986, 1987, 1990, 1991, and 1994; winning the Governor General's Award for *Forms of Devotion* in 1998; publishing three more books since then—he could say without hesitation which prison, including Kingston Penitentiary, he'd been in at the time. He'd been shipped back and forth across the country so many times, I lost track of how many institutions he'd been in. Inmates are moved frequently, sometimes due to a change in security level, sometimes because of conflict with another inmate, and sometimes, he said, just because it seemed like CSC didn't want anyone to get too comfortable.

WE TALKED ABOUT GROWING OLDER. Shane was in perpetual mourning for the loss of his young, strong vigorous body. He lamented the damage done by all that high-school hockey and football he'd been so good at, his right knee broken, all his teeth knocked out. Those perfectly straight white teeth of his that I had admired and secretly envied were, in fact, false. He worried that back in those days, helmets were not required and what if he'd suffered brain damage from multiple untreated concussions? He was bitterly resentful about the whole irreversible process of getting old. I said that was understandable, given that he'd spent all of his adult life in prison.

Rankled by my comment, he was quick to correct me. "*Most*," he said. "I've been in prison for *most* of my adult life. Not *all.*"

He spoke often of the glorious day to come when he'd be "living on the street." This phrase puzzled me at first. To me it meant being homeless, sleeping at a shelter or in an alley or a park, panhandling downtown in front of Shoppers Drug Mart or the Dollar Store, eating lunch at Vinnie's and supper at Martha's Table, one of the other hot meal programs in Kingston. But to Shane, I soon realized, it meant being out of prison, no longer incarcerated, living out here with the rest of us in the so-called free world.

WE TALKED ABOUT OUR CHILDHOODS, me growing up in Thunder Bay, him in Kenworth, a small town thirty kilometres northwest of

Kingston, both of us in working-class families, me an only child born relatively late in my parents' lives, him the eldest of three. Both our mothers had left something to be desired in the maternal nurturing department, his considerably more than mine. His mother still lived in Kenworth; mine had died twenty years ago of cancer. Both our fathers were dead now, his of heart failure sixteen years earlier and mine of Alzheimer's just two years ago. They were both Second World War veterans, having fought as young men in Italy, Holland, and Germany. According to the established mythology of Shane's family, it was the war that had turned his father into a brutal, violent, alcoholic philanderer who terrorized his wife and children. He wanted me to say the same was true of my father. Yes, mine was also a heavy drinker, but we never thought it had anything to do with the war, and he was never violent, instead receding deeper and deeper into himself with each glass of rum and Coke.

Despite the drinking, the beatings, and the affairs, Shane's father had been posthumously elevated to the role of good parent, while his mother, still alive and acrimonious, had become the monstrous root of all familial evil.

In his telling of it, the neighbourhood where he grew up was a nightmarish *Deliverance* territory in which all the mothers were whores, all the fathers were violent drunkards, and all the children were physically and sexually abused. Like he was. He figured my neighbourhood in Thunder Bay must have been the same, and he called me naive when I said no, it wasn't like that at all, and none of my friends were ever abused. He laughed grimly, saying just because I didn't know about it didn't mean it wasn't happening.

He told me about his first marriage, to a girl named Penny, when he was only twenty-one. He'd already been in some trouble by then: breaking and entering, petty theft, drugs. He said Penny only married him because she wanted to piss off her father, who was a cop. They had a son, and then Penny left him, left them both. He said he was happy looking after his son alone. He worked steadily and stayed out of trouble for five years. After Penny remarried, she sued for custody and won. Since then, he'd had only intermittent contact with the boy, had now not been in touch with him for ten years or more. He said the last he'd heard, his son, now in his late thirties, was in prison too, doing time on a drug charge.

It was the loss of his boy, Shane said, that had turned him back to drinking and drugs and crime, more serious crime this time, and before he knew it, he was twenty-seven years old and serving a four-year federal sentence for bank robbery. The difference between provincial and federal time, he explained, is based solely on the length of the sentence. Anything under two years is provincial, anything over is federal. And so he went to the big house.

WE TALKED ABOUT SEX. Actually he talked about sex, and I listened. Sometimes it seemed he was trying to shock me with his stories of multiple and frequent sexual encounters with other men in prison, furtive acts he called "oil changes." I was not shocked. He had also had a long relationship with another inmate named Victor, who became his accomplice in murder. I was not shocked by this either. He said he had never loved Victor. I said there was no reason to deny loving this man. Still, he insisted.

HE TALKED ABOUT THE MURDER. I already knew the details from the CSC paperwork he had handed around at Vinnie's in the spring. It was the summer of 1981, and he was thirty-one years old. Just two months before warrant expiry, when his sentence for bank robbery would have ended and he would have become a free man, he escaped from Bath Institution, then a minimum-security prison. He couldn't explain why he'd done such a thing when he was so close to getting out.

"They call it 'poor impulse control,'" he said. "I call it being young and stupid and stoned. I didn't think about the consequences. I couldn't resist the temptation to run." He went to Toronto to meet up with Victor, who'd been released to a halfway house there on mandatory supervision.

After a week-long binge of alcohol and speed, they were picked up in a park by an elderly man named Philip Bailey, who offered them money for sex. They went back to his apartment. Later Shane passed out in the bedroom. Later still, Philip Bailey caught Victor going through his stuff looking for something to steal and threatened to call the police. He didn't know they were convicts on the lam. Victor called out to Shane for help. Shane killed Philip Bailey with a hammer, then strangled him with an electrical cord to be sure he was dead.

Shane was overwhelmed with emotion as he told me the story—the first time and every other time he talked about it in the coming years. He knew he had done the worst thing any person could ever do. He always called Philip Bailey by his full name, first and last. He held himself entirely accountable for what he'd done and would never let himself forget exactly to whom he'd done it.

"Do you think God forgives me?" he often asked.

I knew enough about God to feel confident that the answer to this question was yes. I never doubted the depth of Shane's remorse, but I didn't know if he would ever be able to forgive himself.

⊂⊃

SHANE HAD BEEN TELLING ME EVERY DAY for weeks that he loved me. I had not yet reciprocated. I wanted to say it. I thought it often enough. I'd spent many sleepless nights trying to sort out my feelings for him. In the end, it was something like what he had said about manslaughter: I didn't plan to fall in love with him, I didn't intend to fall in love with him, but I did.

The reasons I shouldn't become involved with him were self-evident—even to me. I sometimes wonder now if I took Dorothy's advice—don't judge, don't assume—too far in his case. Perhaps in my time at Vinnie's I went overboard in perfecting my practice of acceptance without judgment or assumption. My own better judgment should have told me not to get involved with him. I should have assumed, as everybody else did, that falling in love with a man in prison, let alone a man in prison for murder, was not a good idea. It would be easy to say that I was blinded by love. But I wasn't. I knew this was a risky thing to do.

In retrospect I also wonder if the intensity of his desire for me meant more to me than it should have. Perhaps I didn't realize at the time how much I wanted to be wanted, how deeply I needed to be needed.

Tossing and turning all night, I asked myself many questions. If he'd killed Philip Bailey three years ago instead of thirty, would I get involved with him? No. If he'd killed a woman? No. If he was a sex offender, a rapist, a child pornographer, a pedophile? No. If Alex was a little boy instead of a twenty-one-year-old young man? No. If I was a young woman myself, with my whole life ahead of me? No. If I hadn't already come to know him as a person before I knew he had committed murder? Maybe not.

I drew lines around what I would and wouldn't have been able to accept. I had to arrange it all in my mind in a way I could live with. Did getting involved with him mean I condoned, overlooked, or otherwise minimized the gravity of what he'd done in taking another person's life? No. Absolutely not. The day my son was born I knew that I would kill for him. This is still true even though he's now six foot four. Having acknowledged my own capacity to kill someone meant I could understand how murder happened. Was it possible to love the man while hating the crime? Yes. Did I wish he hadn't killed Philip Bailey? Yes. Did I wish he wasn't in prison? Yes. Could I change either of these things? No. Did I forgive him for what he'd done in the past? Yes. Did I believe he was no longer the same person who'd killed Philip Bailey? Yes. Did I believe people could change? Yes. Did I believe in second chances? Yes.

Only convicted criminals (and perhaps a few celebrities) are forever defined and labelled by the worst thing they have ever done in their lives. The rest of us can be more than one thing. We can be both good and bad. We seldom ever even have to reveal the worst thing we've done in our lives, except maybe to our therapists. What if the next time you went to the grocery store everyone filling up their carts with apples, juice, and Cheerios was wearing a sign stating the worst thing they'd ever done in their lives? What would your sign say?

Yes, he was a murderer. But he was not *only* a murderer.

Did I believe he loved me? Yes. Did I love him? Yes.

I did not look at him every day and see MURDERER. I looked at him every day and saw SHANE, the man I loved.

When faced with a romantic situation where I must choose between following my head or my heart, I have always chosen the latter. I have always been able to override the rational voice in my head. I have never been able to—and could not this time—silence or dismiss the obsessive clamouring in my heart.

Did I sometimes wonder if I was crazy? Yes.

REGARDLESS OF HOW BIZARRE IT MIGHT BE that I'd fallen in love with a murderer, I also knew that with Shane, more than with any other man in any other circumstance, when I told him I loved him, I would be making a commitment that was bound to be complicated—a commitment that was going to change my life. I was sure I loved him, but I also had to be sure I was ready for what lay ahead. As it turned out, it did change my life, but by then what I was living was not my life, bore little or no resemblance to any life I had expected or intended to live.

Even when I was ready to tell him, I didn't do it directly. I wrote it in a card. Not surprising for a writer, I suppose. *To my dear devoted Shane,* I began. It didn't take long to write—I knew what I wanted to say. The problem then was figuring out the best time to give it to him. I could have mailed it, but I knew all incoming and outgoing inmate correspondence was checked, and I didn't like the idea of an officer reading it before he did. The only time we were ever alone was in the car.

When I picked him up the next morning, I intended to give it to him as soon as we were on our way. But he was upset because someone in his unit had drunk all the juice and didn't replace it and wouldn't admit it either. This led to a full-scale rant about how nobody else, including Lenny, ever did anything, and he was the only one who ever cleaned the fucking toilet. He wasn't housed on the range in a regular cell but in one of a number of special units in which five or six inmates lived communally, each with his own bedroom, sharing the kitchen, the living room, the chores. These were the Phoenix units, intended to provide the men with an experience of everyday life more like that which they would have to navigate once they were released—once they, like the mythical bird, had risen from the ashes of their criminal lives and been reborn.

I let him complain until we got to Vinnie's. Once inside, I slipped him the card. The other volunteers were already coming in, so I suggested he take it to the basement and read it alone.

When he came back upstairs, his face was red and he was obviously upset. I couldn't understand it; I had thought he would be thrilled. After stomping around the kitchen in his apron for a few minutes, he said angrily, "Demented! I am not demented. You called me demented."

I had no idea what he was talking about. He took the card out of his pocket and shook it at me, pointing to the first line. "There," he said, "right there."

I looked closer. I still didn't get it. He read his interpretation of the offending line out loud: "To my dear *demented* Shane."

I've often been complimented on my neat handwriting, but apparently it wasn't clear to him. "*Devoted!*" I cried. "It says *devoted*, you idiot!"

Five hours later, after we'd served lunch to more than eighty people, wiped all the tables, done all the dishes, and put them away, we went to the basement to hang up the wet dishtowels. Leaning up against the freezer, he put his arms around me and kissed me. He'd tried before, but I had always pushed him away. This time I didn't. The kiss was deep, passionate, and thrilling—but sadly cut short by the sound of someone else coming down the stairs.

I said it out loud. "I love you."

He said, "Demented or not, I love you with all my heart."

I said it again. "I love you too."

BEFORE I GAVE SHANE the I-love-you card, I'd asked him more than once if he was sure he wanted to be with a woman. The first time, he seemed surprised by the question. I reminded him that he'd been open about his previous sexual encounters with men. He said yes, he was absolutely sure. He was also sure that woman was me.

After I gave him the card, I said, "You are my person," a line I'd lifted from an episode of *Grey's Anatomy*. "But if you go back to drinking and drugs, I will leave you. If you go back to doing crime, I will leave you. If you ever cheat on me, I will leave you."

Love is not supposed to be like parole, is not supposed to come with conditions. But those were mine. As time went on, it became clear that we both had trouble with the concept of "unconditional love."

∞

I HAD DECLARED MY LOVE TO SHANE. We'd had our first kiss. It had taken almost a year to get to this point. Now things began to happen quickly. It appeared that those three little words could have as much of a snowball effect in the prison world as anywhere else.

Despite newly-in-love couples everywhere feeling they are encased in a bulletproof bubble of happiness, no romantic relationship takes place in a vacuum, and this is never more true than when one of those would-be lovers is a prison inmate. Our relationship could not possibly develop according to its own natural timetable. Taking place under the auspices of the Correctional Service of Canada, it could only proceed as they permitted, step by step, rule by rule, document by document, at a pace that proved over the coming years to be sometimes much too fast and other times maddeningly slow, more often the latter than the former.

Relinquishing my position as Shane's approved escort and becoming his regular visitor instead was not without its difficulties. When he informed his parole officer, Janice Mackie, that I wanted to make this change so we could pursue a romantic relationship, she was not impressed. She was sure he must be coercing me, muscling me to suit his own devious purposes, most likely grooming me to become his drug mule. I did my best to convince her that this was not the case, that I had fallen in love with him and was making this decision of my own free will. She remained skeptical. This conversation took place on the phone. I hadn't yet met Janice in person, but I was sure that once I did, she'd see that I was not a likely candidate for either being muscled or lugging drugs. When I did meet her later that week, her attitude had not softened any, and meeting me seemed only to aggravate her mistrust of us both.

Janice reprimanded me for having let Shane call me while I was his escort. She said it was absolutely against the rules for an inmate to be calling his escort for personal reasons. I said I didn't know it was against the rules. She said Shane obviously *did* know, and he should have told me that. He didn't. Nor did I recall this rule having been mentioned when I attended the volunteer training session to become his escort in the first place.

This was the first time, but definitely not the last, that I wanted to say, "I would be more than happy to follow all your rules if only you would tell me what they are. Preferably before, rather than after, I've broken one."

I am, generally speaking, a rule-abiding person. I don't jaywalk or cross the street on a red light even if it's pouring rain or forty below. I never park my car where I'm not supposed to, even if it means driving around the block three or four times to find a spot. I obey the watering restrictions imposed by the city in the summer, and I don't shovel my snow onto the street in the winter. I'm careful about my garbage and recycling, keeping both the collection schedule and the details of what goes in which box posted on the side of my fridge. I have no problem with rules.

I didn't make my comment on the rules to Janice that day, but I did say it later, to another officer at another prison. He snorted cheerfully and said, "Nobody knows what *all* the rules are."

Later still, I would have occasion to say, "I would be more than happy to follow your rules if only they stayed the same from one day to the next."

DESPITE HER MISGIVINGS, Janice Mackie took my name off the escorts list and let me submit my visiting application form. It was a simple enough document, requiring my basic personal information, an emergency contact, and the type and number of the piece of identification I would use when visiting. In the section regarding the nature of my relationship with the inmate, the choice of boxes to be checked included Father, Mother, Spouse, Common-Law Spouse, Brother, Sister, Son, Daughter, and Other. I checked Other, which then required me to specify the type and length of the relationship. After some deliberation, I wrote *girlfriend*, despite this striking me as rather juvenile when we were both in our fifties. In the next box, "Explain if extenuating circumstances," I summed up the situation as best I could in one line while contemplating the implications of the word *extenuating* in this context.

My signature at the end of the form was my consent to a criminal background check, which they'd already conducted when I became an escort, and my acknowledgment that I understood I would be subject to searches of various types whenever I entered the institution, including a frisk search or a strip search should it be deemed "necessary to find contraband or evidence" and that my "oral, visual or telecommunications with an inmate may be subject to interception."

The completed form was to be accompanied by two current photographs (full face view, head and shoulders only) of a specified size. I went to the downtown camera store where they did passport photos. The man behind the counter was someone I'd known for years, although not especially well. His wife was also a writer, and we often ran into each other at literary events. When I told him I needed to have my picture taken, he asked if it was for a passport. I said, "No, it's for a prison visiting application," and showed him the form. I expected him to make some comment on this request. Perhaps I wanted him to. But he betrayed no interest whatsoever, no curiosity, no concern, no nothing. He pointed me towards the backroom, where I was met by another man, one I didn't know, who glanced at the form and took the photos quickly, again with no questions asked. Because this step from escort to visitor felt so momentous to me, I was disappointed to discover that the eccentric quirks of my love life were of such little import to the men at the camera store.

WE HAD OUR FIRST OFFICIAL DATE on Friday, December 8, 2006, Feast of the Immaculate Conception. I'm not Catholic, but I did write a novel about the Virgin Mary, so I knew this was the day Catholics gathered to celebrate the immaculate conception of Mary, who then remained free of original sin for the rest of her life. December 8 was also my mother's birthday. She would have turned ninety that day.

Also on December 8, back in 1980, John Lennon was shot and killed by Mark David Chapman on the steps of the Dakota Hotel in New York City. Lennon's murder twenty-six years earlier had no bearing on our story beyond the fact that it seemed to have happened so long ago, back when Shane was already in prison for bank robbery but had not yet committed murder, not yet commenced serving a life sentence;

and I was already living on my own in Alberta, working as a bank teller, but had not yet published my first book, not yet become a mother, not yet imagined myself moving back to Ontario, not yet begun inching anywhere near the fateful intersection of my life and his.

Shane had an ETA to attend the evening celebration at St. Mary's Cathedral downtown, and I had permission to meet him there. I gave a lot of thought beforehand as to what I should wear, not sure what might constitute appropriate cathedral attire. This would be the first time Shane would see me all dressed up. For the entire eleven months we'd known each other, he had only ever seen me in my Vinnie's clothes: baggy old pants and plaid flannel shirts from the warehouse, a full-length apron looped around my neck and tied at the waist, a backwards blue baseball cap with a Planet Hollywood logo that I'd bought for Alex a dozen years ago during a trip to Montreal.

Finally I decided to wear what I called my "power suit." Purchased some years earlier for an American book tour, it was of a slightly shiny grey fabric with a calf-length pencil skirt and a fitted jacket decorated with jet beading at the collar and cuffs. Paired with my knee-high black leather boots, it was the most stylish and sophisticated outfit I had ever owned.

St. Mary's Cathedral, built in the mid-nineteenth century of limestone quarried by Kingston Penitentiary inmates, is a magnificent example of religious architecture in the Gothic style, with soaring buttresses, stone pillars and statues, dozens of stained glass windows, and a ninety-foot vaulted ceiling. But beyond an overall impression of grandeur and godliness, I was not taking in the splendour of the crowded cathedral as I walked straight down the centre aisle, my boots echoing on the stone floor. I was focused on the back of Shane's head, which I'd spotted midway up on the right-hand side. I would have recognized that bald spot anywhere. Just as I reached his row, he turned his head. Looking more than a little flustered, he stood up and welcomed me in to sit between him and his escort. Afterwards, he said he'd heard the

clack-clack of my boots as I came up the aisle but was afraid to look—
afraid it was or wasn't me.

His escort was a small smiling woman named Hannah, who was
clearly enjoying the prospect of being our chaperone for the evening.
On the other side of her sat Fred from Vinnie's and his wife, Rita. They
too were beaming parentally as Shane reached for my hand.

After mass we all went to the basement for coffee and treats. Shane
knew many people in the crowd and took obvious pleasure in intro-
ducing me to every single one of them. I was overwhelmed but happy.
Outside afterwards, we lingered in the street saying goodbye, Hannah,
Fred, and Rita still beaming as we kissed chastely in the cold night. For
a moment, I thought they were going to applaud. Then we walked to
our cars and drove away, Shane with Hannah back to the prison, Fred
and Rita to their home, and me to mine, grinning and giddy all the
way there.

I have never been religious, but still I felt reassured by the church setting of this first date. In my own version of magical thinking, I couldn't
help but feel our relationship was being sanctioned, if not sanctified,
by history, the Catholic Church, and the Virgin Mary herself. I let this
outweigh any niggling misgivings I might have. What could possibly
go wrong?

As with all couples, this first date became one of the signposts of
our relationship, an essential part of our mythology, a happy memory
we could take out often and relive in detail, as if there were a file box,
something like the little box in which my mother had kept her recipes,
a collection of all the best moments that we could refer to whenever we
needed to remind ourselves how much we loved each other.

As time went on, there came to be a second file box too, a collection
of all the worst moments—the pain, the anger, the tears, the destruction, and the despair. Those memories were taken out often too, relived,
rehashed, and returned to the box unresolved.

⁐

MY VISITING APPLICATION WAS QUICKLY APPROVED just before Christmas. Perhaps the warden didn't share Janice's reservations. I never did meet that warden. In fact, I never met or spoke to any warden at any prison at any time during my years with Shane.

The day after my application was approved, Shane had a seventy-two-hour Unescorted Temporary Absence, a UTA, to his mother's in Kenworth. A higher-level privilege than an ETA, a UTA means the inmate is allowed to be away from the institution for a specified purpose at a specified location for a specified period of time without a certified escort. I found it odd that he required an escort to be at Vinnie's for just a few hours but he did not require one to be away from the prison for a whole weekend. Not only that, but now there were no rules about who was permitted to drive him back and forth. So, although I was no longer an approved escort, I could pick him up at the prison at three o'clock and take him to Kenworth. It was Friday, December 22. He had to be back at Frontenac by three o'clock on Monday, Christmas Day.

He was waiting on the front steps with his duffle bag when I arrived. I didn't even have to go in to the horseshoe and sign for him. He was the same person, and I was the same person, but now the rules were different.

Before we left Kingston, we had to check in at the Parole Office, which was very near my house. There, his community, or "outside," parole officer, Jerry Anderson, would check his paperwork and go over our plans for the pass, which Shane had written out in detail. Whenever he was away from the prison, he had to carry his paperwork at all times, one document identifying him as a federal offender

41

serving a life sentence for murder, the other indicating that he was on an authorized temporary absence from the institution.

A month later, Jerry Anderson would come to my house to do a Community Assessment. This was something like a job interview, during which he checked out my house and asked many questions about my past and present life to determine if my home was an appropriate environment in which Shane might spend time and if I was a suitable "prosocial" person with whom he might associate. I got the job.

This word *prosocial*, so important in the prison world, was not familiar to me. I only knew its opposite. I've often described myself as being "antisocial" when I don't feel like going out, want to stay home in my pyjamas and read or watch TV, preferably while eating popcorn or ice cream, or both. The word *antisocial* is often used to describe the writing life in general, involving as it does long stretches of solitude during which the writer tries to remain focused on writing while fending off the demands and distractions of daily life. Indeed, one definition of the word does mean feeling not sociable, not wanting the company of others. More often than not, this describes me perfectly. But it is the other definition of *antisocial* that is implied in its opposition to *prosocial.*

antisocial. *adjective.* Contrary or averse to the laws and customs of society; devoid of or antagonistic to the practices, principles, and instincts on which society is based: as in *a dangerous, unprincipled, antisocial type of man.*

Although Shane was an avid reader, he didn't share my obsession with language or my fascination with the finer points of definitions and usage. Why would he? He didn't need to know any of this to be proud of his FUCK SOCIETY tattoo.

That first day in his office, Jerry Anderson was casual, relaxed, and cheerful. Shane was anxious, agitated, and defensive. A large vein in his forehead was bulging, and he was grinding his teeth and having trouble forming coherent sentences. I had never seen him like this before. As we left the office, Jerry reminded us that Shane was restricted to a range of forty kilometres in any direction from Kenworth and that I was to call him after the pass and let him know how everything had gone.

Back in the car, Shane calmed down. He said he was just paranoid that something was going to go wrong at the last minute, that Jerry would suddenly cancel his pass for no good reason.

After we arrived in Kenworth, before going to his mother's, we had to check in at the provincial police detachment, the town not having a municipal police force. Shane had to show them his paperwork, verify where he would be staying, show them our itinerary, and so on. I assumed they'd have some questions for me too, would at least want to know who I was and check my ID, but they didn't. We got back in the car and drove on to his mother's apartment.

Now I was nervous. It had been at least twenty years since I had met the mother of a man I was seeing, and that mother didn't much like me, said I was "prickly." This mother, Vera, lived on the ground floor at the back of a seniors' complex, so we went in through the door of her small patio. We stepped directly into the living room, at the far end of which was a small table and three chairs set against a half-wall, and beyond that was the tiny open kitchen. Not part of the kitchen but not part of the living room either, a large upright freezer stood halfway between. To the left were the bedroom and the bathroom, the only two separate rooms in the apartment, the only rooms with doors. Compact and crowded with furniture, the whole place could not have measured more than five hundred square feet.

Shane had made it abundantly clear that he wanted me to stay overnight, but I had insisted on leaving my options open. I'd packed a small bag in case I did decide to stay, but I'd left it in the trunk of the car. I had also insisted that he bring condoms from the prison, where they were freely available to all inmates. He had said he was tested—they were all tested—for AIDS every six months. I had said I wanted to see the paperwork, and until I did, we would have to use condoms. He'd requested a copy of this paperwork but had not yet received it. That day his jacket pockets were optimistically stuffed with condoms, as well as with similar little shiny packages of lubricant, which were also freely available to all inmates, he said, no questions asked.

His mother seemed happy to see us, hugged us both and welcomed us in. She had been in ill health with multiple medical issues for many years, although it wasn't clear to me exactly what was wrong with her. She talked a lot about her bowels, her kidneys, her headaches, her nerves, and she walked with a cane, stiffly bent over and in obvious pain. She looked much older than her seventy-three years. She was only sixteen when Shane was born.

Vera made a pot of coffee and offered us some lemon meringue pie. I declined because it was getting on to five o'clock, and we were planning to go out for dinner just the two of us to a Chinese restaurant downtown, a place called The Imperial that Shane remembered fondly from his youth. He had two pieces of pie anyway.

We sat around the kitchen table, where a collection of at least a dozen prescription pill bottles sat like a centrepiece along with the salt and pepper shakers. This gave me a jolt of *déjà vu* because my father in his last years had also kept his medications on the kitchen table.

We made some small talk: the weather, the winter, Christmas. Vera didn't seem much interested in anything about me, but she did say she was glad to see I wasn't like any of the other women Shane had been "mixed up with" over the years. She made disparaging comments about him and his bad behaviour, referring to him in the third person as if he weren't sitting right there too. Calling her a "heretic," he responded in kind, and they went back and forth across the table, baiting and insulting each other.

She had a list of things she wanted him to do including clean the ceiling fan that hung between the living room and kitchen areas. She said her cleaning lady had done it just last week, but it didn't look clean enough to her. We talked about household matters for a while. Vera said you couldn't get the floor really clean unless you got down on your hands and knees and scrubbed it properly. I agreed. Vera said once you'd opened a block of cheese, you should wrap it in plastic *and* put it in a Ziploc bag to keep it fresh in the fridge. I agreed. These were the only two things Vera and I ever actually agreed on.

Although Shane seemed to be signalling me to be quiet, I remarked on the photograph of a bug-eyed brown pug pinned to the wall above the kitchen table.

"That's my sweet Popeye," Vera said, and, groaning, she hobbled over to the TV set. She returned with a little wooden box in her hand, a smaller version of the same photo taped to the lid. She opened it to reveal what could only be the ashes of the little dog. "I miss him every day," she said tearfully. "I loved that dog more than anybody else in the whole world." Shane snorted. "Sometimes I don't know why I even bother trying to go on without him," she continued. "Every night when I go to bed, I turn my troubles over to Jesus. But then every morning when I wake up alive, I take them back again."

Shane snorted again and stomped to the bathroom. When he returned, he announced that it was time for dinner. Vera waved us out the door, saying not to worry about her, she was too upset to eat; she'd just have a piece of toast or something.

We drove downtown to The Imperial, which turned out to be like any old Chinese restaurant anywhere, a veritable twin to the Bamboo Garden where I'd hung out as a teenager back in Thunder Bay, right down to the faded paper lanterns, the giant plastic menus, the booths upholstered in cracked red plastic patched with duct tape. We took a booth at the back and held hands across the table. The food when it finally came was so greasy and salty as to be almost inedible. This didn't deter Shane, who filled his plate three times. I picked at mine, but he didn't notice and I didn't complain. The novelty of this being our first restaurant meal together more than made up for the deplorable food. The fortune cookies were stale, but the dispatches inside were encouraging, if not grammatically correct. Mine: *Your life is be peaceful and fulfilling.* His: *Good news are on their way.* I tucked them into my wallet for safekeeping. Shane ordered a piece of pie, Boston cream this time. I could see he had a prodigious appetite for pie.

It was still early—too early, we agreed, to go directly back to Vera's apartment, so we drove around town for an hour. Shane played tour guide in the darkness, pointing out places of interest including the elementary and high schools he had attended; the Baptist church where he said the organist had molested him when he was eight, and when he told his mother, she said he was lying; the rink where he played hockey and had all his teeth knocked out; the football field where he had broken his knee; the intersection where his cousin, sixteen years old and driving drunk, had been killed; the corner store he'd once robbed and the owner forgave him without pressing charges; the cemetery where his father, his grandparents, and miscellaneous other relatives were buried. He was very matter-of-fact about all of it.

By the time we arrived back at his mother's building, I had made up my mind without realizing I'd done so. I took my overnight bag out of the trunk and followed him inside. Vera was still up but in her housecoat now, getting ready to retire to her bedroom and watch TV. Her favourite shows, *Law & Order* and *CSI*, were always on some channel, somewhere. To me, Shane said, "She loves watching killers on TV, but she doesn't much like having one in the family." To her, "I hope you're going to shut the bedroom door." She insisted that she absolutely could not shut the door, because she'd feel like she was suffocating, and then she'd have a panic attack. To me, Shane said, "Suffocation. We can only hope." To her, "Never mind."

Vera's final bedtime preparations took a very long time and included tidying the already tidy kitchen and rearranging her pill bottles on the table. Then there was a lengthy and fruitless search for a missing earring and a protracted stay in the bathroom. Also apparently fruitless. When she finally emerged, she grunted, "Still constipated," and went into her room without closing the door or saying good night.

Meanwhile Shane and I had been sitting side by side on the little sofa pretending to watch TV. Mostly we'd just been clicking through the channels. Now we were just waiting for her to fall asleep. This also took a very long time, but finally her TV was turned off, her light turned out. Her door remained open.

We pulled out the sofa bed and made it up with the sheets, blankets, and pillows Vera had left stacked on an armchair. We were both giggling. I used the bathroom first, then waited in the bed in my nightgown while he took his turn. Despite my habitual concern with wearing the right clothes for any and every event, it somehow hadn't occurred to me to buy new lingerie for this occasion, so I had packed the same nightgown I always wore at home: white jersey printed with a pale blue toile pattern, mid-calf length, sleeveless, with a scoop neck and a buttoned placket down the front. Shane made no comment that night but forever after referred to it as my "granny nightie," the perfect accompaniment to my "granny panties."

He came out of the bathroom in his boxers and a pair of white prison-issue plastic flip-flops and went into the kitchen. He took out his false teeth and put them in an empty margarine container on the counter. He had a glass of water, brought me one too. Then he got into the bed beside me, and we waited some more just to be sure Vera was asleep. We pretended to watch the late-night news while he rubbed my feet and I examined his tattoos, all of them visible now on his arms, legs, back, and chest.

Over his heart was the name BRANDY in letters at least an inch high. I threatened to cover it with duct tape, which, I said, I would very much enjoy ripping off afterwards. Later he looked into having this tattoo removed but was told it would be a lengthy, painful, and expensive process. I said never mind. It didn't matter. After a while, I didn't see it anymore anyway. Like a lot of things.

That first night at Vera's he distracted me from Brandy's name on his chest by whipping out his penis and waving it at me.

Eventually we couldn't wait any longer.

It was a very small bed. He was a large man. We were both nervous and out of practice. I had never kissed anyone without teeth before. Much to my surprise, it was extremely sensual and arousing. There were accommodations to be made for his recent surgery, and for my vertigo, which meant there were certain ways I couldn't move my head. But all things considered, it went very well. I had an orgasm. He went on. I had another orgasm. I thought he had one too, but he went on. I was more than satisfied, and still he went on. Finally I was so exhausted I had to ask him to stop. As we lay there panting, he grinned and admitted that condoms and lubricant weren't the only things he'd brought with him from the prison. He had also managed to buy some Viagra from another inmate. He confessed that he'd been so worried about not being able to perform that he had taken not one, not two, but three of them.

We were both gasping and giggling when a loud voice came from the bedroom. "Shane," Vera hollered, "there's still some pie in the fridge if you're hungry!"

Without hesitation, he got out of the little bed and limped to the kitchen, our exuberant activity having aggravated his bad leg and, apparently, also his appetite. He opened the fridge and stood naked in its cold white light. He offered me a piece of pie, but I said no thanks. He stood there and ate the rest of it right out of the box, went to the bathroom, and then came back to bed.

As I tried to fall asleep beside him, there was a kind of tugging in the back of my mind. A small hand wiggling for attention. An anxious voice whispering, What have I done? Oh God, what have I done?

But I steadfastly ignored it.

THE NEXT MORNING I DROVE HOME ALONE and spent the rest of the day finishing up my Christmas preparations. The following day, Sunday, was Christmas Eve, and we planned to attend evening mass at the convent. Alex was off, so he would come too. Late in the day, I drove to Kenworth to get Shane and bring him back to my house. Because his forty-kilometre range included Kingston, he could come to my house but, because he had permission to stay overnight only at his mother's, he could not sleep there.

This would be the first time he'd be inside my house. He always called his cell his "house," but my house really is a house—an almost sixty-year-old white stucco bungalow with turquoise shutters, about 1,200 square feet with three bedrooms, a partially finished full basement, and a large bright kitchen at the front facing the street. It is located on a short block of ten single-family homes, two triplexes, and four low-rise six-unit apartment buildings.

My neighbourhood is what we like to call "diverse," with residents of all ages, backgrounds, incomes, and ethnicities. We are straight, gay, single, common-law, married, divorced, widowed, other. We are employed, unemployed, self-employed, retired. We are middle class, working class, hard to say, somewhere in between. We have many dogs and cats among us—even our pets are friends. We are collectively very fond of our little street, have all mastered the fine balance of caring about and looking out for each other without sacrificing our privacy in the process.

I bought the house in the fall of 1987, when Alex was two years old. We'd been living in Kingston for a year then, in a rented house on the other side of town. My mother died earlier that year and left me enough money to make a good-sized down payment. I was proud of the fact that I'd managed to buy a house on my own as a single mother at a time when such an accomplishment was uncommon. I had now lived in this house almost as long as I'd lived in my childhood home in Thunder Bay.

That Christmas Eve, after Shane was happily reunited with Sammy the kitten, I gave him the tour, trailed by Nelly, who was friendly enough but keeping a close eye on him, barking wildly every time he touched me. Shane wandered from room to room admiring everything, especially the inviting expanse of my queen-size bed made up with a gold-patterned bedspread and many colourful cushions.

We went into the living room, where, as usual, our old cat Max was asleep on the couch. When Shane reached down to pat his head, Max opened one eye and growled at him. "Grumpy old bugger," Shane said, laughing. "Just like me."

Five years earlier, I had fulfilled a lifelong dream by having wall-to-wall floor-to-ceiling bookcases built in on the west wall of the living room. Eighteen feet long, this wall now houses at least a thousand books. There are bookcases of varying sizes in all the other rooms too, but this one is the showpiece. When I had it built, I foolishly thought I would never need more book space again. When we moved from Alberta to Kingston, I brought a hundred boxes of books with me. Thanks to another twenty years of unbridled book buying, there are now books everywhere, some, for want of a shelf, packed in bankers' boxes under the bed and in the back room. I've often defended my book habit by pointing out that it could be worse: it could be heroin. As a former heroin user himself, Shane found this especially amusing.

Originally I had used the bedroom at the back of the house as my office. But when Alex was a teenager, I moved my desk into the living room, getting as far away from the rap music, the video games, and the endless telephone conversations as I possibly could without ending up on the front lawn. My desk was now positioned in the middle of the wall of books.

Shane stood staring at the books, and when he turned to me, there were tears in his eyes. "I will read every single one of them," he said. "And then I'll die a happy man."

Back in the kitchen, I made a pot of coffee, and he and Alex sat chatting at the table while I got ready to go to the convent. When I came back into the room, he pointed down and said, "Next time I'm here, I'll wash this floor for you."

I was irritated and insulted by this, which I took to be a criticism of my housekeeping skills. He said he only intended it as an offer of help, knowing I had to do everything by myself. But it reminded me of the time thirty years earlier, when my parents drove all the way from Thunder Bay to Canmore for a visit, a trip of more than two thousand kilometres, and within half an hour, my mother was back in the car crying because she said my apartment was a filthy mess. My standards of cleanliness were not up to hers—nobody's were. "You didn't even wash the kitchen floor!" she wept.

But both these moments from Shane's first visit to my house, his emotional reaction to the wall of books and his offer to wash the kitchen floor, were soon added to our file box of happy memories, a part of the story we told each other over and over again, laughing.

WHEN I STARTED GOING OUT WITH SHANE (I realize "going out with" is not exactly the right term to describe having a relationship with a prison inmate) and took my first steps into his world, I soon discovered that prison is both like a secret society with its own rules, written and unwritten, and a foreign country with its own culture, customs, and language. Whether you're going into prison as an inmate, a volunteer, or a visitor, you are entering a singular alien territory, a private and perplexing enclave, a previously forbidden and perversely exotic kingdom: mysterious, unmapped, and frequently absurd.

I made my first visit to Shane at Frontenac on the Wednesday evening between Christmas and New Year's. Until now, all of our interactions had taken place outside of the prison. As his escort, I'd been as far as the horseshoe often enough, and I'd been to the programs building for the volunteer training session. But I had never been to the visiting room. Like most people, what I imagined was based solely on what I'd seen in movies and on TV. I was eager now to see it for myself. I had a sense of being granted access to the inner sanctum—which, of course, it was not.

I am a curious person by nature. Some people, including Shane, would more likely call me "nosy," and I might even agree. Being perpetually observant and a chronic eavesdropper are traits that have always served me well in my writing life. I would learn soon enough that curiosity is not a desirable trait in the prison world, where asking too many questions and paying too much attention is frowned upon, and especially not in the visiting room, where Shane was always telling me to mind my own business and quit gawking around.

It was snowing as I made the ten-minute drive from my house to the prison, soft wet flakes dropping straight down in the early dark. The faces of the guards around the horseshoe were friendly and familiar. Shane was standing behind the locked glass doors with a cluster of other inmates impatiently awaiting their visitors. All that I could ever know about what went on behind those glass doors was what Shane told me. Separated as it was from the actual interior of the prison, the visiting room gave little indication of the realities of incarceration.

I had locked my purse in the trunk of my car, was bringing in only my driver's licence, some change for the pop machine, my cigarettes and lighter. Back in those days, smoking was still permitted outside. A guard led me down the hallway into a separate room, where I had my first encounter with the ion scanner, a machine used to detect the microscopic presence of drugs. As Shane had advised, I'd thoroughly washed my driver's licence before leaving home. I have no involvement with drugs of any kind, but this machine, he warned me, was notorious for giving false positives. Besides, he said, I could never know what I might inadvertently have come into contact with.

The guard put on a pair of blue latex gloves and wiped both sides of my licence with a small square of white cloth, then inserted the cloth into the mouth of the machine. Much later, the ion scanner would become the bane of my existence, but that night it had nothing to say, and the guard waved me on to the visiting room. Commonly called V&C, which stands for Visits and Correspondence, it is also the place where the inmates are given their mail after it has been opened and checked.

I stepped into a bright open room with windows on three sides and concrete-block walls painted a soft grey blue, a room filled with large square wooden tables, three or four padded wooden chairs pulled up around each. In one corner were the washrooms, and in the opposite corner, the vending machines for pop and chips and chocolate bars. On a small table beside the machines sat a microwave, a toaster oven, and an electric kettle. The Christmas decorations hanging around the room looked forlorn and bedraggled in that way they always do, anywhere, once the big day has passed.

I don't remember if there were already other visitors in the room when I entered. I don't remember which table I sat at as I waited for

Shane to be called down. I don't remember the moment he walked into the room and my visiting life began.

All the details are lost now in the repetition of future visits, in the accumulation of the hundreds of hours I spent in that room over the next nine months. The remarkable strangeness of finding myself in a prison visiting room in the first place has been replaced now in my memory by all that came after, by how easily I became accustomed to the routine, by how soon I forgot about the cameras in the ceiling and the guards in their glass-walled corner office called "the bubble," by how quickly it all became normal. By the miraculous power of adaptation, we humans are masters of the ability to get used to almost anything, for better or for worse, at once a blessing and a curse, both our salvation and our undoing.

Contrary to what I'd seen in movies, the guards were neither menacing nor armed, and there was no sign of scary-looking men in orange jumpsuits behind glass, talking to their visitors on metal telephones. Here, scary-looking or not, the inmates were dressed in either ordinary street clothes or ill-fitting prison-issue jeans and T-shirts, long- or short-sleeved depending on the season, of a particular colour Shane called "joint blue." Over time, I noticed that, whether by coincidence or on principle, none of them ever wore orange.

Although chatting with people at other tables was not encouraged, it was not forbidden either. Most of the women I met in that room didn't fit the stereotype any more than the inmates did. There was the teacher, the secretary, the retired college professor, the nurse, the personal support worker, the yoga instructor. And me—the writer—now part of a sisterhood to which I had never imagined I would belong.

DURING THE REGULAR Tuesday- and Friday-evening visits, there was seldom more than a handful of visitors. But on weekends, with all-day visiting on both days, the room was usually close to full. There were the mothers and fathers (but mostly the mothers) who came to see their sons. Next to Christmas, Mother's Day is said to be the busiest prison visiting day of the year. There were the blue-haired grandmothers who came to see their grandsons, hugging them fiercely and scolding them gently, or vice versa. There were the aunts, uncles, nieces, nephews, cousins, sisters, brothers, and friends. There were the girlfriends, the wives, and the children.

Along the back wall, adjacent to the bubble, was the children's play area with colourful wooden benches, two Fisher-Price high chairs, dozens of toys including a pink plastic stove, a noisy ride-on car, a miniature tea set, and a Talking Elmo. A double bookcase was stocked with books, magazines, and board games. On weekends, there were always children in the room: sleepy or squalling babies, unsteady toddlers just finding their legs, giggling little girls with ribbons in their hair, rambunctious boys galloping around the tables until their parents made them stop. The inmates played cards or Scrabble with their older children, sometimes spreading out books and papers on the table and helping them with their homework. A television set was mounted near the ceiling in one corner, and once the children had tired themselves out, they settled in to watch Disney movies and cartoons—unless it was hockey season, and then we all watched the game. In the evenings, we watched *Jeopardy!* just like I did at home.

For all those hours in the visiting room, I was not distracted or interrupted by all the things constantly clamouring for my attention at home: no phone calls, no emails, no to-do list, no chores or errands, no pets needing to be watered, walked, or fed. I can think of no comparable circumstance in the free world in which a couple has so much time simply to be together and talk.

Week after week, we told each other the intimate stories of our lives—our hopes and dreams, our fears and failures, our doubts and disappointments. Shane was, after all, a captive audience, and I soon felt he knew me better than anybody else in the whole world. And he loved me anyway. I had always been fearful of being my full strange self. I had always felt so unlike other people, so abnormal, such a misfit. A friend used to encourage me to "have the courage of my eccentricities," but I had never really managed it. Now, with Shane, I finally felt I could.

Perhaps it meant more to me than it should have that he seemed to adore everything about me, that he told me every day—several times a day—that I was beautiful and smart and sexy, and he couldn't understand why nobody had snapped me up years ago.

When he asked me what I wanted most in a relationship, in a *man*, I said, "I want someone I can count on, someone who will never let me down."

He said, "I will always keep you safe."

When I said I had no desire for adventure or excitement anymore, that all I wanted from whatever remained of my life was to be peaceful and creative, he agreed wholeheartedly. He said that was exactly what he wanted too. I had no reason then to doubt him.

When not continuing our intense extended conversation, we did crossword puzzles and played Scrabble, cribbage, or other card games. I was allowed to bring my own Scrabble game from home, also a deck of cards and my crib board. I had never been much interested in cards, and, despite Shane's persistent efforts to teach me, my card-playing skills did not improve. He was especially good at bridge and took the regular prison tournaments very seriously. I snickered every time he mentioned them. I had trouble imagining a bunch of convicts sitting around playing bridge, a game I thought of as the bailiwick of refined elderly women in floral dresses, sensible shoes, and pillbox hats.

He was also extremely good at crossword puzzles, to the point of being able to do the entire *New York Times* puzzle in ink every week. I have to confess I was very impressed by this. I also have to confess that before we did that first crossword puzzle together, I figured I'd have to hold back some on filling in those little squares, so as not to seem like I was showing off how smart I was and possibly making him feel bad.

For months I couldn't beat him at Scrabble, not even once, not even close. A ruthless and relentlessly strategic player, he began to accuse me of letting him win, until finally he realized I just wasn't very good at the game. He said he couldn't understand how someone so in love with words could be so bad at Scrabble. It was true that I took the greatest pleasure in playing unusual or interesting words regardless of how few points they were worth. Eventually I realized that Scrabble is not a game of words but of numbers. Then I started to win more and more often. Much as Shane wasn't a gracious winner, he was an even worse loser.

DEPENDING ON WHO WAS ON DUTY, there were varying degrees of intimacy allowed—or at least overlooked—in V&C. Holding hands, sitting close, resting my head on his shoulder, sometimes even kissing. Shane loved kissing more than any other man I'd known. He said this was because although he'd had a lot of sex in his life, not much of it was of the sort that included kissing. I also liked it very much. But when I began frequently breaking out in cold sores, I wondered if maybe we were overdoing it. I've been prone to cold sores since I was a child, but never like this. Shane wondered sheepishly if it might be the bleach. The what? The bleach he used to clean his false teeth, he said, the bleach in which he soaked them every night because the Polident they sold at the canteen was too expensive. Most food items there were discounted, he said, but personal products like vitamins, toothpaste, Gillette razor blades, and

Polident were sold at the full street price. Horrified, I shrieked. If the bleach was giving me cold sores, imagine what it was doing to his insides. He promised he would stop.

Residual bleach was arguably the most dangerous thing I ever encountered in the visiting room. Although I was surrounded by men who had committed an array of serious crimes, some violent and horrific, I never once felt uneasy there. It was a very controlled environment, and the atmosphere was generally comfortable and convivial. This was perhaps an illusion, but it was real enough for all the hours I spent in that room. Visits were a privilege, and all the men were on their best behaviour. If anyone caused trouble, Shane said, V&C would be cleared, and all the visitors would be sent home. Then the trouble-maker would have to face not only whatever punishment might be meted out by the guards, but also the wrath of the inmates who had lost their visits because of him.

We were all living out important parts of our lives in that room, and like all relationships everywhere, ours were not without drama and melodrama, tension and tears, the main difference being that there, privacy was at a premium.

One evening a young woman cried through the entire visit, while her inmate boyfriend tried to comfort her. Her mother had just been diagnosed with terminal cancer. A few weeks later on a Saturday afternoon, two officers stood at the table of this same young couple, spoke quietly to the pair, then led them out of the room. By the end of the day, we all knew that the young man's older brother had been killed in a car accident that morning on the highway east of town.

Sometimes one couple or another would be arguing at their table, him speaking through gritted teeth, her crying and blowing her nose, him reaching for her hand, her pulling away and refusing to look at him. The agitation emanating from any one table rippled around the entire room, while the rest of us tried not to look. One afternoon we happened to be seated right beside a couple in distress and could hear their conversation. She was breaking up with him. She said she'd met someone else, someone not in prison, someone she could have a real life with. This time he was the one crying. It was a short visit. Later that night he walked away from the prison and made the news. He was arrested in Toronto a few days later and sent to a higher-security institution.

I did not imagine then that I would ever be the one crying in the visiting room. But yes, my turn would come.

ONCE VINNIE'S REOPENED IN THE NEW YEAR, we began to settle into our new configuration as a couple. Shane's status as a volunteer had changed, and he was now coming every day on a "work release" rather than on a series of weekly ETAs. This meant he no longer required an approved escort. I drove him back and forth on the days I was volunteering too; otherwise he was transported by someone else from Vinnie's, usually Laura, or Russell, the man who hadn't been allowed to become an escort because of his old criminal record.

The regular lunch patrons were the least surprised by and the most supportive of our romance, teasing us mercilessly, wanting to know if they'd be invited to the wedding. The reaction of the other volunteers was mixed. Laura and Fred from the convent were pleased. But one woman warned me that though he was handsome and charming, he was bound to be a handful, and I'd have to keep him on a short leash. Another said it was all well and good to be nice to him, but what kind of crazy bleeding heart liberal was I to go ahead and fall in love with him? The one who was most bothered by our relationship, Sylvia, said it wasn't appropriate for two volunteers to be romantically involved, as if we were employees of a high-powered corporation breaking a no-fraternization policy. She frequently chastised us for acting like a pair of lovesick teenagers and being too "friendly" in the kitchen, which, she said, was disturbing for everyone. She was especially bothered the day Shane walked to a nearby convenience store and returned with a single red rose for me.

Thanks to Sylvia and the wonders of modern technology, the news of our romance made it all the way to Patagonia. My friend Dorothy and her husband were there visiting their son and his girlfriend, who were teaching English in Chile for a year. Dorothy was not pleased. I knew she wouldn't be. She said maybe her left-wing broad-mindedness didn't go as far as she had thought it did—maybe didn't go all the way to being able to accept that one of her dearest friends had fallen in love with a murderer. She was also hurt that I hadn't told her myself, that she'd had to hear it by email from Sylvia. I said I didn't tell her myself because I knew she'd be upset, and I didn't want to disrupt her time with her family in South America. Also, because I didn't want to listen to her try to talk me out of it. I have never been one to appreciate unsolicited advice, not even from my closest friends.

Once Dorothy had adjusted to the idea some, she seemed as disturbed by the fact that I was going to church every Sunday as by the fact that I was involved with a convict. She had a deep and abiding aversion to organized religion. I had been given permission to meet Shane for mass at the convent. Arriving there each Sunday with the other inmates, once inside, he stayed away from them. We always sat on the other side of the chapel with Laura from Vinnie's, where, he said, he could feel like a normal person. If one of the other inmates dared to get too close to me, Shane would promptly skewer him with his best mean-convict glare.

Dorothy was disturbed again when she called one night and caught me watching a hockey game. It was true that I'd seldom (never) watched a hockey game of my own volition before I met Shane. But he was a committed hockey fan, and I didn't see anything wrong with taking an interest in what mattered to him. After all, I expected him to take an interest in my writing, didn't I? I also reminded her that I had once published a book of stories called *Hockey Night in Canada*, so it wasn't entirely bizarre that I might watch a game now and then. I had to agree, though, when she pointed out that the title story of that book wasn't exactly about hockey, was more about a young girl learning that much as the rules of the game are clear enough on the ice, the same cannot be said of real life.

Shane was a dedicated Detroit Red Wings fan, and for my team, I chose the Chicago Blackhawks, because they were my father's favourite. I cheered for them on his behalf, with fond nostalgia for those childhood Saturday evenings when I watched the game curled up on the couch beside him, eating popcorn, whooping when they scored, groaning when they didn't, trying to understand what "icing" meant when not on top of a cake.

I DIDN'T EXPECT THAT MY OTHER FRIENDS would be overjoyed about my relationship with Shane, and they weren't. Some kept their opinions to themselves, some didn't. Some had already met him, some hadn't. Only one friend, Lily, seemed cautiously pleased, willing to give us the benefit of the doubt and hope for the best.

Evelyn, who also volunteered at Vinnie's for a time, said he was needy and demanding. Given that the exact same thing was once said of me by another woman as one of the reasons she was ending our ten-year friendship, perhaps I didn't pay as much attention to this comment as I should have.

Monica, who knew me when I first moved to Kingston, pointed out that I had always been fond of the bad boys. She had a point. Put me in a room with a hundred men. Imagine that ninety-nine of them were handsome and clean-cut, obviously successful in their expensive tailored suits and Italian leather shoes. Imagine that the hundredth man had long straggly hair, many tattoos, and was wearing a battered black leather jacket and cowboy boots. The hundredth man would always be the man for me, the only one I was interested in and attracted to, the other ninety-nine barely registering on my desirability radar.

Shaking her finger at me, Monica said there was just one thing I had to remember about bad boys.

With trepidation, I asked, "What's that?"

She said, "They're bad."

Walter, another writer, said I was asking for trouble—how could I be so smart in my writing and so stupid in my real life? Walter was the only person who said the word *stupid* out loud and to my face, but I suspect there were others who thought it too. Walter was laughing when he said it and I laughed too, but I never quite forgave him.

Patricia, also a writer, said she didn't understand why I wanted to be with someone like Shane when I'd always been so afraid. She too had known me for a long time, and she too had a point. Yes, I am a frequently fearful and anxious person. Many years ago, at the end of a telephone interview for a national newspaper, the interviewer, a man I knew slightly, said he had one more question, off the record. "What," he asked, "is your default position?" What was my baseline frame of mind when I was neither up nor down but just somewhere in the ordinary middle?

My immediate answer: "Anxiety."

For those of us inclined to it, there is no end to the number of things to feel anxious about. Once anxiety is churning full-steam, it is hard to let go of. After the original source has dissipated or even disappeared

altogether, the anxiety itself lingers, often just shifting over to something else, to whatever presents itself, like a blood-sucking parasite
moving on to a more hospitable host. I find my own anxiety tiresome
(not to mention *tiring*—I am always exhausted in the aftermath), and I
try, not always successfully, to refrain from inflicting it on anyone else.

I seldom feel entirely safe. If I wasn't anxious, stressed, or worried
about something, I would hardly recognize myself. I'm always bracing
myself for the next thing. Try as I might to abide by Susan Sontag's
wise dictum "Do not suffer future pain," I can seldom manage it.

It would seem to be completely counterintuitive for a person like me
to fall in love with a murderer.

Think of it this way. For fifteen years, I had a pure black cat named
Cleo who crossed my path a dozen or more times a day. This, I figured,
was like a vaccination, rendering me immune to all the other black
cats in the world who might accidentally cross my path, towing all that
proverbial bad luck behind them. Shane was my black cat.

Think of it this way. When my son started school, he was timid,
sensitive, small for his age: a prime target, I feared, for bullies. But it
never happened. He was also immensely likeable, and within weeks,
he'd befriended all the bullies he could find. At the time I thought, Oh
no, he's just like me, all too fond of the bad boys. He tells me now that
he did it on purpose, figuring that nobody else would ever bother him
if all the bullies were his friends. He was right.

Shane was an intimidating-looking man, and that convict glare of
his was mean enough to peel paint. All those jailhouse tattoos made
it obvious where he'd been—although there was once a sweet elderly
lady at Loblaws who asked him if he'd been in the navy—and for anyone who knew the language of tattoos, that teardrop made it clear what
he'd done. Perhaps I believed that as the baddest of the bad boys, Shane
would cast a force field around me that would keep all the other bad
boys away, not to mention all the other things there were to be afraid

of in the world. He looked strong and possibly dangerous. With him beside me, I would be too. He would be my protector. This didn't mean I would be his simpering fawn-eyed damsel in distress. It meant he would always look after me. He would always take care of me. No one else ever had.

After many years of unhappy relationships, I'd come to mistrust the feeling of intoxication I always had when falling for a new man. I'd come to the conclusion that this feeling had only ever led me straight down the road to misery. Although I found him attractive, I didn't have that feeling when I met Shane. We were friends first, just like everybody says you should be. This time I thought I had my wits about me. This time I thought, hilarious though it might sound now, that I was proceeding in a mature and reasonable manner. This time I thought I was safe.

There I was, at the age of fifty-two, still believing in dark horses, long shots, exceptions to the rule, swimming against the tide, betting against the odds. There I was, still looking for love in the unlikeliest of places (prison) with the unlikeliest of people (him).

SHANE WAS ALWAYS FORTHCOMING about his criminal history. Soon after we became involved, he presented me with a large package of paperwork. Hefty though these files were, they comprised but a small sampling of his oeuvre. He seemed proud of the vast amount of paperwork he'd accumulated over thirty years in custody, as if it were proof of his importance in the world.

In addition to the AIDS test results I'd insisted on seeing, there were reams of official CSC documents detailing the whole story of his incarcerated life. I was impressed by his candour and his apparent desire to lay all his cards on the table so that I knew exactly what I was getting myself into, as if he were giving me the opportunity to do my due diligence before signing the deal. I joked about it with my friends, pointing out that this was one of the advantages of dating a convict: not only did I always know where he was, but he came with paperwork outlining all the terrible things he'd done in his life, whereas with a regular guy you just had to find out what was wrong with him as you went along.

It occurs to me now that we both came with paperwork: him with all those files and me with all my books. Much as I thought I knew all about him from reading those documents, he thought he knew all about me from reading my books. In the final analysis, perhaps we both looked better—or at least different—on paper than we did in real life.

PATRICIA ALSO SAID SHE HATED TO SEE ME once again falling for an "unavailable" man. But despite being incarcerated, Shane was hardly unavailable. Most weeks we saw each other every day except Thursday, when Vinnie's was closed and there was no visiting. Most weeks I visited him on Tuesday and Friday evenings and on Saturday afternoon. On Sundays I met him at the convent in the morning, and then, after treats in the basement, he and the other inmates were taken back to the prison while I went home, changed my clothes, then went to the prison for the afternoon.

I'd also been given permission to join him at the AA meetings he attended on Wednesday evenings. Each week he and half a dozen other inmates from Frontenac, as well as another group from minimum-security Pittsburgh Institution, were escorted to and from a church in the west end where the meetings were held in the basement.

I quit drinking on my own on May 1, 1992—May Day, May Day! By then I'd had a serious drinking problem for many years. When I finally made up my mind to quit, I didn't go to AA for several reasons: I am not a joiner, I was shy, I was embarrassed, and I knew little about AA, was leery of what I *did* know, all that talk about a Higher Power, the Twelve Steps, and the Big Book. I couldn't imagine myself sitting around with a bunch of strangers, saying, "Hi, my name is Diane, and I'm an alcoholic." I had now been stone-cold sober for almost fifteen years, was long past feeling tempted to have a drink or worrying about a relapse. At first I only went to the AA meetings because I was curious, and Shane wanted me to. But I soon found myself wishing I'd gone there in the first place.

What I found in that basement was a compassionate community of people to whom I didn't have to defend, justify, or otherwise explain myself; people with whom I shared a great many personality traits regardless of how different our lives might be; people who were as ready to laugh as they were to cry, on their own or someone else's behalf. At AA it didn't matter where I came from, how many books I'd published, what I was wearing, how much money I made, or how many times I'd messed up my life. All that mattered was that I was there. Each week I went home after the meeting feeling strengthened and sustained, filled with new ways to think about not only my relationship with alcohol, but also my relationship with the world and myself.

The following spring, Shane and I both celebrated our sobriety birthdays at AA, fifteen years for me, seven for him. He credited a prison doctor with getting him off alcohol and drugs, including heroin. She was, he said, the best doctor he'd had in thirty years inside, and he owed her his life. I was touched by the birthday cards we received from the other members and the Black Forest cake we were served at coffee time. In my other life, only Dorothy had ever acknowledged the importance of each successful year of my sobriety and shared the pride I took in this accomplishment. She had never missed sending me a congratulatory card and did not now.

LESS THAN THREE WEEKS after Shane began working at Vinnie's in January 2006, Stephen Harper was elected the twenty-second prime minister of Canada, his Conservative Party squeezing into power with a minority win. A large part of Harper's platform was his "Tough on Crime" agenda. Despite the fact that the overall crime rate had been declining for at least a decade, this agenda was relentlessly advanced as what was needed to keep Canadians safe: tougher sentencing, tougher punishment, tougher conditions inside, and tougher release restrictions. Bringing sweeping changes to almost every component of the criminal justice system, these measures would do nothing to address the root causes of crime nor to actually prevent crimes from being committed. Much of what Harper proposed was based on the American correctional system as it had evolved during the expansion of its own "War on Drugs" campaign—a process by which the United States had become the world leader in incarceration, with more than two million prisoners nationwide. Even the American Department of Corrections had since admitted that this had done nothing to prevent or reduce crime, and they were now changing direction. The Harper government would continue with this increasingly punitive agenda undeterred by the empirical evidence of its obvious and expensive failure in the United States.

In early 2007, before the implementation of these changes began in earnest, visitors were allowed to bring home-cooked meals to be eaten in V&C. In those days, which we later came to think of as the halcyon days, I could cook a delicious and nutritious meal at home and bring it to the prison in my insulated cooler.

Knowing how much Shane enjoyed food, I brought him familiar

favourites like meat loaf, beef stew, chili, lasagna, perogies, or pork chops. I've never thought of myself as a good cook, but he was impressed. Sometimes I surprised him with dishes he had never tried before: basmati rice, chicken tortilla soup, Greek barley salad, and Chinese pork, one of my mother's recipes featuring stir-fried pork tenderloin, green pepper, and mushrooms. Looking back on it now, I wonder why I never took him a pie.

Shane could bring cutlery and plates from his unit to V&C. In the summer, he could also bring fresh salads made from the produce grown in the large garden tended by the inmates on the prison grounds. I brought cloth placemats from home, and some women brought tablecloths. Once inside, we all went about setting our tables and warming up our dinners in the microwave as if it were the most normal thing in the world to be dishing up dinner in a prison. Soon enough it was. Much as we speak of someone "being" in prison, in fact, the inmates *live* there, and, especially for lifers like Shane, the prison becomes home. It also becomes home away from home for their wives and girlfriends. And me.

IN THOSE DAYS, I WAS ALLOWED to bring books to Shane, five or six every couple of weeks. He had already made his way through most of the small library at Frontenac, where, according to him, the fiction collection was composed mainly of tattered paperback copies of murder mysteries and horror novels. He often lamented the lack of serious literary fiction, especially by Canadian writers. I was more than happy to rectify this problem and spent hours choosing books for him from my shelves. I was disappointed that he didn't much like Alice Munro, pleased to find he shared my love of *The Book of Negroes* by Lawrence Hill, so much so that he passed it on to several other guys before returning it. I was not surprised that he was especially fond of *No Country for Old Men* by Cormac McCarthy. Soon to be sixty years old, he'd often commented on the regrettable fact that jail was no country for old men. Once he requested a copy of *Waiting for Godot*, but returned it unread and without comment.

Each time I arrived at V&C with my bag of books, they were thoroughly checked, not for their literary merit or their suitability for prison consumption but to ensure I hadn't hidden any money, drugs, or weapons between the covers. After they were approved, Shane could keep them in his unit and read them at his leisure. He had a lot more time to read than I ever did. Whenever he would heave a big sigh and say, "I've got nothing to do this afternoon, I guess I'll have to read," I could barely contain my envious annoyance.

IN THOSE DAYS, AT THE END OF EACH VISIT, the inmates were permitted, under the watchful eyes of the guards, to walk out of the building with their visitors, down the front steps, and partway into the parking lot, where they stood behind a yellow line painted on the pavement, waving as their loved ones returned to their cars. One summer Sunday afternoon, after looking back to wave goodbye one more time, I found a woman slumped sobbing against the car next to mine. I was a seasoned visitor by then, and I'd noticed her inside, a new face in the visiting room, a well-dressed woman with stylish blonde hair and expensive-looking jewellery, there to see her son, who looked about the same age as mine. He was tall and slender, clean-cut with big brown eyes and a shy grin. They could have been brothers, her son and mine. Shane said the boy had arrived just a few days before, apparently on a drug charge.

Shane had warned me many times not to get too friendly with the other visitors, not to get involved in their problems. He said you never knew who might be up to something, bringing in drugs or money, and CSC was big on guilt by association. There was also something he called "We think, we feel, we believe"—meaning suspicions were enough for CSC. They didn't have to *prove* anything before punishing you for it. But I could not, in good conscience, just walk past this crying woman, get into my car, and drive happily away.

I glanced back at the building. Both Shane and her son had gone inside. All the inmates had. Only a single guard still stood on the steps watching us. I fully expected him to come charging out to the parking lot and send me on my way, but still, I had to say something.

"Are you okay?" I asked, for want of a better opening. Obviously she was not.

"No, no, no," she sobbed. "I can't bear it. I can't bear to see him in there. I can't bear to drive away and leave him."

I made comforting noises and patted her arm. The guard remained on the steps, watching but not moving towards us.

She said, "He told me not to worry. He said, 'I'm okay here, Mom. I'm making friends here already. Don't worry about me, Mom. I like it here.'"

Telling me this made her cry even harder. I felt tears prickling my eyes too.

She looked at me desperately and said, "How can you stand it? How can you do this over and over again, just driving away and leaving your fellow in there?"

I said, "He is not my son."

IN ADDITION TO ALL THE TIME WE SPENT TOGETHER, Shane was also sending me cards and letters two or three times a week. I didn't hear the term "love-bombing" until much later. His love letters were usually handwritten but sometimes typed. There were a few computers available for inmate use. Each inmate had his own floppy disk containing his files and a few games, but they did not have Internet access at any time. Stamps, envelopes, writing paper, and cards could be purchased at the canteen. There was a limited selection of free cards in the chapel too. I wondered if the guards who checked the outgoing mail were amused to find, behind the religious sentiment with lilies and cherubs on the front, the less angelic and more lascivious declarations of Shane's love and passion.

I didn't have time to send him cards and letters. Our relationship was making for a much busier schedule than I was used to. I was always trying to find time for housework, errands, cooking, and laundry, not to mention my son, my pets, my friends, and my writing. I was often tired, cranky, and overwhelmed, a messy state of mind Shane called "frazzled." Generally speaking, I prefer to do the same things every day in the same way, and I am mightily resentful when my routine is disrupted. I was now so busy that I couldn't remember the last time I'd had a quiet routine day.

Sometimes I considered cutting down on the number of visits, but I knew how much they meant to Shane. I was his only visitor. His mother and other family members lived nearby, but I'd never seen them visit him. He said they used to, but over the years their visits had dwindled down to nothing. He thought they couldn't be bothered and had given up on him. He thought they were ashamed of him.

I was not ashamed of him. I'd like to say I never hid my relationship with Shane from anyone. But that's not strictly true. I was well aware that there was a stigma attached to having a relationship with a prison inmate, and that even in a prison town like Kingston, it wasn't something everyone would find acceptable.

I had entered this territory as a neophyte, but I soon developed an instinct for knowing who and who not to tell. This wasn't because I was ashamed of him, but because there were awkward conversations I preferred to avoid. In certain situations where I didn't know the people involved, I thought it best to prevaricate. Once, at a book club gathering made up of snobbish wealthy conservative matrons, I mentioned his name a few times when we were having coffee afterwards.

One woman then asked the classic small-talk question: "What does your husband do?"

Have I mentioned that I do not suffer snobs gladly? Give me a fool any day.

Without saying he wasn't my husband and without consciously deciding to skirt the issue, I said, "He's with Corrections." (True.)

She said, "Oh, that's interesting. How long has he been with them?"

I said, "Thirty years." (Also true.)

She said, "He'll be getting ready to retire soon then."

I said, "Yes." (More or less true, depending on how you interpret the word *retire*.)

THE ONE THING THAT MADE THE HECTIC SCHEDULE of that first year bearable, if not any less stressful, was that we believed it wouldn't last long. Shane was almost out. His next parole hearing would be in August or September. Having been turned down for day parole to an Ottawa halfway house last year, he had now set his sights on a house in Peterborough, a small city about two hundred kilometres west of Kingston.

Despite the number of correctional institutions in Kingston, there is only one federal halfway house for men in the city, and it was mainly taking sex offenders, was no longer accepting lifers. The

Salvation Army's Harbour Light facility accepted a limited number of federal parolees, but after Shane applied and met with them, it was determined that he was not eligible, because he didn't have a current substance abuse problem. He was born and raised in the Kingston area and his entire support network was here, but because he was neither a sex offender nor a drug addict, he would have to go elsewhere to complete his day parole, which would take at least a year, possibly longer.

Although we weren't entirely sure how we'd manage a long-distance relationship, he assured me repeatedly that once he got to Peterborough, everything would be wonderful. I wanted to believe him. So I did.

∞

LIKE ANYBODY WHO FALLS IN LOVE with someone who has a child, even a child who is twenty-one years old and technically an adult, Shane struggled to figure out the nature of his relationship with Alex. Should he be his father figure? Should he be his buddy? Should he be some combination of both or something else entirely? Having been a single parent from the beginning, I didn't know either.

Alex's father was a man I'd been with very briefly out west. By the time I found out I was pregnant, he had disappeared, and I was glad of that. Alex had never met him, nor ever expressed any desire to do so. Shane had once jokingly offered to have someone find him and "dump him." In my world, getting or being dumped meant the sudden end of a relationship. In his world, it meant something else. I said, "No thanks, we're good."

Now, in an effort to spend more time with Alex, Shane suggested that he submit a visiting application too. Once he was approved, we chose a Tuesday evening near the end of February to visit Shane together. I made a pot of chili, put it in a Tupperware container in the cooler along with sour cream, grated cheese, fresh buns. Once inside, I set the table, while Shane and Alex heated up the chili and the buns. Shane had two large bowlfuls. For dessert we had peanut butter cookies baked by one of the other guys in his unit. The rest of the evening passed quickly with conversation and Shane trying to teach Alex how to play cribbage. He, like his mother, has no natural aptitude for cards.

Near the end of the visit, Shane had the prison photographer called down. For a dollar a photo, inmates could have their pictures taken in V&C by the inmate who'd been given this job—a job more sought after than many, I supposed, and one, I observed over the years, filled by men with varying levels of ability or lack thereof.

There we were in the photograph, all three of us grinning at the camera with a still life of three placemats, three cans of Coke, a pair of salt and pepper shakers, and the crib board on the table in front of us. Behind us was the microwave and three large uncurtained windows blank with winter darkness.

Whether taken inside V&C or out in the yard, these photos were always carefully posed to be sure that no other people were accidentally included in the frame and to be sure there was nothing in the shot to identify the setting as a prison. Perhaps this was done so the pictures could be put in the family album without embarrassment or explanation, or perhaps it was another instance of CSC protecting its own privacy.

The next morning, when I picked up Shane to go to Vinnie's, we agreed the visit had been a great success. But he said he wasn't feeling well; his stomach was upset and he had terrible gas. He joked that perhaps I'd poisoned him with my chili. I said no, I hadn't, but I'd keep that idea in mind for future reference. By mid-morning he was feeling worse and asked me to take him back to the prison.

After I did, I returned to Vinnie's to finish serving lunch. Because we were left short-handed on what proved to be an exceptionally busy day, I didn't get home until well after two o'clock, at which point I headed directly for the couch. I was almost asleep when the phone rang. I could see by the call display that it was him. Annoyed at having my nap interrupted, I let it ring. He called right back. This time I answered it, even more annoyed.

"I'm bleeding like a stuck pig," he said without preamble. He was going to KGH, Kingston General Hospital. The ambulance was on its way.

I knew this must be serious. If it was anything less than life-threatening, he'd be taken to the hospital at Kingston Penitentiary instead. He had time to explain only briefly that after sleeping for a couple of hours, he had decided to have a bath. In the tub, he started vomiting blood. He was barely conscious when Lenny barged in and found him in the blood-filled tub. Lenny pulled him out and called for help on the emergency phone to the horseshoe. The guards came on the run, he said, and then I could hear them pulling him away from the phone. The ambulance had arrived.

I spent the next hour pacing around the house. As a visitor, I was only supposed to call the prison in the event of an emergency. Surely this qualified. I was put through to the keeper on duty. The person in charge of the daily operations of the prison, the keeper, next to the warden, is the boss of the place and much more accessible. Today it was one of the female keepers, Irene Henry, of whom I was especially fond. Kind and concerned, she said Shane was still in Emergency, but I could not go there or contact him by phone. All I could do was wait. Irene said if he was admitted, then I'd be allowed to visit him, but this would have to be arranged through Regional Headquarters.

After I'd spent a long sleepless night with no news, the phone rang early the next morning. I didn't recognize the name or number in the call display. When I grabbed the receiver, a male voice introduced himself as Father Monaghan calling from KGH. I assumed the worst, that Shane was dead or dying, and the priest was there to perform the last rites. But no, he was quick to assure me he was at the hospital to minister to someone else, and Shane was still very much alive, recovering in Emergency from what they'd now determined was an esophageal bleed.

Shane had told me he had something called Barrett's Esophagus. When I'd looked it up, I'd discovered this is a complication of GERD (gastroesophageal reflux disease) in which the normal tissue that lines the esophagus changes to tissue resembling that of the intestinal lining. Considered a premalignant condition, Barrett's Esophagus significantly increases the risk of esophageal cancer, for which the mortality rate is over 85 per cent. Most patients diagnosed with esophageal cancer survive for less than one year.

Father Monaghan said that although it was against the rules, Shane had begged him to call me and let me know he was okay. "He's a very persuasive man, your Shane," the priest said, chuckling.

By the next morning, Shane had been discharged and taken back to Frontenac. He called as soon as he got there, his usually deep strong voice so weak I could hardly hear him. He said if I called Irene Henry again, maybe she'd let me come for a visit that afternoon. Irene was agreeable to this, and I was allowed to go and sit with him for an hour. One of the prison nurses led him into V&C and sat at the table with us. He was pale and shaky but already trying to make light of it.

"Don't worry," he said. "I'm going to live to be a hundred."

"He will too," joked the nurse. "He'll live forever just to spite the rest of us."

Shane said with a weak smile, "Only the good die young."

SHANE CONTINUED TO HAVE MONTHLY seventy-two-hour passes to Kenworth. Although I'd passed the Community Assessment, this series of UTAs was approved to his mother's, and he was still not allowed to sleep overnight at my house. Vera had dropped the niceties of the Christmas pass. Now when we came through the door, she no longer welcomed or even greeted us. Now she started talking where she'd left off the previous month, with a long litany of complaints about her health, her neighbours, her cleaning lady, and Shane.

The hostility between them escalated each month, as did the list of things she wanted done. Our first task each time was to go grocery shopping for her. She had her extensive list and the money ready. This despite the fact that I seldom saw her eat anything except toast and pie. She already had enough food jammed into her freezer to feed a family of twelve for a year, as well as enough toilet paper packed ceiling-high in the hall closet to last well into the next decade.

The first time Shane and I went together to the Loblaws in Kenworth, we briefly lost track of each other in the sprawling store. I found him in the produce department, standing stock-still in front of an artful display of red and green apples stacked in a perfect pyramid, so shiny they were fairly glowing. It wasn't even apple season.

Transfixed before them with his head slightly bowed, he looked as if he were praying. "They are so beautiful," he said softly, and he kissed me.

Not every grocery shopping expedition was as poignant as that first one. Vera was very particular, and her lists were very specific. Once, next to the word *milk*, in brackets she'd written *like homo*. In front of the dairy case, we studied the many varieties of milk for several minutes.

"There it is," I said finally, pointing to a carton that announced in large letters with an exclamation mark, TASTES LIKE HOMO!

"Tastes like homo?" Shane said loudly, grinning. "How does my mother know what a homo tastes like?"

"How old are *you?*" I snarled.

A man standing near us snickered. I turned on my heel and stormed away, charging down the aisle with the half-filled cart in front of me and Shane with the milk in his hand and his mouth hanging open behind me.

Regardless of how careful we were with Vera's shopping, she was never satisfied. We always got something wrong: the wrong soup, the wrong crackers, the wrong pie. After each shopping trip, there were harsh words, directed not at me but at Shane, who, according to Vera, could do nothing right, never had been able to, never would be able to, and it was no bloody wonder he ended up in prison.

I had problems with my mother too, but not to this extreme. Long after her death, my aunt Clara, congratulating me on my Governor General's Award win, said it was a wonder I'd ever accomplished anything at all, considering how hard my mother had been on me. But her methods of denigration were usually more subtle, if no less insidious, than Vera's. Except when we hit puberty and meno-pause in the same year, and she began telling me often that I was a mistake and she had never wanted me anyway. Except when I told her I was pregnant, unmarried with no man in sight, and she temporarily disowned me, would not answer my letters or speak to me on the phone.

By the time Alex was born, she was over it enough to spend some time with him, her only grandchild, before she died of cancer eighteen months later. When Alex and I flew to Thunder Bay for her funeral, I discovered that she had not told a single person about him, not even her best friend, with whom she had coffee almost every afternoon. Her friend was so hurt and angry that she refused to go to the funeral. She stayed home and looked after Alex instead.

SOMETIMES VERA'S SHOPPING LIST EXTENDED beyond groceries, involving then a trip to Walmart for a rubber mat for the patio door (because Shane never wiped his feet properly), a vegetable steamer (there was never fresh produce of any kind in her kitchen), or a dozen washcloths (which must not be too fluffy, she said; she couldn't stand the fluffy ones). I chose the thinnest washcloths I could find.

One day she requested a new bedside lamp, because her old one was broken. I could see how much, despite everything, Shane still wanted to please her. I could also see this was never going to happen. I realize now that me trying to please him was a mission as impossible as him trying to please his mother or me trying to please mine. That day, when he led Vera into the bedroom to show off the new lamp he'd chosen and installed, she said it wasn't as good as the old one, but it would have to do. He was angry and unreachable for the rest of the day, mired in the miserable state of mind he called "twisted."

Vera often tried to engage me in a rousing round of Shane-bashing, but I wouldn't play. She told me stories of the awful things he'd done as a child, the way another mother might have shown me his baby pictures. Soon her nastiness was extended to cover me too. I ignored her. Easy for me—she wasn't *my* mother. I tried to help Shane by suggesting that instead of going over to the dark side with her, he should stay in the light with me. This made sense to him, and it almost worked. But he could never resist her cruelty for long.

When the weather warmed up, we spent as much time away from her apartment as possible. We went for walks, we washed the car, and occasionally we stopped in to visit his relatives who lived on the other

side of town. These visits were unpredictable and often included someone saying, "I'll never speak to you again. You are dead to me." I told
Shane that much as I was prepared to take on him and all his issues,
I was *not* prepared to take on his entire dysfunctional family. He said
that was fine with him.

We fell into the habit of having picnic lunches in the park beside the
river in the shadow of the train bridge. One afternoon we saw a great
blue heron standing on one leg on a rock in the middle of the river.
I had never seen one before, and was awed by its dignified stillness.
After eating our lunch, we would spread a blanket on the grass beneath
one of the big trees and read together in the shade. Usually Shane fell
asleep beside me. Sometimes we had ice cream cones and pretended
we were carefree and young again. Now, whenever I happen to be on
the train going over that bridge, I look down and try to see us sitting
there, innocent and peaceful. But nothing looks familiar.

After a few months I stopped sleeping over at Vera's in the little pull-
out bed. Instead, after we made love, I got up, got dressed, and drove
home. I couldn't bear to be around her any more than I had to, nor
to watch how Shane changed in the face of her abuse. His responses
to her taunts and jibes became increasingly rancorous and vindictive.
The two of them would then became so furiously embroiled in painful
episodes from their shared past that it was as if these things had happened last week, not fifty years ago. I could do nothing to stop them
and usually fled to the patio, where I'd sit smoking and feeding peanuts
to the squirrels while inside they continued attacking each other. At
the end of a weekend of such venomous acrimony, I could not bear to
watch Vera hug him, slip him some money, and tell him she loved him.
I could not bear to hear him say he loved her too.

Soon we were spending more and more hours of our pass days
in Kingston instead. Each time, our itinerary was approved by Jerry
Anderson. As long as Shane slept at Vera's, we could spend some of our

time in Kingston. The day after each pass, I called Jerry to report that all had gone well. He didn't seem to require a lot of detail, and I didn't say much about the difficulties with Vera other than that she was hard to get along with. Now when I took Shane to or picked him up at her apartment, I didn't even go inside. I just dropped him off and drove back home or waited in the car for him to come out.

Having so little time alone together, we tended not to socialize much during the hours we had in Kingston. Mostly it was just the two of us playing house, delighting in these short stretches of freedom. On the days we spent together at my house without guards, security cameras, or his mother, we were finally able to make love alone when Alex was at work. We were getting to know each other's bodies and the unbridled pleasures of my queen-size bed. There was time now for tenderness, playfulness, and the perfection of his already excellent foot-rubbing and full-body massage techniques.

Each time we went into the bedroom and shut the door, Nelly stood on the other side barking the entire time. When we opened the door afterwards, she'd come bounding up onto the bed, licking my face and then Shane's until he squealed like a little girl. I imagined she'd eventually get used to our closed-door sojourns, but she never did.

SHANE'S PERSISTENCE IN PURSUING A PLACE at the Peterborough halfway house was paying off. He was invited to go and stay there for a seventy-two-hour UTA in May. This would be an audition of sorts, on the basis of which they would decide whether to accept him for residency. Just as if he actually lived there, he would be required to sleep there at night and otherwise abide by the rules of the house. During the day, we'd be free to explore the city together, Shane having to check in by phone every four hours. He would also have to be interviewed at the police station and the Parole Office. I made a reservation at the Best Western and took my car in for a tune-up.

Because I am afraid of driving on the 401, said to be the busiest highway in North America and stretching up to eighteen lanes across at some points, I mapped out a more northerly route on the secondary highways. It was a warm and sunny spring day, with only light traffic on an early Tuesday afternoon. The trip took exactly three hours door-to-door from the prison to the halfway house.

Our visit began with a guided tour of the facility. Situated close to downtown, it was a large well-kept two-storey house near the end of a one-way street. Run by the St. Leonard's Society, it was a Community Residential Facility (CRF), meaning that it was under contract to, but not operated directly by, CSC. This house specialized in working with older lifers like Shane and generally did not accept those inmates they referred to as the "young warriors." It contained eighteen beds for the residents, two per room, and two cots for visiting inmates, one of which had been set up for Shane in the basement common room.

On the main floor, across from the office area, was a comfortably shabby living room. Sitting on the couch watching TV was a grey-haired man Shane recognized from some prison somewhere decades ago. They greeted each other with much back-slapping and grinning. The large bright kitchen, homey despite its commercial-sized appliances, was the domain of not one but two cooks, both middle-aged women named Alice. Around the corner was the eating area, where snacks and coffee were available throughout the day and evening. Enjoying coffee and muffins at one of the tables were two more grey-haired men Shane recognized. More back-slapping and grinning. "It's like an old-age home for convicts," Shane said happily.

While he met with the director and the supervisor, I went to the Best Western and checked in. The room was on the ground floor at the back, with a sliding glass door to a wooden patio just steps away from the banks of the Otonabee River. Waddling along the edge of the river was a Canada goose with six yellow goslings toddling along behind her. After coaxing them one by one into the water, she proceeded with what looked like a swimming lesson, and within minutes they were all bobbing in circles on the river. On the grassy bank were a dozen mallard ducks that came quacking towards me in straggly single-file the minute I slid open the patio door. Obviously they were used to being fed by the hotel guests.

When I picked Shane up later in the afternoon, he was pleased with how his interview had gone, was almost sure he'd get in. On the way to the hotel, we stopped and bought a loaf of bread for the ducks. Just as we got into the room, my cell phone rang. It was Dorothy. I got comfortable on the bed for a chat, and Shane went outside to feed the ducks. When he came back in fifteen minutes later, I was still on the phone. I could see by his face that he was angry, but I couldn't imagine why. I wound up the conversation and said goodbye to Dorothy.

As often happened, he wouldn't tell me what was wrong. He repeatedly denied being upset, but his voice was slippery with recrimination, and he would not look at me. Eventually I wormed it out of him. Knowing that Dorothy had her reservations about our relationship, he didn't like the fact that she'd called "to check up on me," that she was worried about me being out of town alone with someone like *him*. By this time I knew that whenever anybody, including Shane himself, said "someone like *him*" what they meant was a murderer.

It didn't matter how many times I assured him that this was not the case, that Dorothy *always* called me when I was out of town because we were *friends* and because she knew I didn't like being away from home. He did not believe me. We'd been a couple for six months now, and I already knew that once he had a thought in his head, it would stay there, no matter how much evidence was offered to the contrary. Unlike the rest of us, who have come to realize that not all our thoughts are right, reasonable, or even sane, Shane seemed to give complete credence to every single thought that came into his mind, and no amount of reality would dislodge it. He also found it hard to believe that not everything was about him.

This time I was the one who went outside to feed the ducks.

As darkness fell, he came and stood beside me on the riverbank. He put his arm around my waist and sighed. I knew this was as close as he was likely to come to an apology. I thought about how easy it would be to push him in the river. That old Talking Heads song "Take Me to the River" was playing in my head. The rocks were slippery. It was dark. He had a bad leg. He didn't know how to swim. It would look like an accident. No one would ever suspect someone like *me*. After all, *he* was the murderer.

We got in the car, and I drove him back to the halfway house hours ahead of his curfew.

Two weeks later, Janice Mackie requested a meeting with both of us. As soon as we sat down, she handed Shane a letter. Reading it, he began to grind his teeth in the disturbing way he did when trying to control his emotions. The Peterborough house had accepted him.

Janice congratulated him, reminded him that now he'd have to start thinking of himself as an ex-con instead of a convict. Then she got down to business. His hearing would take place in early September, and she would support him in his request for day parole. We had about three and a half months to prepare. Of course, I had no experience with parole hearings. The closest thing in my world to which I could liken it was having to defend your thesis, but the topic, in this case, was your criminal life and the outcome was not a degree but an increased measure of freedom. And it was a thesis you would have to defend not just once, but over and over and over again.

Janice went through the details of how we might prepare. Then she said, "Here's a tip. Whatever you do at that hearing, don't grind your teeth like that!" and asked him to leave the room.

As soon as the door closed behind him, she looked at me grimly and asked, "Do you know what he did?"

I said, "Yes, I do."

She said, "Tell me."

Apparently she was satisfied with my reply. She asked if I intended to move to Peterborough, it being common practice for the wives and girlfriends of long-term prisoners to follow them from place to place. I said no, I wouldn't be moving. My life was established here in Kingston, my son still lived with me, I owned my own home. For whatever length of time Shane had to live in Peterborough, we would manage long-distance, with him coming home on weekend passes. She seemed to approve of this plan.

She called Shane back in. "This woman loves you," she said. "I don't know why, but she does. If you screw this up, I'll have you back in jail so fast you won't know what hit you." As if, for a lifer, failing at a relationship was a criminal offence.

Then she showed us the door.

WHEN VINNIE'S CLOSED FOR THE SUMMER, we told them we wouldn't be coming back in the fall, because Shane would be in Peterborough. At least we hoped he would. This was how it went when attempting to plan your life around CSC. We didn't know for sure what was going to happen, but we had to plan ahead as if we did.

He began working as a groundskeeper at the Cataraqui Cemetery. Established in 1850 and now designated as a National Historic Site, the cemetery occupies over ninety acres, designed with curving intersecting avenues like streets in a town. It is the final resting place of many historically significant people including Sir John A. Macdonald; John Creighton, once mayor of Kingston, also warden of Kingston Penitentiary from 1871 until his death in 1885; William Cloverdale, architect and master builder of KP; Henry Traill, son of author Catharine Parr Traill, nephew of Susanna Moodie and Agnes Strickland, and the first Kingston prison guard to be killed in the line of duty, beaten to death by two convicts in July 1870 as they made their escape from KP. In a city as old as Kingston, first capital of Canada, history is everywhere, and prison is always part of it.

Although it was sometimes difficult with his bad leg, Shane was much happier doing physical work outdoors than he had been cooped up in the crowded kitchen at Vinnie's. Besides, as he pointed out, it was much quieter there. I too like cemeteries for their restful qualities. Our pass days that summer included several visits to the cemetery, where he showed me the gardens he'd worked on, and we explored the avenues. Most of the 46,000 people buried there were not historically significant at all but just ordinary people who had lived out their assorted lives for better or worse, then ended up here, their stories buried with them.

We discussed where we'd like to be buried. From early on, Shane had often talked about how he wanted us to be buried together, side by side in a double plot. Peculiar as this might have been, it was comforting too. He also talked from early on about getting married. After he was divorced from Brandy, of course. They were still legally married but hadn't seen each other in seven or eight years.

He arranged his July pass to Vera's to coincide with my birthday. I turned fifty-three that year, and he surprised me not only with a cake, but also with a ring. With Vera's help, he'd ordered it from the Sears catalogue, a slim silver band with a setting of imitation diamonds and rubies, ruby being the gemstone for July. I must have hesitated when he gave it to me, because he was quick to assure me it was *not* an engagement ring. When the time came for that, he said, he'd buy me a real diamond, a big one. If I did hesitate, it was not because of the ring or the difficulties of the relationship itself, but because I wished Vera had had nothing to do with it.

At Frontenac, visiting felt freer in the summer, because we could now go outside to the visiting yard, an area just like any other family park anywhere, except maybe for the chain-link fence around it. But it was an ordinary chain-link fence, not more than four feet high, the kind you see all over the city. We sat at one of the wooden picnic tables arranged around the edges beneath large leafy trees. There was no air conditioning inside, so the shade was much appreciated, as was the fact that in the yard we could smoke. We watched the groundhogs ducking into and out of their burrows, tunnelling under the field adjacent to the yard, popping up by the bulrushes in the swampy area on the other side, comically perched on their haunches, swivelling their heads and sniffing the air in all directions.

A large flock of Canada geese lived on the prison grounds. Driving in towards the parking lot, I often had to wait while a gaggle of them waddled nonchalantly across the road. They didn't venture into the visiting yard when it was in use but evidently spent some time there when no one was around. Walking across the tidily mown lawn to the picnic tables was an intricate exercise in tiptoeing through the goose poop.

If we sat with our backs to the stone wall of Collins Bay, we could look across the yard to the baseball diamond and the wooded area beyond the swamp. There we sometimes spotted a single white-tailed deer poised at the edge of the trees and, once, a coyote loping down to the swamp. The fragrance from the cow barns often drifted into the yard, pungent but not unpleasant. From this vantage point, it was easy enough to forget we were in a prison—easy enough, for that matter, to forget we were in the middle of a city at all.

Occasionally a pair of guards came outside and strolled around the yard, but mostly they left the surveillance to several cameras installed in strategic locations around the grounds, cameras so high-powered, it was said, they could see all the way to the far parking lot, perhaps all the way to the shopping mall across the street, which wasn't even visible to the naked eye from where we sat.

The outside children's area was a small playground in the middle of the yard, compact but complete with a combination slide and climbing structure, a sandbox, and a swing. Near each picnic table was a small cast-iron barbecue mounted on a metal post cemented into the ground. In those days, visitors could bring in a bag of charcoal, meat for the grill, and all the other requisite ingredients for a tasty afternoon barbecue. We could even bring our own lawn chairs from home.

Alex joined us a few times for these barbecue visits, he and Shane together overseeing the grilling of the hamburgers or hot dogs, or even steaks if I'd found some on sale. Fortunately Alex was not there the day one of the wives was caught giving her husband a blowjob at the table in the far corner of the yard. After we ate, we often played a few rounds on the overgrown nine-hole mini-golf course just outside the yard, something inmates were only allowed to do when they had visitors.

Seeing how much we all enjoyed the barbecuing, I decided to buy a barbecue for home. I'd once had a small gas one but was afraid of the propane tank and seldom used it. Eventually I gave it away. Now I certainly didn't want and couldn't afford one of those fancy gas barbecues that look almost as big as my car. At Canadian Tire, I bought a bag of briquettes and an old-fashioned round metal grill on legs, much like the one we had back in Thunder Bay when I was young. In addition to its nostalgia value, the little barbecue was also a nod to the future, to the day when Shane came home to stay, and we could barbecue in the backyard together, the three of us, just like a real family.

SHANE'S HEARING WAS SCHEDULED for a Friday morning in early September. I submitted my Request to Observe a Parole Hearing. Anyone over the age of eighteen can apply to observe a hearing provided they have a valid reason for wanting to be there and pass the standard background security checks. An application would not be approved if the Board determined that the observer's presence would disrupt the hearing or otherwise jeopardize "the security and good order of the institution."

I wrote my letter of support to the Parole Board. Janice said it shouldn't be more than two pages—given the enormous volume of Shane's accumulated paperwork, she said, they already had more than enough to read.

I worked on that letter for days. I described the development of our relationship over the past twenty months. I told them about my writing career and about my son. I assured them that while Alex, like many young men, may have harboured some delusions about the "glamour" of the criminal life, Shane had gone to great lengths to demonstrate that this was not the way to live and there was nothing glamorous about it. I told them I understood that, as a lifer, Shane would always be under the supervision of CSC. I assured them that I understood this would have an impact on my life too and that I would help ensure that he met all the requirements of parole.

I moved myself to tears as I wrote the final sentence: *Shane and I share a joyful vision of our future together, and we intend to do everything we can to make these dreams come true.*

ON THE MORNING OF THE HEARING, I met Shane and Stuart from LifeLine in the visiting room at eight o'clock. Stuart would serve as Shane's assistant, helping him through the panel process and speaking on his behalf at the end of the hearing. We were joined by Fred from Vinnie's, also attending as a supportive observer. I was glad I wouldn't have to sit by myself. As observers, Fred and I were not allowed to speak unless the Board chose to address or question us directly.

Of course we were all hoping for the best, but we had no idea how today's decision might go. Last year Shane had handled being turned down quite well, and I knew he would again this year if he had to. It was all part of the process. Much as this was the first parole hearing I had ever attended, he'd already been through many. I reminded him one more time that no matter what the outcome of this hearing, I loved him and our relationship would continue.

Just before eight-thirty, Janice Mackie took us upstairs to the hearing room. Shane sat between her and Stuart at a long conference table facing an identical table across the room at which the three Board members were already seated, two men and one woman. I took my place in a chair at the side, Shane to my right and the Board members to my left. Directly across from me sat the hearing officer, who outlined the details of how the hearing would proceed.

Janice spoke first and was very positive about Shane's progress in the two years she had been his parole officer. She noted that Jerry Anderson was out of town but had expressed no concerns and supported Shane's request to go to Peterborough as well.

The lead Board member then began by referring to Shane's first criminal charge for break and enter back in 1969. I had been warned that a hearing could go on for hours. Now I was thinking, Good God, how long is this going to take?

The questions continued, coming primarily from the lead Board member, with the other two interjecting with questions of their own. They were serious but not unpleasant as they progressed fairly quickly to his index offence, the murder of Philip Bailey in 1981. After covering this in graphic detail, they moved on to questions about his marriage to Brandy in 1994 and his subsequent escape in 1996. In his thoughtful lengthy answers, Shane displayed sincerity, honesty, and considerable insight into his own past actions. He remained focused and composed, and he did not grind his teeth. Eventually they made their way to the present and our relationship.

To Shane the lead Board member said, "She's here. Be careful what you say." There was quiet laughter around the room. Shane began to cry as he talked about me. The hearing officer passed him a box of Kleenex.

The lead Board member noted that Shane had received a number of strong support letters and singled mine out as being "exceptional and very well-written." This time we all laughed out loud.

After an hour and a half, we were asked to leave the room, all of us except the Board members and the hearing officer. Janice went to her office, and Shane, Stuart, Fred, and I went back down to V&C to await the decision. We were anxious, hopeful, and prepared to be disappointed all at once. Within ten minutes, Janice reappeared to take us back upstairs. She said the speed of the decision could be a good sign or a bad sign. Only one way to find out. Returning to the hearing room, we again took our seats.

When the lead Board member said, "Day parole is granted," it was all we could do not to leap up and cheer. Then he explained the conditions they had imposed: in addition to abiding by all the rules and requirements of the halfway house, Shane must not consume, purchase, or possess alcohol or drugs; must not enter any establishment where the primary source of income is alcohol; must not associate with anyone involved in criminal activity; must follow any psychological counselling as arranged by his parole officer. These are standard conditions for most federal parolees.

In conclusion, smiling, the lead Board member said, "You are a very fortunate man to have found someone who will help you in your return to society. You must cater to and develop this support. You must cherish this woman who loves you."

PART TWO

September 2007 to October 2008

We'd been warned that it could be a month or more before there was room at the halfway house, but only a week after the hearing, a bed became available. He was to be there on Wednesday at noon. We had four days to get ready. He didn't have much to pack: clothes, toiletries, shoes, lamp, CD player, paperwork, photographs, a few keepsakes he'd managed to hang onto over the years. Also his three-ring binder full of certificates in plastic sheet protectors—from the university courses in sociology, philosophy, and anthropology he'd taken by correspondence; from the Bible studies he'd done through the convent; from the dozens of CSC programs he'd completed over the years: Anger and Emotions Management, Alternatives to Violence, Cognitive and Living Skills, Community Integration, Personal Development.

Trying to think of things that would help keep him occupied on his own in Peterborough, I put a selection of pens and blank notebooks into the box I was making for him. I also added two paint-by-number kits.

He once said Lenny did these and he'd like to try it too, so I bought him a pair of lighthouse scenes to signify the light at the end of the tunnel and a pair of wolves in the forest because the wolf was his favourite animal.

For sentimental value, I gave him the old pillow from my childhood bed that I had kept safe with me for over thirty years and the carved wooden cane I once gave my father, returned to me by the nursing home after his death.

THE EVENING BEFORE I WAS TO DRIVE Shane to Peterborough, I made what I believed would be my last visit to Frontenac. One of the officers on duty was Lorne Matheson, a man who'd been with CSC as long as Shane, on the opposite side of the fence, as it were. I found it ironic and oddly touching that inmates and officers alike invariably phrased it in the same way: "I've done thirty years." To hear Shane and Lorne tell it, they were both angry and aggressive when they were young, their conflicts frequent and intense. But now they had both mellowed considerably and were friends, or at least as close to friends as they could be in this context. Lorne was a member of Shane's Case Management Team, and he'd even written a support letter to the Parole Board in which he described him as "a model inmate." I had already noticed that in prison, the standard of what constituted model behaviour was set quite low. Still, this was a valuable recommendation, perhaps the prison equivalent to having your favourite famous author write a glowing blurb for the back of your new book.

When I went in that evening, Shane was waiting impatiently behind the glass doors as usual, and Lorne seemed especially glad to see me. He and Shirley, one of my favourite female officers, led me down the hallway to the ion scanner. I handed Lorne my driver's licence for testing as usual. He swiped it and put the little square of cloth into the machine.

Within seconds, it sounded the alarm indicating that the presence of drugs had been detected, an alarm loud enough to be heard all the way back to the horseshoe and beyond, all the way to behind the glass doors where Shane was standing.

In more than a hundred visits during the past nine months, I had never once hit positive on the machine. How could it be happening *now*? How could it be happening *tonight* of all nights? I was well aware of the dismal array of possible consequences of a positive hit: this visit denied, all future visits denied, a permanent black mark on Shane's record. It could even be enough to cause the postponement or cancellation of his move to the halfway house.

When I turned to Lorne in shocked disbelief, he and Shirley started to laugh, slapping their thighs and giving each other high-fives. Then Lorne twisted a knob on the machine so the alarm went off again, even louder this time.

"My goodbye present to Shane," he said. "I set it to go off. I just wanted to piss him off one more time."

Shane was not exactly amused.

∞

THE NEXT MORNING, I ARRIVED back at Frontenac at eight o'clock. Shane was waiting inside at the horseshoe with his duffle bag, backpack, and boxes, clutching his paperwork and a small brown envelope. If there had been no one to drive him, they would have paid for his bus ticket. But I was there, and the envelope contained the twenty dollars that had been left in his account and the eighty dollars each inmate received upon release. Shane said they held this eighty dollars to cover the cost of your body bag if you died inside, but I was never sure if this was true or the carceral equivalent of an urban legend.

Lenny was waiting with him. Janice Mackie was there too, and after we'd put the last of his belongings in my car, she shook his hand and said with a grin, "Good luck, Shane. I hope I never see you again." He and Lenny shook hands too but said nothing.

With no further fanfare, we got in the car and drove out of the parking lot. No balloons, no cake, no gold watch, no brass band, no fireworks—but we were on our way.

In the car we listened to the CDs I'd made for him. At his request, I'd started with sounds of nature for relaxation and Buddhist chants for meditation. Then I asked him for a list of songs he'd like to have. It turned out to be a very long list, including "The Air That I Breathe" by The Hollies, "Smoke Gets in Your Eyes" by The Platters, "Memories Are Made of This" by Dean Martin, "Never on a Sunday" by Connie Francis, "Little Green Bag" by George Baker, "Talk Back Trembling Lips" by Johnny Tillotson, "Crying" by Roy Orbison, "Time in a Bottle" by Jim Croce, and, of course, "Unchained Melody" by Sam Cooke.

Although Shane was only five years older than me, clearly we had very different tastes in music. Some of these songs I'd never even heard of, and the rest I thought of as "old man music," songs my father would have enjoyed. The only ones I liked too were those by Roy Orbison and Jim Croce. I was mystified by this list, until I realized these old songs were all from the years before he went to prison. This was the music he'd loved when he was in his teens and early twenties, when he was a healthy young man excelling at football and hockey, a handsome young man married at the age of twenty-one, soon to be a father. Yes, he'd been in some trouble by then, and yes, he'd started down the wrong road with drinking and drugs, but it was not too late. His life, still full then of potential and possibility, could have gone in any direction. When he was that young man listening to this music, the word life did not yet mean a life sentence.

For good measure, I'd also made a CD of some of my favourite music from the past, and we listened to that too: The Rolling Stones, Janis Joplin, Little Feat, Eric Clapton, Meatloaf, John Lee Hooker, B.B. King, Joan Armatrading, "Wild Thing" by The Troggs, "I Am Woman" by Helen Reddy, "Total Eclipse of the Heart" by Bonnie Tyler, "Walk on the Wild Side" by Lou Reed, "Let's Give Them Something to Talk About" by Bonnie Raitt.

Following the same route we'd taken back in May, we arrived at the halfway house just before noon. Shane would be sharing a basement room with another man. Visitors not being allowed in the residents' rooms, I only stepped in briefly while we carried in his belongings. With a window on the far wall, two built-in closets on the opposite wall, and two single beds with storage lockers beneath them, there was, as my mother would have said, barely enough room to swing a cat. But Shane was overjoyed with his new accommodation, the best thing about it being what it *wasn't*: prison.

While he unpacked, I waited in the office area upstairs, chatting with the supervisor. Several of the other residents passed in and out, most of them older men like Shane, some looking more like criminals than others, all of them pleasant and polite. I studied two large bulletin boards, one covered with notices—of job openings, church services, AA and NA meetings, bus schedules, a lost dog—and the other covered with lists— of lunch and dinner menus, upcoming passes, a chore list for the next two weeks. Shane had already been assigned to clean the bathrooms, a task I knew he would actually enjoy. As for passes, after he'd been there for two weeks, he too would be able to come home for the weekend—to *my* home, not his mother's—and, fittingly, it would be Thanksgiving.

I had once again booked a room at the Best Western. I planned to spend Wednesday and Thursday nights there and then drive home alone on Friday afternoon. In the meantime, there was much to be done to help Shane start getting settled in his new city. First he had interviews with the police and his new parole officer. Although the supervisor told him to get used to the place for a week or two before looking for a job, he checked in at two different employment agencies and picked up pamphlets on how to prepare a proper resumé.

We went to the library so he could get a card and start borrowing books right away. One of the problems with having been in prison for so long was that Shane had none of the standard pieces of identification: no driver's licence, no credit card, no health card. He didn't even have a birth certificate anymore, it having been lost somewhere along the way. All he had was his federal inmate ID card—and me. Whatever reservations the librarian may have had about him, they were banished once I introduced myself and she recognized my name. If there's any place where being a writer can come in handy, it is a library. We came out an hour later with a library card, a stack of books, and an invitation for me to give a reading there when my new novel, *At a Loss for Words*, came out in the spring.

On Friday morning, I picked him up at the halfway house, and we went back to the Best Western for breakfast. On the patio outside our room, we sipped our coffee and fed the ducks. I took pictures of them clustered around Shane's feet, quacking for more bread, took a picture too of the boldest duck, who waddled right into the room and sat looking out at us from beside the bed, as if he might like to hop up there and have a nap.

We'd done what we could to get Shane organized, and the halfway house staff would help him with the rest. I got out pens and a notepad, and we set about making a list. We were both never happier than when making a list.

Shane rolled up his sleeves and said, as he often did, "You and I are a lot alike."

Our tastes in music and the fact that he was a Coke drinker while I preferred Pepsi notwithstanding (was it even possible, we joked, to be a two-cola couple?), yes, we did have more in common than you might expect. Making lists, making plans, making lists of plans. Reading, of course. Crossword puzzles and all word games. Bookstores. Cemeteries. Afternoon naps. Perhaps these were small things. But there were deeper things too that we shared. Don't we all do this when we fall in love—don't we all search for signs of ourselves in the other? You can always find them if you look hard enough.

There was our mutual connection to banks, of course: he was once a bank robber and I was once a bank teller. Shane tended to think of bank robbery as a "victimless crime" as long as no one got shot. After I told him how frightening it was for me the day a foolish old man stepped up to my wicket at the bank in Canmore, cocked his hand like a gun, stuck his index finger in my chest, and said, "This is a stick-up, give me all your money," he revised his opinion. Having once noticed him looking a little too long (and a little too longingly) at a Brink's truck idling beside us at a red light, I had taken to hollering, "Cover your eyes! Cover your eyes!" every time we passed one. Much hilarity ensued. We both liked to laugh.

We both tended to obsess about things, and we were both inclined to depression and anxiety. We were both thin-skinned and easily hurt, although he tried harder to hide this about himself. We both sometimes felt sorry for ourselves. We were both very emotional, although he was uncomfortable with what he called his "soft feelings." He did not trust kindness, caring, tenderness, happiness, harmony, love. He had the same emotional repertoire as anyone else, but any negative feelings—fear, disappointment, anxiety, regret, embarrassment, loneliness, shame—always came out as anger. Later I discovered that sometimes his soft feelings came out that way too.

We had both struggled for years to feel we belonged somewhere, anywhere, with someone, anyone. Shane said that when he went to prison, it was the first time he'd ever felt a true sense of family and fraternity. And me? I felt I belonged with him.

We both had fond memories of having fried baloney for supper when we were kids. This perhaps meant more to me than it should have. For me it was the baloney of belonging. Once when I was waxing nostalgic to Dorothy about the delights of this delicacy, the circles of baloney brown and crispy around the edges, curling up like little cups on the plate, she said she'd never heard of such a thing. She said, as she had on several occasions about other topics, "It's a class thing."

Shane liked to say we'd both been in prison before we found each other. He said that although my prison had been much cozier than his, still I'd been living a sexless, loveless, unfulfilled life until he came along, and that no matter how many books I read or wrote, no matter how comfortable my house was, still I was all alone. I pointed out that I was not alone, I had Alex. He meant alone with no one to lean on, he said, no one to help me, no one to hold me, no one to rub my feet or wash my back. There was some truth to this, but I didn't agree with the prison metaphor. I knew, though, that it was part of how he liked to tell himself the story of our relationship, that it wasn't just me helping him, that he'd helped me too, rescuing me from my sad lonely life and setting me free.

We both had what my friend Evelyn called "busy brains," our minds never still, our thoughts constantly galloping around in all directions at once. When she first said this about me, I instantly recognized it as the perfect description of what sometimes felt like static in my head or the sizzling snow that used to fill the TV screen when the station went out. Recently I heard a radio program about memory in which it said the average person has seventy thousand thoughts a day. How do you count or measure a thought anyway? Is thinking, I love you, I don't know why I love you, I wish I didn't love you, one thought or three?

The researcher went on to say this number is much higher for "the very thoughtful and painstakingly neurotic among us."

I like to think my busy brain is an integral part of my creativity. But I know it has its dark side too, is a prime contributor to my anxiety, my neuroses, my obsessions, my chronic insomnia. On a good day, I get along well with my busy brain and appreciate its inexhaustible energy. But there are other times when my thoughts are swarming uncontrollably, my brain seems to be filling up with psychedelic zigzag lines rocking to some horror movie soundtrack, and all I want to do is turn it off. As for Shane, the fractious firestorm that sometimes erupted in his brain was even worse, and it could be contagious. I already knew that if he started a conversation by saying, "I've been thinking," there was a stretch of rough road directly ahead, possibly laced with land mines.

That morning at the Best Western, after we'd completed our list, run out of bread for the ducks, and taken advantage one more time of having a room with a bed in it all to ourselves, I delivered Shane to the halfway house in time for lunch and headed for the highway. I drove home with a sense of relief and anticipation. Our prison days were done, and we had stepped now into the next chapter of our story. I was looking forward to having more time to myself, to resuming my regular routines, to no longer feeling frazzled all the time, to being able to get some writing done.

∞

LONELY OR NOT BEFORE I MET SHANE, I count solitude as one of the basic requirements of daily life, right up there with air, water, food, shelter, and books. To paraphrase Gibbon, who paraphrased Cicero, who recorded what was said by Scipio to Cato: "I am never less alone than when by myself." This has been true since I was very young, perhaps because I was the only child of older parents and had to learn to amuse myself. It is a good character trait for a writer, and I'm not one to complain about the "isolation" of the writing life. If anything, I am more likely to complain about not having enough isolation. This was one way in which Shane and I were not alike. He most often took my need for solitude as an affront.

One of the mistaken preconceptions I had about a man who'd been in prison for thirty years was that he too would be good at being alone and keeping himself occupied. In hindsight, I realize I should have given more thought to the fact that prison is a place where being forced to be alone is one of the ultimate punishments. Call it "solitary confinement," "segregation," or "the hole," it is now widely considered a violation of basic human rights and a form of psychological torture when continued for too long.

Shane did not like being alone. But he also might as well have had a tattoo that said HELL IS OTHER PEOPLE. Most of us interpret this sentiment from Jean-Paul Sartre's play *No Exit* as meaning that all the pain in our lives is caused by other people, and the world would be a much better place if there weren't so many of them in it. For Shane, this matter of other people was a double-edged sword. He didn't much like them either collectively or individually. His friendships seldom lasted for more than two weeks. Lenny, it seemed, was his only long-term friend. But he couldn't stand to be alone either.

Sometimes before his move to the halfway house, I'd felt suffocated by his constant attention. When I once said, "You know, when you get out, we're not going to be joined at the hip, we're not going to be together 24/7," he replied incredulously, "We're *not*?"

EARLY ON SUNDAY MORNING, I was jarred awake by the sound of banging and crashing in the kitchen. It was Thanksgiving, Shane's first weekend home. The bed beside me was empty. I stomped into the kitchen grumbling. He was making a lemon meringue pie. I said I didn't see the need to make a lemon meringue pie *at six-thirty in the morning.* He just laughed and carried on. I poured myself a cup of coffee and flounced into the living room in my housecoat. I tried to do my usual morning reading, but with the racket in the kitchen, reading was no more possible than sleeping. I have never made a pie in my life. Did it have to be this *noisy?*

Perhaps I'd underestimated how hard it was going to be for me to have another person in the house. Perhaps I'd underestimated how cranky I could be. But that day I managed to get over it quickly enough, and by dinnertime, my silly morning meltdown had already been added to our file box of happy memories.

Yes, it was Thanksgiving, and we were indeed thankful for many things, including being able to cook dinner together using my new pots and pans.

When Shane was still at Frontenac, he had been a diligent peruser of the many sales flyers that showed up in the prison—the same flyers that filled up my mailbox at home and that I tossed into the recycling box without looking at. He liked to read the best bargains to me over the phone. Sometimes I found this charming, his way of trying to participate in the household when he couldn't actually be here. Other times it just made me impatient, especially if the bargains were on things I'd never buy anyway.

One day he spotted an excellent deal on a ten-piece set of KitchenAid cookware. Now this was something I could use. Usually retailing for four hundred dollars, the set was now on sale for half price. Shane had a pass that weekend, so we went directly to the Canadian Tire store near my house.

Including three saucepans of various sizes, a five-quart Dutch oven, a ten-inch skillet, and a steamer insert, all stainless steel with break-proof glass lids, it was indeed a beautiful set. We stood proudly in the checkout line with our cart, holding hands, imagining what we'd cook first, feeling closer and closer, ever closer to normal. Shane set the box on the counter, and I got out my credit card. It felt like a commitment, that big box of pretty pots and pans, a step towards the future in which we would live happily ever after together in the free world.

And now here we were on Thanksgiving, using the new cookware together just as we'd imagined we would. Our dinner was delicious, especially the pie.

The next day, we were thankful to be able to sleep in, then putter around the house all morning. After a lunch of turkey sandwiches and the rest of the pie, we went outside and started getting the yard ready for winter. We raked leaves, put away the lawn chairs and the barbecue, and regretfully emptied the flowerpots we'd planted together in the spring.

On his pass to Vera's in May, we'd gone to the garden centre and loaded up the car with impatiens for the window boxes, a gigantic pink and purple fuchsia to hang at the front, assorted other annuals to be planted in decorative containers, and a few perennials for the shade garden I'd been trying to establish at the back.

Shane had done some landscaping work at the prison, and that day, if he'd had his way, we would have bought much more. But when we got to the cash register, he could see why I'd been so prudent about my choices. At the prison, of course, he didn't have to pay for the plants and had no idea how expensive they could be. We did, however, buy one special thing I'd always wanted to try: a smoke bush.

This is not my life

GUNN, AN

We spent the rest of the day happily planting and playing in the dirt. We selected a spot for the smoke bush in the backyard. Then Shane dug the hole, and together we gently tucked the little plant in, filling all around it with compost and new soil and watering it generously. Not much more than ten inches high, the smoke bush was another nod to the future, to *our* future, as we imagined how lush and beautiful it would be in five years, ten, twenty.

He said he'd rip out the weeds coming up through the cracks at the edge of my driveway. I said, "They're not weeds, they're bleeding hearts. They come up every year, and I like them." Having been called a bleeding heart often enough myself, I felt compelled to defend and protect them.

He laughed and said, "I get it. Don't worry, I won't touch them." He contented himself with digging up some dandelions instead.

Later we sat back in our lawn chairs and admired our day's handiwork. Full of ideas for other projects we might tackle when he got home to stay, Shane outlined complicated detailed plans that would amount to a full-scale outdoor makeover. I resisted the urge to ask who was going to pay for all this. I could already see that sitting around making elaborate plans for the future, however grandiose and unrealistic, was a salient and vital part of prison life. Whether these plans were likely ever to come to fruition was not the important thing. What mattered was believing in the future and one's own existence in it—a future of freedom, happiness, and success where the word *security* would mean something altogether different than it meant now. Telling the story of the future was the important thing, even if it was a future that might never come.

And now here we were, thankful to be wrapping the smoke bush in burlap for the winter. It had already grown to twice its original size in just one season.

All weekend we were thankful for one thing after another, especially being able to spend the whole night together in my queen-size bed. Not just one night, but three. Yes, I'd forgotten how loudly he snored. No matter what position he was in, no matter how many times I nudged, poked, or tried to roll him over, no matter how many Breathe Right strips I stuck across his nose, nothing would make the snoring stop. But it didn't matter. I would get used to it. I would buy earplugs. Between the snoring, the sex, and the fact that I was completely unaccustomed to sharing the bed except with little Nelly, I didn't sleep much all weekend. But it didn't matter. I would get used to it.

FOR THE TIME BEING, Shane would have a pass home every other weekend. Come January, provided all had gone well, his status at the halfway house would be changed to "five and two," meaning he would be required to spend five nights a week there with two nights at my house in Kingston.

In the two weeks between our Thanksgiving weekend and his next pass, he accomplished a lot. Because he'd been having UTAs, ETAs, and work releases in the community for several years, the outside world was not entirely foreign to him. He was not, after all, Rip Van Winkle. He knew what needed to be done, and, of course, he had that list we'd made together. He called often to keep me updated, usually three or four times a day, sometimes as many as seven or eight. I knew he was lonely, and I tried to be patient, figuring that once he got used to us living in different cities, he wouldn't feel the need to call so often. Within a few months, Lenny too would be granted day parole and move to the Peterborough house. This did not help with the loneliness as much as I'd hoped.

In his first two weeks in Peterborough, Shane had his first meeting with the CSC psychologist, Dr. Quinn, whom he would continue to see once a month as required by the Parole Board. He bought a bus pass and was learning the routes around the city. He began working out and swimming at the Y, a free membership being provided by the halfway house for each of the residents. He spent many frustrating hours on the phone trying to replace his lost birth certificate. As it happened, the office he was directed to was located in Thunder Bay (not my fault), and the person he was dealing with didn't speak English very well (also not my fault). After several calls in which Shane repeatedly explained where he'd been for the last thirty years, this person said he could find no record of him anywhere. Given that Shane had effectively been "a ward of the state" for more than half his life, this was absurdly ironic. When he sarcastically said, "Does that mean I'm innocent after all? Does that mean I've been pardoned?" the man on the phone didn't laugh.

He had already found a job. He would be working at the Saint Vincent de Paul Society Thrift Store, primarily on the loading dock. He would work thirty-six hours a week, with Friday afternoons off so he could come home for the weekend. He would be paid minimum wage, which, compared to the amount he made inside, sounded like a veritable fortune. Now he needed to open a bank account into which his paycheques could be deposited. He still didn't have the proper ID to be able to do this easily, so when I picked him up the next weekend, we went together to the bank. Because I was a long-time customer of that bank myself, opening a joint account in both our names was the simplest solution. He wouldn't have access to any of my individual accounts, but I would be able to withdraw from this one. In this way he could contribute to the cost of gas and groceries for our weekends together.

Knowing how anxious I was about winter driving, he said he would start taking the bus back and forth at the end of November. This was not expensive and would make things easier for me. On each pass weekend, I was spending twelve hours on the road, clocking eight hundred kilometres with the two round trips. For a person who doesn't like driving even when the weather is good, this was a challenge. He planned to get his driver's licence in the spring.

AT FOUR IN THE MORNING ON Remembrance Day, the ringing phone woke me from a deep sleep. It was not a pass weekend. Shane was calling from the Peterborough hospital. He'd been rushed there by ambulance, he said. It might be a heart attack. He'd had one many years before. He admitted that he hadn't been taking his blood pressure medication. He'd been feeling so good, he said, that he thought he didn't need it anymore.

I was up and dressed and on my way by four-thirty. The roads were all but deserted in the pre-dawn darkness. In the parking lot of the Tim Hortons in Kenworth, there was a cluster of pickup trucks and a dozen men in red and orange vests and hats. I saw similar configurations of men and trucks at other spots along the highway. It was deer hunting season.

One of the (many) ways in which Shane and I were not alike was in our attitudes towards hunting. An avid hunter when he was young, he still reminisced fondly about how wonderful it was to be out in the woods enjoying nature. To which I invariably replied, "Couldn't you just enjoy nature without killing something while you were out there?"

Just the previous weekend I'd splurged and made a special dinner featuring one of my favourite dishes: grilled lamb chops. He tried but couldn't bring himself to eat them, said he kept picturing those innocent little lambs gambolling in a meadow, oblivious to the fact that they were soon going to end up on somebody's plate. He said it made no sense at all that I loved lamb chops while being so against hunting. I said it made no sense either that he, the tough-guy hunter, couldn't eat lamb chops. I said it was a good thing that since he was under a lifetime weapons ban, this would only ever be an academic argument. Regardless of what I thought about it, there would be no more hunting for him.

In the end, I made him a peanut butter sandwich and ate his lamb chops as well as mine. He said we humans are nothing if not a mess of contradictions. I said, "*Mass.* The saying is 'a *mass* of contradictions.'" He said it was true either way. And that that was another way in which we were a lot alike.

I arrived at the hospital at seven-thirty. He was still in Emergency, and they took me right in. I could hear him snoring before I got into the room, so I knew he was still alive. The nurse said they were waiting for the last test results, but it now looked like he'd had a severe episode of angina, not a heart attack. He drifted in and out of sleep for the next two or three hours, while I sat beside his bed.

Once the test results were in, the doctor had checked him again, and the halfway house had been consulted, he was released into my care for the next twenty-four hours. He was still groggy and loopy from the medication they'd given him, but I managed to get him out to the parking lot and loaded into the car.

We went to the Best Western, where, luckily, there was a room available, and I got the discounted hospital rate for one night. The rest of the day and the night passed peacefully with no further problems.

In the morning, after breakfast at the hotel, I took him back to the halfway house. Kissing me goodbye, he said, "Don't worry. I'm not going to die. I'm going to live to be a hundred." This was the same thing he'd said nine months ago after the esophageal bleed.

This time I said, "Is that a promise or a threat?"

CHRISTMAS TOOK UP MOST OF the month of December, just as it always does. In addition to the usual hoopla, this year it also involved a lot of back-and-forthing on the bus. Shane was home for the weekend in the middle of the month. He would be back a week later on Christmas Eve for four days, then again for four more days at New Year's.

Shane and I decided to do the decorating on the mid-month weekend. Now that Alex was older, usually we just set up a small tree on a table in the corner of the living room. But this year, in honour of Shane being with us, I thought we should resurrect the big tree. I'd bought this six-foot artificial tree when Alex and I first moved to Kingston, the prospect of getting a real one every year by myself being more than I could handle at the time. This year I hauled it up from the basement along with the three plastic tubs of decorations we had accumulated over the years, these being a testament to the fact that although I'm not keen on Christmas myself, I had made a concerted festive effort for Alex's sake. Shane and I put up the tree on Saturday night so Alex would be surprised when he got home from work.

I took great pleasure in sharing the stories of all our special ornaments with Shane, who couldn't remember the last time he'd decorated a Christmas tree. By the time we were finished, I was feeling quite nostalgic and sentimental, so I got out Alex's baby book and the photo album of his first year back in Canmore. We sat together on the couch, and I spread the books open on the coffee table. Alex was an exceptionally well-documented baby from the very first ultrasound photo all the way to his first birthday in the backyard, him in a jaunty red and gold party hat grinning and waving his arms, with the blue and grey mountains keeping watch in the near distance behind him. I was so swept up in sharing my memories of Alex's babyhood with Shane that I didn't notice until I stood up to get the next album that he was scowling and grinding his teeth.

"I wasn't there," he said angrily. "I should have been there. I should have been in those pictures too. But I wasn't there."

I didn't know what to make of this. Should I be touched, angry, disappointed, disturbed? I put the baby book and the photo album away. Maybe it was just too much all at once—Christmas, the tree, the decorations, the pictures, the memories—too much emotion for him to handle, too much of another life, *my* life long before he came along, my life with my son, the kind of life he might have had but didn't.

Maybe there would be another time, I thought, a better time to show him the rest of the albums, a time when he'd be able to enjoy sharing my earlier life with my bouncing brown-eyed baby boy. But there wasn't.

NOW THAT HE WAS WORKING, Shane was excited to be able to buy me a Christmas gift. He couldn't resist dropping hints. It was an item of clothing, he said. He'd picked it out himself, he said. I was afraid to imagine what he might have chosen.

Ever since we'd started sleeping together, he'd been trying to convince me to wear sexy lingerie. But I was happy with my granny nightie and did not oblige. When I did buy new sleepwear, it was an oversized T-shirt with a drawing of a large fish, a pair of red smooching lips, and the words KISS MY BASS. I bought him a pair of matching boxers with the same sentiment across the back. This pretty much summed up how I feel about a lot of things, including sexy lingerie. I find the idea of wearing such getups ludicrous, not because I think them offensive or demeaning or shameful, but because they just seem silly to me, the embodiment of a kind of cartoon sexiness better suited to the nocturnal tuggings of teenage boys than to the mature sensual pleasures of grown men. I was sure that if I ever did try wearing such a costume, I'd be overcome with a very unsexy fit of hysterical laughter. And maybe I was fonder of my fifty-something body than I realized. Maybe I thought it was alluring and sexy enough without the props.

At Vinnie's, Shane had often brought things from the warehouse to me in the kitchen, clothes he said he thought I'd like—more accurately, clothes he would have liked me to like. Considering that it was a religious organization run by elderly nuns, a surprising number of slinky nightgowns were donated. There was also once a donation of a large purple dildo. It too was brought into the kitchen, thankfully not by Shane but by one of our regular lunch patrons, who carefully arranged it on her table as a centrepiece. She was quite indignant when we made her put it away.

Over time Shane had brought me, among other things, a pair of black pleather pants that would have been skin-tight even on an anorexic supermodel, a metallic silver top with a neckline that would have plunged all the way to my navel, a teeny tiny red bikini made of a shiny slippery material somewhere between plastic and rubber. He'd also often expressed a deep longing to see me in stilettos.

He was crestfallen when each time he brought me an offering, I rolled my eyes, guffawed, and said, "You're kidding, right?"

But I knew he wasn't kidding, and now when he tucked the store-wrapped box under the Christmas tree with the rest, I was worried. The box was too large to be underwear and too small to be shoes—but beyond that it offered no clues.

In our family, we have a tradition of opening one gift each on Christmas Eve. That night, Shane placed the box in my hands before I could even sit down on the couch. Usually a wrapping paper ripper, this time I peeled off each piece of tape very slowly as Shane hovered over me. Alex, I was glad to see, was occupied with opening his own present and paying no attention to mine.

Nestled in layers of red and green tissue paper was a jacket. A gorgeous jacket. A black blazer decorated in a random pattern with bits of fabric, ribbon, seam binding, and rickrack. I gasped, not with horror as I was afraid I might, but with pleasure and relief. It was truly original and elegant. It fit me perfectly. Shane said he thought it was something I could wear for the upcoming readings when my new novel came out. He was right. And I did, receiving many compliments every time.

OVER THE HOLIDAYS, SHANE CALLED BRANDY, now living in Windsor, to tell her he wanted a divorce. He still maintained that he had never really loved her, that it was only a marriage of convenience, not a question of love but merely a matter of drugs and sex. I knew this wasn't true. I didn't need it to be true. I knew he had loved her, and I had no problem with that.

I still chuckled whenever I thought of the time he was in the flower section at Loblaws while I browsed through the nearby greeting card racks. Amazed to discover a bouquet of bright blue carnations, he turned to me and called, "Brandy! Come and look at this!" I snorted and, pretending to be mad, stalked off in the other direction. I found him later in the checkout line clutching the blue bouquet. He said the sales clerk told him he pretty much had to buy it in hopes of not getting killed for having called me by the wrong name. I tucked this incident too into our file box of happy memories.

Shane seemed to feel he had to deny ever loving Brandy or anybody else before he met me. He expected the same from me. *Thou shalt have no other loves before me.*

I have never been married, although I came close twice when I was young. In both cases, I was the one who backed out. I've had many other relationships, though. The truth is, I have loved often and obsessively, randomly and recklessly, never wisely or well. The truth is, I have frequently been a fool for love. The truth is, I have an abysmal rap sheet for romance.

One of Shane's favourite sayings was "This is the bottom line." He was always delivering the bottom line about something. In this case, the bottom line for me was that I'd never had a good relationship in my life. Why did I think I could have one now? Was this one somehow the culmination of all the rest? Was I perversely trying to outdo myself in the "bad choice" department? Perhaps bad choices are like lies. Perhaps one invariably leads to another—until eventually you're caught in such a knotted web of them that you can't escape.

Had I learned absolutely nothing from all my previous romantic disasters? Apparently. Shane was extremely proud of the fact that he had failed the psychopath test, but if there were a similar diagnostic tool to determine a person's self-destructive romanticism, I would have earned a perfect score.

∞

IN JANUARY, SHANE BEGAN COMING HOME every weekend as planned. He took the bus home on Friday and back again on Sunday, usually on the last bus out at five-thirty. Months passed in this pattern, with some variations due to bad weather, long weekends, or work commitments on my part.

With both Friday and Sunday being travel days, in fact we had only one full day at home each weekend. We still tended to keep to ourselves. Before Shane came along, I had seldom seen my friends on weekends anyway. They were always busy with their husbands and families then. If there happened to be a book launch or a reading scheduled on a Friday night or Saturday, Shane and I would usually attend. He grew comfortable at these events, and people seemed to like him. There would be time later, I imagined, to expand our social life and make some couple friends, but for now, this was a good beginning.

Mostly on our weekends together, we did ordinary couple things like shopping, laundry, cooking, cleaning, yardwork. Of course, none of these was ordinary for Shane, and doing them as a couple was not ordinary for me. In retrospect, I think we were both working hard at pretending to be two normal people just going about their normal everyday lives. We wanted so much to be like everybody else. But we were not. We were like tourists exploring an exotic foreign land or maybe like aliens discovering the manifold joys of being human—one of which, of course, was sex.

I like sex as much as the next person—unless the next person is a man who has been in prison for thirty years. Shane didn't believe me when I told him that for almost the entire decade of my forties, I had been celibate by choice. He often said he was a physical person while I was more cerebral. He was probably right.

He became fixated on a brief passage in my first novel, *In the Language of Love*, a single long sentence in which the main character ruminates about guilt, sin, and confession, especially "the sin of having fucked a married man, not once, not twice, but probably two hundred times, once seven times in a single day."

I reminded him that the book was a *novel*, and that although the main character did bear some resemblance to me, still it was a work of *fiction* and should not be read as autobiography. He was having none of that. I pointed out that if a person, *any* person, was going to have sex seven times in one day, it would likely be a person much younger than we were. I said that if we had actually done all the things in bed that he'd like to do, he would be dead by now. He was having none of that either—clearly he would have liked to take his chances and give it a try.

While sex was always at the very top of his to-do list, it usually barely registered on mine. This became an ever-increasing problem between us. The more he insisted, the more I resisted. If we weren't in bed within an hour after arriving home from Peterborough, he sank into what I called his "big bad mood." This might well last the entire weekend. It seemed that no matter what sex we might have later, for him it was too little too late.

Once back in Peterborough, he would call over and over again apologizing. He blamed his big bad mood on the weather. It was too cold. It was too hot. It was raining. It was windy. It was humid. But that wasn't it. He was tired, he said. His stomach was upset, he was constipated, he had a headache, his leg hurt, a guy at the halfway house had eaten all the bacon and he didn't get any. But that wasn't it. None of that was ever it. It was simply that he didn't get what he wanted the minute he wanted it. Throwing a temper tantrum over not getting one's way is not charming in a five-year-old child, let alone in a fifty-eight-year-old man.

Whatever he'd said to the halfway house supervisor and his parole officer about these arguments, we were soon required to have a meeting with them. We sat in the supervisor's tiny office, me and three large men discussing our sexual problems. I was embarrassed and humiliated. By the end of the meeting, we had more or less reached the consensus that my sex drive was lower than his and that he would stop throwing what his parole officer called "a hissy fit" when he didn't get what he wanted.

If only it were that simple.

Over and over again, I allowed myself to accept his apologies. Over and over again, I allowed myself to believe him when he promised he'd never act like that again. Over and over again, I believed him because I wanted to.

∞

FOR SIX MONTHS, Shane had been seeing the CSC psychologist, Dr. Quinn, once a month in Peterborough. He found these sessions helpful and asked if we could see Dr. Quinn together to receive some couples counselling. Dr. Quinn had an office in Belleville and another here in Kingston. Unfortunately his office here was located at KP, and Shane refused to go there. Dr. Quinn, rather obligingly, I thought, said he'd come to my house instead.

We arranged our first meeting for a Monday afternoon in April. Shane had an extended pass that weekend. On Saturday he took the bus from Peterborough, I took the train from Kingston, and we met in Ottawa, where I was giving a reading that evening. Since the publication of my new novel two months earlier, he had been coming to as many of my book events as possible. He was now working at the recycling plant, and they were quite flexible about giving him time off. The writing community seemed to be accepting of him, and apparently none of the many people he met at these events knew the meaning of that teardrop tattoo—or if they did, it didn't faze them.

We returned to Kingston together by train on Sunday afternoon. Shane couldn't remember the last time he'd travelled by train, and as a special treat for both of us, I had upgraded our tickets to first class. We would be driving back to Peterborough on Tuesday.

Dr. Quinn's serious but gentle manner put me at ease immediately. I could see why Shane liked him so much. He seemed like the kind of person you could tell anything to, and he would understand: just what you want in a psychologist, I suppose, and not at all what I'd expected in one who dealt with violent criminals all day every day. After we got comfortable at the kitchen table, he went over what Shane had already told him about the difficulties of trying to maintain our long-distance relationship. He noted that as a long-term prisoner now reintegrating into society, Shane had a lot to deal with in addition to our relationship. I told Dr. Quinn that having been on my own for almost as long as Shane had been in prison, there was a great deal of adjustment required on my part as well.

"We are open," I said, "to any help you can give us."

Dr. Quinn said we both seemed to believe that Shane's chances of getting full parole were dependent on us having a healthy relationship. Yes, we said, we did believe that. His release plan hinged entirely on our relationship. Plus we were both still haunted by what Janice Mackie had said when he left Frontenac: that if our relationship failed, he would be sent back to prison. Dr. Quinn said this was not true: we needed to keep the two issues separate.

When he asked me what in particular I considered a significant problem between us, I told him I was having trouble balancing our relationship and my work. With Shane coming home every weekend, I was now trying to accomplish in four days what I used to in seven. I was more frazzled than ever. Much as Shane loved the fact that I was a writer and was proud of me, especially when we could attend literary events together as we'd done just that weekend in Ottawa, he seemed unwilling or unable to understand that the writing itself requires a lot of time and concentration, that writing a book is a lot harder and takes a lot longer than reading one. He was always excited about the having-written, not so much about the having-to-write.

Dr. Quinn said, "I don't read much myself, but my wife does."

I've heard this said by many men many times over the years. Dr. Quinn looked surprised when I laughed.

I talked about the phone calls, how I couldn't get my work done when I was constantly being interrupted. I told him that no matter how many times I explained this and no matter how many times we argued about it, still Shane did not respect my writing time and persisted in making it almost impossible for me to work.

"I've been publishing books for over twenty years," I said, "and it's awfully late in the game for me to be fighting for time to write. I'm sure if I worked in an office, if I was a teacher or a doctor or even a sales clerk, Shane wouldn't think it was okay to call me all the time when I was at work. I'm sure your wife doesn't call you when you're working."

By this point in our relationship, I had given up trying to make Shane understand how important my writing was to me personally. He could not comprehend the word *passion* in any context other than sexual. In fact, he had trouble understanding why we people out here do the things we do: what motivations could there possibly be besides sex, money, drugs, or revenge? Given where he'd been for the last thirty years, I could see why he thought this way. He hadn't had the best cross-section of people upon which to base his knowledge of human nature in general or his judgments of people individually. I'd often pointed out to him that if I were as judgmental as he was, I wouldn't be with him in the first place. He didn't seem willing or able to try on a new way of thinking. He persisted in applying all he'd learned about people in the prison paradigm to the rest of the world—including me. I realize now that this was part of being institutionalized.

Sitting at the table with Dr. Quinn that day, I thought maybe reducing my writing to a matter of dollars and cents, food in the fridge and a stove to cook it on, a car in the driveway and gas in the tank would make more sense to Shane. So I turned and waved my arms around to take in the whole kitchen, the entire house, the car outside too, and I said, "It's my work that paid for all this. It's my writing that makes it possible for us to live here."

I should have known that Shane would take this the wrong way. Of course he did. He took it to mean that I was saying he wasn't contributing to the household. I tried to explain that that's not what I meant at all. I was simply saying that my writing was how I made a living, that it was important financially, and for that reason alone, I should be "allowed" to do it. I suggested that maybe he, having been in prison for so long, didn't understand about the importance of work in the so-called free world where nothing is actually free. "In prison, work is optional," I said. "But out here, we people, we work."

This conversation went directly into that second file box, the one of unhappy memories. Later, years later, Shane would still bring up how much it had hurt him when I said he wasn't contributing to the household. But I didn't intend to hurt him, and that day I hoped Dr. Quinn was getting a good look at what I was grappling with.

When our hour together was over, he suggested we continue meeting once a month. To make this easier, we could come to his Belleville office on our way from Peterborough back to Kingston on a Friday afternoon. The direct bus between our two cities had recently been cancelled. Because there was no indirect bus route that didn't take at least eight hours, once again I was driving. We thought the monthly Friday meeting was an excellent idea.

As we were saying our goodbyes at the door, Dr. Quinn's cell phone rang. He took it out of his pocket and looked at it. Then he looked pointedly at me and said, "It's my wife."

ON HIS WEEKENDS HOME, Shane sometimes called his mother, but we only stopped in to see her two or three times during the fall and winter, and then only for a few minutes. Over the spring, Vera's health had declined steadily, and she was hospitalized several times. Shane would not visit her in the hospital, and he insisted that if she died, he would not go to her funeral.

She died in the middle of June on a Sunday afternoon, of congestive heart failure. The funeral, a simple graveside ceremony at the Kenworth cemetery, would be held five days later, on Friday.

In the face of the eventuality of Vera's death becoming an actual event, Shane changed his mind and decided he should go to her funeral. She was his mother after all, so yes, of course it was right that he should go. It seemed right that I should go too, if only to give him moral support. His pass for that weekend was rearranged so he could come home on Thursday. He'd got his G1 licence just the week before, so now he could share the driving as long as there was a registered driver in the car. That would be me.

I drove to Peterborough early that morning, and we were back in Kenworth in time to spend the afternoon helping two of his family members, Roy and Darlene, finish cleaning out Vera's apartment. Every cupboard and closet was jammed with stuff, including, in the bedroom closet, not only the unopened package of washcloths I'd bought for her but many other unopened packages of washcloths, dishtowels, and pillowcases. All of these went into the pile to be donated to Vinnie's. Throughout the apartment, we found items with pieces of masking tape on the bottom indicating who should get what. We found Shane's name on the inside cover of a large dictionary that had belonged to his maternal grandparents and also on the bottom of two delicate china teacups. The dictionary made sense—but what use did she think he could possibly have for the teacups? There was no name on the bottom of the little wooden box containing Popeye's ashes. Why can't I remember what we did with it?

Sometime during the afternoon, Darlene said that she and another relative, Marsha, had had an altercation the day before, a vicious argument that ended with Marsha apparently threatening to kill Darlene for having turned the rest of the family against her. Whether this accusation was true or not, Shane and Roy were not taking Marsha's alleged threat lightly. She was, in their opinion, quite capable of carrying it out or at least trying to. She had been on medication and under the care of a psychiatrist for many years, but it didn't seem to be helping a whole lot. After much discussion, at Shane's suggestion, he and Roy went to the OPP station and explained the situation and their fear that something terrible was going to happen at the funeral. The fact that it was Shane who insisted they go to the police made me realize how seriously worried he was. Any interaction with the police for any reason had to be reported to his parole officer and would be duly investigated and noted in his files.

THERE WERE MORE PEOPLE AT THE graveside ceremony than I had expected. Vera had no friends and was estranged from her own siblings, but her extended family was large: nieces, nephews, cousins, all their spouses, children, and grandchildren. Even the minister who officiated was a relative.

I had met Marsha only once before and didn't immediately recognize her at the cemetery. Shane had to point her out to me. She didn't stand out in a crowd, certainly not as someone who was said to have recently threatened murder.

When she spotted Shane, Marsha rushed over and gave him a big hug, me too. As if nothing had happened, as if we were all one big happy family—or, in this instance, one big *sad* family, now grieving the regrettable loss of one of its own. She was the one who set up a portable CD player at the edge of the grave so there would be musical accompaniment. She was also the only one who cried, letting out intermittent choking sobs and howls as the minister said his piece, assuring us all that Vera had gone to a better place. Perhaps she was the one who wrote the newspaper obituary in which Vera was described as *Loving Mother of.*

After the brief ceremony, we all dispersed to our respective cars and then reconvened in the common room at Vera's apartment building. As Shane introduced me around to everyone, I wondered why they had all travelled to the funeral of this woman they clearly didn't like and hadn't bothered with when she was alive. But I knew I had no right to be judgmental. Shane and I were the same, only there for form's sake, only there out of a sense of obligation rather than any true measure of love or sadness. We would not miss her and neither would they.

Most of the relatives were surprised to see Shane, because they thought he was still in prison. His aunt Winnie was especially happy to see him and kept hugging him around the waist. She told him how much she loved him, how she'd prayed for him every night for thirty years, how she'd never given up on him, how she'd always been there for him. I didn't see how this could be true. Shane had never even mentioned her, and she certainly had never found her way to the prison visiting room.

Darlene was steering clear of Marsha, and the rest of us were keeping a close eye on her as she mingled around the room, moving from one cluster of people to another, chatting pleasantly, occasionally bursting into only slightly maniacal laughter. Not for the first time in my life, I thought that families, especially other people's families, must surely be the greatest unsolved mystery on earth. Also not for the first time, I noted that Shane seemed to be one of the better-adjusted members of his.

After everyone else had said their goodbyes and headed back to wherever they came from, Shane, Roy, Darlene, and I emptied the coffee urn, washed the cups and glasses, tidied up the room. Marsha was friendly enough, giving Darlene a wide berth, helping to clean up a bit too, but then she disappeared. We thought (hoped) she'd gone home. Shane and Roy had wandered off too—to have a smoke, Darlene and I assumed.

We found the three of them in Vera's now-empty apartment. Marsha was crying, clinging first to Roy, then to Shane. Darlene and I went out to the patio and fed the squirrels. Soon the three of them came outside together. Marsha seemed calmer. We all went to our cars. Roy left alone because he wanted to stop downtown to buy a case of beer. Darlene was eager to get home, so she came in my car with us.

Shane said Marsha was upset because she felt left out, said we didn't like her anymore, were ignoring her, having fun without her. I said it wasn't fun, it was a funeral. As we headed down the street, me driving, Shane in the front seat, Darlene in the back, we were congratulating ourselves on having made it through the day without incident. In the rear-view mirror, I could see a large white car coming up fast behind us. Before I could say anything, it swerved wildly to the left, cut back in front of us, and came to a screeching halt in the middle of the street.

Shane said, "Here we go."

Marsha leapt out of the car and ran towards us screaming, "I hate you! I hate you! I hate you!" She was kicking the grille and pounding on the hood of my little car. I was terrified and fumbling for my phone. Shane and Darlene were stunned into silence. Marsha darted to the passenger side and peered in at Shane. Still screaming, she began to pound on his window with both fists. With her fury focused on him now, she seemed to have forgotten all about Darlene, who was shrieking in the back seat. Shane remained utterly silent, staring straight ahead. By now, with shaking hands, I'd managed to dial 911. As I tried to explain to the dispatcher where we were and what was happening, Marsha ran back to her car and began gunning it in reverse. I handed the phone to Shane and started backing up. Marsha kept gunning it, slamming on the brakes, then gunning it some more. I was soon half up on the sidewalk, trying to get away from her. Fortunately there was no one behind us. After one final lunge that brought the back of her car to within an inch of the front of mine, she squealed away, making an out-of-control left turn onto the intersecting street, and then she was gone.

Shane was still speaking calmly to the dispatcher, who said we should now go directly to the OPP station. He then called Roy, who said he would meet us there.

Two officers were waiting in the parking lot when we arrived. Roy pulled in right behind us. We all started talking at once. One officer asked the questions, and the other took notes. Shane handed his paperwork to the questioning officer, who studied it closely, then handed it back without comment.

In the end, they said they could take no action against Marsha. Shane asked what he should do if she came after us again.

The officer said, "Sir, you have the right to defend yourself."

Shane held up his paperwork and said, "No, sir, I do not."

We'd been seeing Dr. Quinn once a month as planned. I was still complaining about the phone calls. Every day was disrupted, often six or seven times. If I answered and reminded him that I was working, he was angry, not at himself for having called but at me for having complained. If I didn't answer, he kept calling until I did. If I unplugged the phone, there was hell to pay when I plugged it back in.

I also tried to talk about the sexual problems. Dr. Quinn looked surprised when I said that the more it became a battlefield, the less I wanted to. He didn't seem to understand when I said I wasn't in the habit of having sex with someone who was nasty to me.

At our July session, Dr. Quinn had two suggestions. First, he said perhaps it would be better if Shane didn't come home *every* weekend, if maybe occasionally we took a break so I'd have time to relax and recharge. Second, he suggested that perhaps I was too engrossed in my work and just didn't have room in my life for Shane. I said this wasn't true. I did have room in my life for him, but no matter how much room I made for him, it was never enough. He seemed to want *all* of my life to be *all* about him *all* of the time.

Shane said angrily, "What am I supposed to do when you're working then? Sit in the corner and be quiet?"

I said, "Yes."

We took a break in August. Shane wasn't happy about it, but I insisted. I felt much better for it, and he said he could see that. I hoped that in the long run, he would realize that if I wasn't feeling so frazzled and pressured all the time, things would be better for him too, including the sex. He never came to this conclusion.

For the first ten minutes of our next session, Shane was playing with his new cell phone and didn't appear to be listening. Finally, I said,

"Shane, please put your phone away. We're here to talk to Dr. Quinn." Then Dr. Quinn scolded me for scolding him as if he were a child.

This time Dr. Quinn had three suggestions for how we might improve our relationship. We already knew that Shane's hearing for full parole would take place in mid-October. Dr. Quinn said that if he did get full parole, instead of moving in with me, he should rent his own apartment and we could "date." He had no suggestions as to how Shane might pay for this apartment. In fact, we discussed this idea later with the halfway house supervisor, who said the Parole Board wouldn't be keen on Shane setting up what he referred to as "his own little fuck shack."

Dr. Quinn's next suggestion was that I should buy a bigger house. He didn't seem to consider that I might be having enough money trouble as it was, never mind trying to buy a bigger house.

Dr. Quinn said that instead of working "unstructured hours" at home, I should rent an office elsewhere, and thus I would be better able to separate my business and my personal lives. I resisted pointing out that if my working hours were unstructured, it was because Shane wouldn't stop calling when I was working.

⚭

SHANE OFTEN SAID BEING IN JAIL was like being on stage. Not only were the guards always watching you, but so were the other guys, checking you out, sizing you up, taking your number. Were you solid, or were you a rat? Were you a tough guy or a wimp? Could they trust you? Could they muscle you? Could they get under your skin? Could they kill you if they had to? Should they respect you? Should they be afraid of you? Should they watch their backs or make sure you were watching yours? Should they just ignore you, and stay out of your way?

When Shane was in it, my home too began to feel like a stage. I became more and more self-conscious with his eyes always on me. For thirty years he'd had no privacy and I'd had plenty, so it was hardly surprising that this was an issue. Personal habits and behaviours I had never thought about before, including closing the bathroom door, suddenly became peculiar, eccentric, possibly suspicious. He didn't seem to grasp the difference between privacy and secrecy. And now I fell prey to another interpretation of Sartre's saying "Hell is other people" and his ideas about "The Look"—that the presence of another person with their eyes upon you causes you to see yourself as an object, to judge both yourself and your world as they might.

Fastidious as Shane was in some ways—I'd often called him "Mr. Clean" when he went on about how he washed down his room at Frontenac with bleach every week—in others he was anything but. I know the same is true of me. I am particular about some things, careless or downright slovenly about others. He was always watching me, commenting on what I was doing and suggesting a better way. His way. He said he was just trying to help. I've had a few too many people in my life eager to tell me what I should do and how I should do it, all in the name of "trying to help." Now he was doing it too. Was this because he'd had people telling him what he could and couldn't, should and shouldn't, do for so long that now he figured it was his turn? Was this because he'd been made to feel helpless for so long that now he had to flex his control muscles in any way he could?

There was room for improvement, it seemed, in pretty much everything I did. I should put the coffee together before I went to bed rather than in the morning. I should wash the dishes immediately after using them, even if it was only a coffee mug or one small plate. I should not be so fussy about hanging the towels and washcloths evenly in the bathroom, and I should wash them after each use. I should put out the garbage right before bed rather than at suppertime. I should not be so fussy about how and when the laundry was done. I should clean the bathtub with bleach after every use. I should not be so fussy about turning off the lights in unoccupied rooms. I should clean the kitty litter box more often (he definitely had a point there). I should not nap with my clothes on because it was unsanitary (perhaps he had an ulterior motive here). I should not be so fussy about the recycling (you'd think someone who worked at a recycling plant would have appreciated my efforts).

In summary, as far as household matters went, I should be less fussy about the things I was fussy about and more fussy about the things I wasn't fussy about. It seemed that as far as my fussiness went, there was either too much of it or not enough. In any event, it needed to be redistributed. We could not seem to coordinate our respective fussinesses. We weren't either one of us easy to live with. Clearly we both had a lot to unlearn.

I'd been running this particular household for twenty years. I'd run other households of my own for another ten years before that. In my opinion, generally speaking, the household ran smoothly enough. Why did a man who'd been in prison for the same number of years as I'd been running households think he knew how to do it better than I did? Was I being a churlish bitch when I pointed this out to him? Was I trying to provoke him when, paraphrasing something I'd read somewhere once, I said one of the best things about living alone is that all your bad habits miraculously disappear? No, I was not. Was I surprised when he did not find this funny? No, I was not.

Whenever I tried to tell him how I felt, he would cut me off and tell me how he felt. When I said, "You make me feel like I can't do anything right," *he* said I made *him* feel exactly the same way. When I said, "You don't listen to me when I talk," he said *I* was the one who didn't listen. When I said I felt like I had no voice in this relationship, he said he was the one who had no voice. Impasse reached in record time. Deadlock.

I had seriously misjudged how hard it was going to be to adjust to sharing my space with another adult. Now twenty-three years old, Alex was technically an adult too, but still he was my child, and we'd had all those years to grow into it together. And although he still lived at home because he couldn't yet afford to get his own place, he was hardly ever there. When he was home, he was usually sleeping, because he worked nights.

Of course I had known making this adjustment would be a serious, perhaps even formidable, challenge, but I hadn't considered that it might be all the way to impossible. Of course I'd known it would be a time of great change, but I didn't imagine that how I made the coffee, hung the towels, or cleaned the bathtub would also be subject to revision. I didn't expect it would be so hard for me to relinquish control over the garbage, the recycling, or the laundry.

When I finally lightened up about the laundry, showed him how the washing machine worked and cautioned him to please use the Medium setting on the dryer, I didn't imagine he would then dry everything on High anyway, thus shrinking my best hundred-dollar jeans so much that I could never wear them again. Nor did I imagine this would be my fault—because how was he supposed to remember everything I told him to do when I was always telling him what to do?

Perhaps I should have taken more seriously the fridge magnet I'd bought some years before I met him: a cartoon woman is talking on the phone, and in the speech bubble it says, I WANT A MAN IN MY LIFE … I JUST DON'T WANT HIM IN MY HOUSE! Next to it now was the magnet Shane had given me, discovered at the Vinnie's warehouse in a donated box of odds and ends: an elegant woman in a purple satin gown and silver high heels lounges on an ornate pink bed, and below her it says,

QUEEN OF FUCKING EVERYTHING. Donated at the same time, surely by the same woman, was a black T-shirt on which it said in large white capital letters, DO YOU KNOW WHO I AM? I desperately wanted this shirt but had to concede when the director claimed it for herself. Instead I settled for one with the movie title MISS CONGENIALITY in pink block letters and below it, in pink script, ARMED AND FABULOUS.

SHANE WAS NEVER HAPPY WITH MY SHOWERHEAD. An old metal standard style, not more than three inches in diameter, it was probably installed when the house was built in 1950. It didn't do anything fancy like the new multifunction ones—it just sprayed water out of the holes. I'd never replaced it, because I prefer baths anyway and Alex had never complained. Shane had been coveting one of the new space-age ones ever since his first pass home.

One day at Canadian Tire, I finally bought a new one. Not one of the four-hundred-dollar chrome models that can do everything but wash the car and water the garden, but a simpler one, a discontinued model on sale for fifty dollars. As soon as we got home, Shane wanted to begin the installation. I said I'd call a plumber and have it done next week. He said plumbers were too expensive. He was sure he could do it himself, no problem. He reminded me that Dr. Quinn had said he should do more things around the house—this would make him feel it was his house too, not just mine. I went downstairs and turned off the water.

The first problem was the removal of the old showerhead. After several liberal applications of WD-40 and many unsuccessful attempts to unscrew it, first with his bare hands, then with a pair of pliers, then with a number of different-sized wrenches, all accompanied by much grunting and cursing, Shane got out the hammer. I said I didn't think this was a good idea. He ignored me. I couldn't bear to watch, went and sat in the kitchen with my hands over my ears. He bashed away at it for a good ten minutes, then emerged triumphant with the showerhead in his hand.

The second problem was that the size and threads of the new shower-head didn't match those of the pipe now sticking naked out of the wall. We went back to Canadian Tire and bought an adapter that looked like it would fit. It didn't. We went back to Canadian Tire and bought a different adapter. It didn't fit either. We went back to Canadian Tire and consulted a salesperson, who, after much discussion of male and female ends, said that if neither of those adapters worked, we'd have to call a plumber. Shane still refused to call a plumber. He said he'd just put the old showerhead back up and leave it at that.

The third problem was that once he'd screwed the old showerhead in place and turned the water back on, it was squirting out in all direc-tions at the connection. I've often been glad I live so close to Canadian Tire. This time we bought plumber's tape and pipe joint compound.

The fourth problem was that once he'd applied both the tape and the compound, there was still more water coming out of the connection than out of the showerhead itself. He finished the job with a complicated construction of duct tape and plastic bags.

On Monday I called a plumber, who charged me a hundred dollars to come over and tell me there was no way a new showerhead of any kind could ever be attached to that old pipe. It and all the other pipes connected to it would have to be ripped out and replaced. Needless to say, I could not afford to have this done.

We never spoke of it again. Shane used the maimed shower with-out further complaint. I began keeping the shower curtain closed so

I didn't have to look at the duct tape and plastic bag sculpture now sticking out of the wall.

I kept telling myself to let it go. I kept telling myself that life is too short to be fussing about a damn showerhead. I kept telling myself it didn't matter. But it did. It mattered to me. How was it that a man who'd been in prison for thirty years had come out with such a sense of entitlement that my old showerhead couldn't possibly be good enough for him? As time went on, he also expressed dissatisfaction with the stove, the fridge, the couch, the reading chair, the kitchen table, the cutlery, the drapes and curtains in every room that I'd sewn myself and was very proud of. How was it that the house he had so loved and admired in the beginning had become so unsatisfactory? Shouldn't a man who'd been in prison for thirty years be a bit more thankful finally to have a nice place to live? A nice, free place to live?

I thought about the difference between the words *grateful* and *thankful*. I didn't mean he should be *grateful*. There was something condescending about that word in this circumstance, casting me as Lady Bountiful and him as the wretched sot who should be down on his knees kissing my feet in gratitude. I meant *thankful* in the sense of feeling fortunate. I meant *thankful* in the way I felt fortunate to live in this house, small and somewhat untidy though it might be. I meant *thankful* in the way I was thankful for my writing, my son, my good health, my life as it was now and as I imagined it would continue to be. How was it that he never seemed to feel thankful for anything, least of all me?

∞

SHANE'S HEARING FOR FULL PAROLE was scheduled for a Wednesday morning in mid-October, just after Thanksgiving. This time I would be his assistant, and Stuart from LifeLine would be an observer. I found it odd that to be an observer you had to submit an application and be approved, but to be an assistant, all you had to do was declare your intention and show up. Because Shane was no longer incarcerated, this time the hearing would be held at the National Parole Board Regional Office in Kingston.

The halfway house rearranged his passes to make things easier. He would come home for the first weekend of October as usual. The following weekend, he wouldn't come home until Sunday, returning to Peterborough on Wednesday afternoon after the hearing. During the week between, I would prepare what to say to the Parole Board as his assistant, bearing in mind the advice we'd received from the halfway house supervisor, who said that what the Board really needed was to be "comforted."

ON THE FIRST WEEKEND OF OCTOBER, I finished up some work on Friday morning, then headed to Peterborough. It was overcast and raining lightly. Shane drove on the way back, taking a more southerly route through the countryside, following the back roads he'd known in his youth. I reminded him perhaps more often than necessary that my car was a Toyota Echo, not the souped-up Mustang he'd been so proud of back then. He slowed down. The clouds began to lift, and the sun came out. By the time we reached the outskirts of Kingston, we had seen six rainbows along the way. I was counting out loud.

Who doesn't love a rainbow? How could a rainbow ever be anything other than a good sign? How could the sight of six rainbows in one afternoon ever be anything other than miraculous? How could we not see this as a promise to the future, a promise to our future together in which we would indeed live happily ever after, amen?

Yes, we were having some problems, but on a good day, on a day with six rainbows, we both believed that once Shane got home to stay and we were relieved of the pressures of a long-distance relationship, then everything would be fine. I should perhaps have given more thought to the fact that a rainbow, even a rainbow multiplied by six, is essentially a trick of the light, an optical illusion that cannot be physically approached or located. On reflection, I can see that we were complicit in our belief that full parole would be the magic key by which all that was wrong would be righted, all that was damaged would be healed, all that was broken would be fixed. Yes, I believed that true love could overcome all obstacles, that the love of a good woman could make him happy and whole. Yes, I believed I was a good woman.

IN BED THE NIGHT BEFORE THE HEARING, while Shane snored on beside me, I found myself thinking about a movie we'd watched together early in our relationship. This was back when I was still sleeping over at his mother's, and it happened that one of his favourite movies was being shown on late-night TV. Made in 1986 and billed as a comedy adventure, *Tough Guys* stars Burt Lancaster as Harry Doyle and Kirk Douglas as Archie Long, two aging bank robbers who have just been released from prison after serving thirty years. They are the last of their kind, the last great outlaws, the last men in America to have robbed a train, the Gold Coast Flyer. It doesn't take them long to discover how much the world has changed since they went to prison back in 1956. It doesn't take them long to get back to doing what they do best.

As we watched the movie curled up together in Vera's sofa bed, I could see that for Shane this was the story of him and Lenny, right down to the body types. He was Burt/Harry, tall, muscular, imposing, and Lenny was Kirk/Archie, small, wiry, a little jumpy. I could also see this was how Shane wanted to think of himself: as an honourable out-law, a noble and good-hearted tough guy who just happened to live on the wrong side of the law.

After trying to put their old gang back together but finding the other guys well past their outlaw days, Harry and Archie decide to go it alone, first stealing an armoured truck, only to discover that all it contains is a single roll of quarters. Learning that the Gold Coast Flyer is about to make its final run, Archie gets the bright idea to hijack the train and drive it straight across the American border to Mexico. Harry tries to talk him out of it, but before you know it, there they are on the train, southbound to freedom, singing "I've Been Workin' on the Railroad" at the top of their lungs. It looks like they're going to go out in a blaze of glory. They don't realize until they're almost there that the track ends just a few feet beyond the border. But there is no turning back now, and they decide to go for it anyway.

In bed beside Shane the night before the hearing, I kept thinking about that train. Seventy tons of shining steel barrelling along at a hundred miles an hour, and when the track suddenly ends beneath its iron wheels, the train keeps going right across the border in a barrage of bullets until it is buried deep and forever in mountains of hot brown sand. The Mexican border patrol appears with their guns drawn.

ON THE MORNING OF THE HEARING, we met Stuart in the parking lot shortly after eight o'clock. We smoked and paced and smoked some more, not only anxious about the hearing, but also alarmed about the results of the previous day's federal election. Inmates had had the right to vote since 2002, but Shane said most of them had been apathetic and usually didn't bother. Now more and more inmates, including him, were exercising their right to vote, trying to defeat the Harper government. Still, the Conservatives had come out on top again, with a stronger minority this time. Those Tough on Crime drums that had been beating in the distance were moving ever closer.

We went inside and upstairs to the second floor. Shane and I sat together at one table facing the Board members at another. Stuart, as an observer, sat in a chair against the wall behind us. This time there were three men on the Board, one of them participating by video conference from Ottawa. Shane's parole officer had recently retired, and his new one would deliver her report via speakerphone from Peterborough. It took some time to get all the technology working properly, but finally we were ready to begin.

The parole officer said that Shane had been compliant with the terms of his day parole, showed a good prosocial attitude and a strong work ethic, and maintained consistent communication with his Case Management Team. She noted that our relationship was stable and prosocial. In conclusion, she stated that CSC recommended full parole be granted.

The lead Board member began the interview by asking Shane about his early years in Kenworth, where he was known as a "tough guy." I tried not to think about that train. I tried to think about six rainbows instead.

Through the questioning about his family, his marriages, and his criminal life, Shane was often barely audible, groping for words and stumbling over them when he did find them. As the questioning moved to the present and our relationship, his answers became clearer and more focused. He said he knew that what he used to treasure was nothing compared to what he had now.

The Board member in Ottawa noted that past problems in intimate relationships had caused him to react in unexpected ways. How would he deal with it if I broke up with him? Shane said he loved me more than he had ever loved anyone, but he also knew there could be life without me. He'd learned to stand on his own two feet, he said, but he'd also learned to ask for guidance when he needed it.

After noting that the parole officer, the psychologist, and the halfway house all thought he was ready for full parole, the Ottawa Board member then asked him, "Do *you* think you're ready?"

Shane's reply was a long and thoughtful explanation of why he thought that yes, he was ready. All three Board members seemed satisfied with his answer. Nobody asked me if *I* was ready.

Finally, after two hours, it was my turn to speak. I began by saying that Shane was a success story. I told them how well he'd handled various situations that might once have triggered him in a negative way. I told them the whole story of what had happened after Vera's funeral, with emphasis on the fact that it was Shane's idea to go to the police, that he had remained calm, reasonable, and cool-headed throughout the entire episode.

I confirmed that in the three years I'd known Shane, he had never shown any interest in drugs, alcohol, or criminal activity. I explained that having been on my own with Alex for almost as long as Shane had been in prison, I was extremely independent and sometimes found it difficult to adjust to no longer being the only one in charge; however, we were both committed to working out these problems as we went along. They did seem "comforted" by what I had to say—and maybe relieved when I finally stopped talking.

We waited with Stuart in the next room while the Board deliberated. After fifteen minutes, we were escorted back into the hearing room. The lead Board member cut to the chase. When he said, "We have decided to grant you full parole," Shane gave a little giggle and so did I. The lead Board member reviewed the conditions they were imposing, which were the same as they'd always been, with the addition that Shane must immediately report all intimate relationships and any changes in our relationship to his parole officer.

Then the lead Board member, by way of goodbye, said, "We hope not to see you again, especially not at a post-suspension hearing."

Shane said, "Thank you, sir. You won't."

PART THREE

October 2008 to August 2009

I was not ready.

After the hearing, we came home and had a quick lunch. Shane made a few phone calls to share the good news. I didn't call anyone, because I didn't know who would consider it good news. Then he called his employer to tell them he would be leaving Peterborough for good on Friday. He was no longer working at the recycling plant but at a company producing plastic car parts. He said he wouldn't be returning to work and wanted his cheque tomorrow. The receptionist said this was not possible; his cheque would be issued at the end of the current pay period as usual. It could not be issued tomorrow. They went back and forth a few times, Shane becoming increasingly agitated. Finally, he said, "Go fuck yourself, you stupid cunt! And shove your fucking lousy job up your fat fucking ass!" and slammed down the receiver.

I stood stunned in the middle of the kitchen staring at him, probably with my mouth open.

He said, "What?" and went to put his duffle bag in the car.

I was not ready.

It was Wednesday night. I was to pick him up on Friday at noon and bring him home to stay. I had one day to get ready. On Thursday morning, I emptied a dresser drawer and made room for his clothes in the closet. I cleaned the bathroom and made a permanent space in the cabinet for his toiletries and his shaving kit. On Thursday afternoon, I got groceries, cleaned the bathroom, vacuumed and dusted the whole house, washed the towels, changed the bed. I didn't know what else to do. I'd thought about a cake, balloons, a WELCOME HOME banner, but he'd said, "Don't bother with silly shit like that."

Why hadn't I started getting ready for him to move in weeks ago, when we first learned the hearing would be in October? I was too busy. I was too tired. I was too frazzled. No, that wasn't it. Maybe I was being superstitious like those people who don't prepare the nursery until after the baby is born. Maybe I was afraid of counting my chickens before they hatched. Maybe I was afraid of getting my hopes up. No, that wasn't it either. The truth was, I didn't believe it was really going to happen. I didn't believe he was going to get full parole this year. I thought that, as I knew often happened, he'd have to try two or three times before he actually got it. I thought we would have more time to get things right.

I was not ready, and I knew it. Shane was not ready either, and despite what he'd said at the hearing, I think he knew it too. Later we would be accused of intentionally setting out to deceive the Parole Board. No, that wasn't it. We weren't trying to deceive them. Stranded somewhere between delusion and denial, we were trying to deceive ourselves, and we succeeded. Briefly.

I WAS NOT READY.

What if I'd said that at the hearing? What if when it was finally my turn to speak, I'd said, "No, I am not ready. No, he is not ready. No, we are not ready." What if—as when the minister says, If anyone present knows of any reason why this couple should not be joined, speak now or forever hold your peace—I'd said, "No, we are not ready to take this step, but we don't know what else to do."

I felt trapped with Shane on that train hurtling forward even with the end of the track in sight. I was the centrepiece of his release plan, the linchpin of his freedom. Despite what Dr. Quinn was still saying to the contrary, it felt true to me that his full parole and our relationship were inextricably entwined. It also felt true to me that there could be no turning back now. I had been dealing with CSC long enough to know there was an all-or-nothing bottom line to their ideology and a conspicuous absence of flexibility. We'd submitted our plan, and we'd best stick to it. They had put all the steps in place in order, and we must follow them, no detours allowed. This was the next step. I didn't know of any other way to proceed. Perhaps I'd caught some of Shane's paranoia, but I didn't trust any of them enough to imagine they would let us step back from the brink and catch our breath.

I was sure that if I'd stood up at the hearing and said, "I am not ready," the whole thing would have blown up in our faces. I was also sure that never in the whole history of the world had a man being granted full parole stood up and said, "Thanks, but no thanks. I am not ready."

ON FRIDAY MORNING, I arrived at the halfway house at eleven-thirty. Shane's belongings were already packed and stacked in the parking lot. Two items were missing: my old pillow, which had disintegrated when he put it in the washing machine, and my father's cane, which he'd lost. He and Lenny were on the front steps waiting for me. We loaded the car, then Shane went inside to hand in his key. Lenny and I stood there smoking. I could see tears in his eyes.

I hugged him and said, "Don't worry, everything will be all right. Don't worry, I'll take good care of him."

Lenny sighed and said, "He's a heavy load, you know."

I said, "I know."

Shane came back outside, they had a manly hug, and then we got in the car and drove away. In the rear-view mirror, I could see Lenny alone in the parking lot, waving. We turned the corner and headed home.

We lived together for forty-nine days.

∞

I THOUGHT WE WOULD AT LEAST HAVE a honeymoon stage before getting down to the business of figuring out how to live together. I thought he would be happy just to be home. Looking back, I realize I didn't know then and don't know now what "happy" would have meant for him, what exactly this condition we call "happiness" would have entailed. How often do we make this mistake, assuming we know what these words mean for someone else, for someone we love? How often do we assume their definition of happiness must be the same as our own?

He was now as close to total freedom as he, a lifer, was ever going to get. I thought freedom would be enough for him. Being with him had reminded me of how precious it was—and of how those of us who've always been free simply take it for granted. But once he had it himself, it seemed an impossible gift he didn't know what to do with. I thought I would be enough for him. But I was wrong about that too.

Shane had said so many times that all he wanted was a quiet, peaceful, ordinary life—with me. In retrospect, I can see how utterly naive I was, imagining he would know how to do that. Perhaps I should have given more thought to the fact that there seemed to be a pattern in his previous behaviour—that every time he'd come close to having that, he had done something to make sure it didn't happen. In retrospect, it was as if by granting him full parole, the Board had given him to me, just handed him over and said, "Here you go, ma'am. We've looked after him for thirty years. Now you do it."

He was miserable from the minute he walked in the door that first Friday afternoon. I helped him unpack and put away his things. I noticed but didn't mention that the paint-by-number sets I'd given him were still untouched, and the blank notebooks were still blank. What I remember most of that first weekend is him sitting on the couch scowling at the TV. Scowling at me too every time I went near him. The cold he'd had before the hearing was back, and it was much worse. I remember saying I'd go to the drugstore and buy some NeoCitran. I remember him saying he needed some lotion too, because his skin was dry and itchy. I said I'd buy some Keri lotion. I knew it was his favourite. He said it was too expensive. Then we had an argument about the cost of lotion.

I understood that he wasn't feeling well. But I didn't understand why he was so angry at me. This was when he started calling me "the new warden" and himself my "pet convict." I did not yet understand that he had to have someone to fight against—that he had been for so long in the "me versus them" mode that he couldn't find another stance, another way to be in the world. When he was at Frontenac, he could fight against the staff, his parole officer, the warden, all the other guys. When he was in Peterborough, he could fight against the director and the supervisor, his employers, his co-workers, all the other guys. Once he came home to stay, there was nobody to fight against except me. He did not know how to stop fighting *against* and start fighting *for*. I did not yet understand that he was only comfortable when he was miserable, that he was only happy if he was making someone else miserable too.

I did not yet understand that he was afraid. That for him, jail felt safer than being on the street. That contrary to what Janis Joplin had said, *freedom* was just another word for everything left to lose.

ON MONDAY MORNING, we went to the Urgent Care Centre at Hotel Dieu. After two or three hours in the waiting room, Shane was diagnosed with bronchitis and given a prescription for antibiotics. We went to the drugstore. He was appalled at the cost of the prescription. Until now, all his medications had been covered, first by CSC, then by the halfway house. This was not something he'd taken into consideration about life in the so-called free world. The antibiotics improved his bronchitis but not his disposition.

In the first week, we were busy every day, too busy with the practicalities to consider the full implications of our new circumstance. We moved my desk to the back room, where it had been originally, thus returning the living room to its proper function as a shared family space and giving me a separate room to work in. We made trips to the employment agency, the cell phone company, the parole office, the police station. I wondered about going to see someone at the John

Howard Society, a national organization whose mission is to provide "effective, just, and humane responses to crime and its causes." One of its important services is to assist released prisoners with integration back into society, but for reasons he never explained, Shane did not want to contact them.

Instead we went to see the community chaplain, a person we'd learned about by accident from a business card Shane had been given by another inmate when he was still at Frontenac. At the time, he had said he wasn't interested and stashed it in the glove compartment. Now I retrieved it. We called and made an inquiry. I hadn't known that the community chaplain was someone who helped newly released inmates. Her name was Valerie, and yes, she could see us tomorrow afternoon.

Our appointment was brief. She said she usually started working with a man when he was still inside, beginning the preparation for his release. She said she didn't know why Shane hadn't asked to see her then. He made no reply. I said I didn't know why no one on his CMT had ever suggested that he, or we, should see her. She had no answer. She asked about housing. We explained that he was living with me, so that wasn't an issue. She asked about employment and gave us the address of an agency where he could take his resumé. He had already done that. She said he should make an appointment with Ontario Works, which provided start-up money for newly released inmates and could help him until he found a job. She said she would set up what she called "a healing circle," a group of people who could help us as Shane found his footing in the community. She made an appointment for our first meeting with the circle at the beginning of December.

I left Valerie's office feeling hopeful. We were not so alone after all. We had found someone to help us, and she would find more people to help us, and everything would be all right.

Back in the car, Shane opened the package she'd given him—a release package, she said. It included a toothbrush, a three-pack of condoms, six city bus tickets with a map of the routes, a list of Kingston AA and NA meetings, and another list of local agencies providing food hampers and hot meal programs including Vinnie's.

I WAS SCHEDULED TO ATTEND BookFest Windsor on the weekend of November 1. Back in the summer, when Shane was still in Peterborough, it had been arranged that he would come with me. He thought we should get together with Brandy while we were there. I was noncommittal about that idea. The Windsor trip must now be approved by his Kingston parole officer. Jerry Anderson was temporarily working elsewhere. He'd be back in early December, and until then Shane was added to the caseload of an older woman who seemed none too pleased about it. But she approved the plan.

The weekend before the Windsor trip, I wanted to stock up on Nelly's favourite treats, dried pork lung pieces, something to ease her separation anxiety some. We went to the large pet store directly across the street from the prison. While I looked for the treats near the front, Shane wandered to the back. A few minutes later, I heard him calling my name. I found him with his face nearly pressed against the glass of a large cage in which there sat one tiny forlorn brown puppy. She looked much like Nelly had when I got her: irresistibly adorable, not much more than two or three pounds, with big brown eyes and large perky ears. Nelly looked like a fox kit when she was small. This one looked more like a wolf cub.

We went home with two bags of pork lung treats and another dog.

This was not an entirely impulsive decision on my part. I knew how much Shane loved animals, but our pets were so bonded to me that they mostly ignored him. With Nelly in particular, it was blatantly obvious that although she was tolerating his presence, she was *my* dog, and he could never be anything beyond at best a diversion and at worst an outright interloper, a now ever-present rival for my affections. I'd thought before that it would be good for him to have a dog of his own, a canine companion who would love him above all others, including and especially me. I also believe in the therapeutic power of animals. Or maybe this is all retrospective dissembling on my part. Maybe getting this puppy was just the canine version of having a baby in hopes of saving a faltering relationship.

In any event, I hadn't imagined that he would have his own dog quite this soon. But here she was, the newest member of our family, a Pomeranian and Miniature Schnauzer cross that we named Maggie. At least she wasn't a German shepherd, a Great Dane, or a St. Bernard. It wasn't until after we got her home and introduced her to the others that I thought about our upcoming trip to Windsor in just six days. I knew Alex would do just fine looking after the other pets, but I didn't think it would be a good idea to leave him in charge of a new puppy as well, especially because he worked such long hours. Shane said he'd be happy to stay home with her; it didn't matter, he would rather have Maggie than a weekend in Windsor any day.

FOLLOWING VALERIE'S SUGGESTION, we made an appointment at the Ontario Works office on Tuesday morning. This proved to be a long, humiliating day at the end of which we were told that because Shane was living with me rather than on his own, he was not eligible for start-up money, and the total monthly amount he could receive from Ontario Works was fifty dollars.

Back home in the late afternoon, we were both so exhausted and angry that we could do nothing but sit at the kitchen table smoking and raving. Shane was determined to interpret my anger as being directed at him. I could not convince him that I was not angry at him. I was angry at "them"—CSC, the Parole Board, and Ontario Works, all three of them. I was angry at the "system," this trifecta of bureaucracies that seemed to be setting us up to fail. I was angry that CSC expected so little of an inmate returning to society that all they offered him by way of support was a list of free-food agencies and a visit to the welfare office. I was angry at Ontario Works, where we were told that if I had declared myself as his landlord, he would have been eligible for both the start-up money and the full monthly welfare amount for a single person of $535. I was angry that the Parole Board had given him to me with the tacit understanding that I would look after him, and now he was being penalized for that. I was angry that I was expected to support him financially, when I had hardly enough money to support myself and my son. I was angry that fifty dollars a month wouldn't even cover the pet food. I was angry at myself for getting into this mess in the first place.

WE MANAGED TO PULL OURSELVES TOGETHER and get through the next day, Wednesday, reasonably well. I was busy preparing for my trip to Windsor on Friday; Shane was puttering around the house, playing with the puppy, doing a few chores, including a load of laundry. Alex had to be at work at five o'clock. I'd give him a ride as I usually did.

Shortly before it was time to leave, Alex discovered his jacket was still damp from his walk home in the rain the night before. I asked Shane if he could please take the clothes out of the dryer so Alex could dry his jacket. He did, then sat back down at the computer where he'd been playing games. I asked him if he could please let Alex use the computer for a few minutes, so he could check his Facebook page before he went to work the way he always did.

It took me less than half an hour to drive downtown and back. As soon as I walked back into the house, it was clear that Shane had suffered a major mood swing in my absence. He had assumed his big bad mood position, sitting on the end of the couch scowling at the TV. Even when I cheerily called, "Hello," he said nothing and didn't even turn his head. I went into the kitchen and finished preparing the meal: ham, fried potatoes, lima beans, salad. When I called that dinner was ready, he came to the table, ate like a pig, then dropped his empty plate in the sink, all without speaking to or looking at me. On his way back to the couch, he said, "I hate lima beans." He had, however, eaten them all.

Okay, fine. I had no idea what was wrong this time and didn't much care. I would not ask him what was wrong, I would ignore him as he was ignoring me. Two could play this game, I thought. We ignored each other for the rest of the evening. He said he'd sleep on the couch. I said, "Whatever."

He kept this up all day Thursday. I did too. I again took Alex to work for five o'clock. Shane and I again sat down to eat dinner without speaking. I had such a knot in my stomach that I couldn't eat anyway. He had no problem, again wolfing it down, again dropping his empty plate in the sink.

And then I lost it. Two *could not* play this game. Only he could. I was done. I set my own untouched plate of food in the sink. As he stalked past me on his way back to the couch, without premeditation I picked up the wooden cutting board on which I'd sliced the leftover ham and smashed it as hard as I could on the edge of the counter. Almost an inch thick, it broke in half, and the pieces flew across the room.

We spent the rest of the evening yelling at each other in the kitchen. No, that's not true. I yelled. He spoke quietly in his syrupy sarcastic voice. I yelled some more. His voice got quieter and even more syrupy. Eventually he explained with great satisfaction that he was upset because I'd asked him to take the clothes out of the dryer so Alex could use it and then to get off the computer so Alex could use it too. He said I had disrespected him. I said he was crazy.

How long did it take me to understand that he actually thought it was reasonable for a grown man to behave the way he had for a full twenty-four hours simply because he'd been asked to accommodate someone else's needs? How long did it take me to understand that he thought it was perfectly okay to come into my formerly peaceful home and turn it into a battleground? How much longer did it take me to understand that he was proud of himself for having won the contest, torn away my dignity and self-respect, reduced me to the lowest common denominator, and driven me into a violent rage?

I got ready for bed, assuming that he'd once again sleep on the couch. But no, he was happy now and crawled in beside me. I turned my back and moved as close to the far edge as I could.

He said, "Don't worry, I won't touch you."

I said, "Good."

He said, "I'm afraid of you."

I said, "Good."

I SELDOM LOOK FORWARD TO LEAVING HOME, but in this instance, I could hardly wait to get on the train in the morning and be gone. We had now been living together for exactly two weeks. It was Halloween. As the train rolled west, I tried to make this into some kind of metaphor: me in disguise as a violent raving lunatic harridan now being let out of the asylum for a couple of days, during which I could return to my former self, my writer self, my *real* self in my real world. But I couldn't make the metaphor work, because I couldn't be sure anymore which was the disguise and which was the real me. In Windsor everyone treated me just as they always had. They had no reason to think I was anyone other than I'd ever been, no reason to wonder about disguises or denominators. As far as they could tell, the person inhabiting my body, standing on the stage, reading from my book, chatting with them at dinner, was still me.

Shane called many times over the weekend. Sometimes I answered, sometimes I didn't. Sometimes he was pleasant, sometimes he wasn't.

When I arrived back home on Sunday around six o'clock, Alex had already gone to work, and Shane was in position on the couch scowling at the TV.

By way of greeting, he said, "Is this it then? Are we breaking up now?"

I should have said yes.

PERHAPS NOVEMBER IS THE CRUELLEST MONTH, not April after all. Every day that Shane and I lived together was cold and grim, and after daylight saving time ended, by five o'clock it was dark. Every evening on the six o'clock news, the weatherman noted how many minutes of daylight we'd lost as we crept towards the shortest day. By the end of the month, the sun was setting at four-thirty. I have always found the onset of the early darkness depressing. Certainly being cooped up together in my little house in November didn't help. I felt invaded, and the house felt so small. Later Shane said it felt so big to him, cavernous after all those years inside. It was too cold to go and sit outside. I could not get away from him. I could hear him breathing even when he was in the next room. Every time I turned around, there he was: looking at me. Every morning when I got up, there he was: sitting at the kitchen table scowling and not looking at me. It unnerved me that he didn't even say good morning.

He had spread his resumé all over town with no results. With the help of the halfway house, he'd never had a problem finding a job in Peterborough. But now, trying to do it on his own in Kingston, he was just an almost-sixty-year-old man with an extensive and serious criminal record, no consistent education or employment history, no marketable skills, a bad leg, and a myriad of other health problems. He seemed to have given up on the job search and was now spending a lot of time sitting at the kitchen table, smoking, drinking coffee or Coke, doing crossword puzzles, reading the newspaper. I tried not to dwell on how this reminded me of my father, who, after my mother died, used to come and stay with us for a whole month at Christmas. He too was disinclined to leave the house without me. He too spent hours sitting at the kitchen table, looking out the window, waiting for the next meal. But Shane wasn't sitting there waiting for the next meal. He was waiting for the next thing to be mad about.

I tried not to dwell on how much it annoyed me that he kept his pills on the table, five or six prescription bottles in a cluster. This reminded me not only of my father but also of Shane's mother, and that was even worse. When I dared to comment on the pills, he waved his hand around to indicate all the other things that tended to take up residence on the table. *My* things—my Day-Timer, books, papers, mail, pads of Post-its, a jar of pens and pencils, a square wicker basket containing all manner of odds and ends including Scotch tape, dental floss, a calculator, and a pencil sharpener in the shape of a shoe. But not *pills*. I keep mine in the kitchen cupboard where they belong.

I tried not to dwell on how he reminded me of my mother too—cold, critical, chronically disappointed in me. Of course I knew about women who ended up marrying their fathers. But I hadn't considered that you could end up with a man just like your mother too.

Just as prison was a foreign country for me when I first became involved with Shane, ordinary family life at home was an alien territory for him. From what he'd told me of his early life and what I'd seen of his mother, even when he was young, he'd had little or no experience of it. Maybe I was being unreasonable to imagine that he would at least try to fit into our family. When we drove through the neighbourhood or took a walk down the street, what did he imagine all the people inside the other houses were doing? It seemed that for him the three pillars of life at home were fighting, fucking, and food. Everything else was just filler.

MY MEMORIES OF THE REST OF NOVEMBER are ragged, disordered fragments, stretches of blankness punctuated by unpleasant incidents. Looking back now at my Day-Timer to jog my memory, I see the pages from the middle of October to the end of November are blank. Except for one day when I wrote in large letters: *Organize my mind!*

This was when I was a basket case. I had only recently learned the origin of this term. It was First World War slang for a soldier who'd lost all four limbs and had to be carried off the battlefield in a basket.

This was when I had to go into the bathroom several times a day and look at myself in the mirror, checking to see if I was still me, if the extent to which I felt diminished and demoralized showed in my face. It did.

One afternoon, flinging open the door and barging into the bath-room, Shane caught me. "What the fuck are you doing?" he said when he saw me leaning over the sink peering into my own face in the mirror.

When I explained, he shook his head and left the room, slamming the door behind him.

Later that evening, I asked him, "Do I look the same as I did when we first met?"

He'd settled down by then and said, "Yes. You are even more beautiful."

"No, no, I'm not," I protested.

Can you see me? Can you see me? No, he could not see me. Perhaps he never had been able to.

"Can't you see what this is doing to me?" I cried.

"Here we go," he said.

He said this every time I got upset, every time I disagreed with him, every time I had the audacity to challenge him.

"Here we go."

It was like shooting a starter pistol, and then we both jumped off the cliff.

I WENT DOWNTOWN FOR LUNCH with Dorothy and Lily on yet another cold damp gloomy day. When I got home, I was so chilled that I decided to have a bath even though I'd already had one that morn-ing. Shane accused me of having gone out *not* to have lunch with my friends but to have sex with another man, of wanting to have a bath *not* because I was chilled but because I wanted to wash away the evidence. We argued in the kitchen. After he finally calmed down, I went and had my bath.

"Are you okay?" he asked afterwards.

This was what he always asked after one of our go-rounds. That was how I thought of them. They weren't exactly arguments, at least not in any way I had ever experienced before. He called them "bumps."

"Are you okay? Are you going to be okay?"

There was no right answer. Obviously I wasn't okay and didn't know yet if I was going to be okay or when. If I said, "Yes, I'm fine," then I was lying and letting him think I didn't mind being treated badly. If I said, "No, I'm not okay," then he was angry all over again.

We have all asked this question when we didn't know what else to say, just the way I'd asked it of the woman crying in the Frontenac parking lot after she'd visited her son for the first time. We have all asked this question as a way of offering comfort, empathy, a friendly ear in a difficult situation. But Shane wasn't attempting to comfort me. It was his signal that the argument was over, that he was feeling better and was now asking me to comfort him. It was never his fault for having upset me. It was only ever my fault for getting upset.

Now he said all this upset was making his already too-high blood pressure skyrocket. He pointed to his eyes, which were bulging and glassy, and to the vein in his forehead, which was protruding and throbbing like a mutant heart—two things that always happened when his blood pressure was spiking. The implication seemed to be that if he had a stroke, that would be my fault too. I backed down. I knew if he could figure out how to cause himself to have a stroke and blame it on me, he would.

The problem was never what he'd said or done. The problem was always that I had objected. He was innocent. I was a bitch. I don't think Shane ever blamed himself for anything, whereas I tend to take the blame for pretty much everything. We were a perfect match.

"Here we go."

And we were off.

"Are you okay?"

And we were done.

WE WERE DRIVING. I don't remember where we were going. It was morning. The roads were bad. There'd been some freezing rain in the night. We weren't talking. I wasn't thinking about anything. I was just trying to drive.

Suddenly Shane said, "I took your light."

He'd always said I had a special light. Maybe now he could see that it was gone. Maybe now he could see me after all. At least that morning in the car on the slippery roads, at least for that moment he could see me.

"Yes," I said. "Yes, you did."

TWO OF MY NEIGHBOURS BOUGHT him a ticket to attend a hockey game with them. He was excited about this, but when the day came, he said maybe he shouldn't go after all, maybe I was upset about him leaving me at home alone for the evening. I wondered why he couldn't see how much I was looking forward to an evening by myself. I assured him that it was fine, I would be fine, I wanted him to go and enjoy himself. I knew his sudden reluctance had nothing to do with me. He was about to go out for the evening with two men he hardly knew, to do something he hadn't done in more than thirty years. I knew he was afraid. But he went. And came home happier than I'd seen him since he moved in.

HE ALMOST GOT A JOB AT A SMALL DINER close to both the house and the LifeLine office. In fact, the LifeLine workers and their clients were all regulars there, and Stuart had arranged his interview with the owner. It went well, Shane said. He felt sure they were going to hire him. When he hadn't heard anything for a couple of days, he started walking over there two or three times a day to pester the owner. Both

Stuart and I suggested this might not be a good idea. He should just be patient. He could not be patient. When he still hadn't received a definite job offer after a week, he once again marched over to the diner. He was back home in less than ten minutes, grinning.

"You look so happy," I said. "Did you get the job?"

"No," he said proudly. "I just told the bastard to go fuck himself."

Whether we care to admit it or not, most of us tend to act in our own best interest. Not so for Shane. Not only was he a master at cutting off his nose to spite his face, but he was equally adept at shooting himself in the foot. Sometimes, by way of a double-jointed acrobatic exercise, he even managed to do both these things at once. I often thought it was no wonder he limped and couldn't breathe at night.

IN LIEU OF AN ACTUAL PAYING JOB, going back to Vinnie's seemed like the next best thing. It would keep Shane occupied and out of the house for several hours a day. Instead of working in the kitchen, this time he'd be helping out in the warehouse, keeping the parking lot shovelled and the walkway salted, and riding in the van with Russell to pick up donations.

He still had only his G1 licence and could not drive the car alone, so for the first few days, I drove him there in the morning and picked him up again later. This seemed like the natural and reasonable thing to do. It was a half-hour walk, it was so cold, often snowing, his leg was always more painful in the cold, and besides, driving him back and forth to Vinnie's was a familiar habit.

But then he said I was treating him like a child, that he was quite capable of getting himself there and back; he didn't want or need a ride. I said fine, I was just trying to be helpful. He said he didn't need my help. He said he would walk, and he did.

Each day he called me three or four times from Vinnie's to see what I was doing, once to complain that they weren't doing the Christmas decorating right. Each day when he got home, he complained bitterly about the cold, the snow, the pain in his leg. I said nothing. He stopped going.

IT WAS SHANE'S FIFTY-NINTH BIRTHDAY. We went out for dinner to the restaurant where Alex worked. He was off that night, had gone out for the evening with his new girlfriend. Between his job and his girlfriend, he was now home even less than he used to be. He was seldom there to see how badly things were going between Shane and me. When he was there, we did a good job of pretending everything was fine—just as we did the two or three times we went to Sunday mass at the convent and the Wednesday evening AA meeting.

That night I had the steak sandwich medium-rare, and Shane had the bison burger, which he didn't like very much. We had deep-fried cheesecake for dessert. Who on earth ever thought of deep-frying a cheesecake, we wondered, and how could they possibly have known it would be so delicious? We didn't linger long afterwards, because Shane was worried about his parole condition that said he must not frequent places that made the majority of their income from alcohol. We had no way of knowing, of course, how much money this restaurant made from food and how much from alcohol. When he'd once asked Janice Mackie about this ambiguity, she said that to be sure, we should eat only at places that didn't have a liquor licence, like KFC or McDonald's.

We'd been here for dinner before with no problems, and there was no problem this time either. But after we got home, he said he wondered if I'd taken him there hoping someone from CSC or the Parole Board would see him and he'd get into trouble. No, I had not.

SHANE WAS SICK AGAIN, COUGHING, CHOKING, GAGGING. He was sleeping on the couch so he wouldn't keep me awake. He got up often in the night. I could hear him wandering around the house. Then he would throw open the bedroom door, flick on the ceiling light, and stand in the doorway asking me questions.

"Are you sleeping?"

"Do you find me repulsive?"

"Why are you sleeping?"

"Why do you hate me?"

"Why aren't you sleeping?"

I was beginning to wonder about the state of his mental health.

Later he said, "I bet you were listening to me choking on the couch and wishing I would die." Later still, I admitted that yes, the thought had crossed my mind.

He went to see his new doctor. Not only had he been lucky enough to find a family physician when they were in short supply, but Dr. Chapman's office was within walking distance of the house. Given that Shane had Barrett's Esophagus, Dr. Chapman was very concerned. He said Shane needed to have some tests. Shane said he was sure he had cancer. Was that the day he drank twelve cans of Coke one right after the other, saying this was as good a way to get high as any?

HE SAID, "WE CAN'T GO ON LIKE THIS. I'm going to get my own apartment."

I said, "I'll help you look."

DR. QUINN WAS HERE AGAIN. He said he could make arrangements for Shane to return to the Peterborough house, where he could live temporarily while he made another plan. Shane said no, he'd already found an apartment. And he had—a basement bachelor in a building only four blocks from my house. I had some doubts about the apartment. The first and only place we'd looked at, it was a filthy disgusting mess featuring a backed-up toilet and a fridge full of rotten food. I had doubts about the building too, it having a reputation as the residence of miscellaneous criminals, drug dealers, and escorts. But Shane was determined, and the Parole Office had already approved it. I still cannot imagine why they approved it.

Shane would take possession of the apartment on December 1. I did not point out that this was the second anniversary of the day I gave him the I-love-you card, the day we had deemed to be the official beginning of our relationship.

The plan, as we explained it to Dr. Quinn, was that while living separately, we would continue our relationship on a "dating" basis, just as he had once suggested. I started to cry when telling him that Shane didn't trust me. When he was still in Peterborough, there was sometimes an undercurrent of jealousy, but he had managed to keep it under control. Now he was accusing me of being with another man every time I left the house. Why had his jealousy become so extreme now that we were living together? What had I ever done to make him distrust me? Later Shane said he was acting that way because he was so afraid of losing me. If he was afraid of losing me, why didn't he treat me better instead of worse?

Dr. Quinn sternly told me to stop crying. "Let it go," he said. "You're hanging onto the past. Stop talking about it. Just let it go. It doesn't matter now."

THE NIGHT BEFORE SHANE MOVED OUT, there was me saying, "I never meant to hurt you. I never tried to hurt you on purpose."

There was him saying, "Me neither."

I couldn't for the life of me see how this was true. Maybe it wasn't true when I said it either.

We were sitting on the couch in our pyjamas holding hands. There had been some crying on both our parts. That morning we'd been to the first meeting of the healing circle Valerie had arranged. But it was too late. In the morning, Stuart from LifeLine would arrive with the small moving van he'd borrowed for the day.

STUART HAD TAKEN SHANE BACK to Ontario Works, and this time he came away with a start-up cheque and the full monthly benefit. As a welfare recipient, he would now have to pay only two dollars for each prescription he needed.

With some of the start-up money, he bought a new mattress and box spring from the Salvation Army Thrift Store. I contributed what I could to furnishing the apartment: a loveseat and a large armchair we no longer used, a wooden folding table, bedding, towels, curtains, a set of dishes. His relatives contributed an old TV set and a VCR, a box of videos, a small bookcase, coffee mugs, cutlery, pots and pans. I helped him arrange everything, and then we went to Canadian Tire to buy the items he was missing: shower curtain, toaster, bath mat, plunger, two Rubbermaid tubs in which he'd keep his clothes until he got a dresser.

We were both more relaxed than we'd been in weeks, months maybe. I went home feeling hopeful. Maybe this new arrangement was going to work.

TWO DAYS LATER, I TOOK HIM THE PUPPY, MAGGIE. This was the plan: she would live with him, while Nelly, Max, and Sammy would stay with me and Alex. I packed up her toys, her bed, her leash, her dishes, some food, a bag of treats. I felt some sadness leaving her there, and when I arrived back home without her, the others, even Max and especially Nelly, were confused and distressed. But Maggie had been with us for only a month and a half—I figured we'd adjust to this change soon enough.

Getting them all settled in at bedtime that night was difficult—they were taking turns wandering around the house looking for her. This was repeated when I got up in the morning. But before I could figure out what to do about it, the phone rang. Shane said he couldn't keep Maggie; I'd have to come and get her. He said she cried all night and peed on the brand-new bath mat four times. I did not point out that she was just a puppy and did that here too—the peeing, not the crying. So I got dressed and went over, bringing her and all her belongings back in the car. At home the reunion with the others was joyful and exuberant, and she was not the only one of them who peed on the floor in all the excitement.

FOR THE FIRST TWO WEEKS OF DECEMBER, almost every day Shane needed a ride somewhere. How was it that when we lived together, he resented me trying to help him with anything, but now he wanted my help with something every day? And how was it that he couldn't just knock on the door like anybody else would? Why did he have to pound on it as if it were an emergency or perhaps the Gestapo?

He needed a ride to the food bank. He needed a ride to the welfare office. He needed a ride to the Salvation Army Thrift Store, because he was cold at night and wanted more blankets. He needed a ride to Canadian Tire, because there was a rat in his apartment, and he wanted to buy poison and a trap. He needed a ride to the police station to do his monthly check-in. He needed a ride to the cell phone store, because his phone was stolen when he left it on the table at the downtown Tim Hortons when he went to the washroom.

I could have said no to any or all of these requests, but I didn't. Although I was no longer clear about our relationship status, whether we were living together or not, I still cared about him, and as far as I knew, he still had no one else to help him. On many levels, I felt responsible for him. I didn't want to see him fail and end up back in jail.

IN THE BUNDLE OF TOWELS I'D GIVEN HIM, I had accidentally included Nelly's towel, the large white one I'd wrapped her in when I had to put her in a kennel for a week when my father died in Thunder Bay. With a permanent marker, I'd printed her name in large letters on the towel. Shane was enraged when he discovered I'd given him the dog's towel. He called and demanded to know what was I trying to say—that he was no better than a dog?

There was the matter of perceived slights. He was always ready to be provoked, seeing insult, offence, disrespect when there was none intended. He would fasten on the smallest thing—an offhand remark, a sideways glance, an inadvertent sigh—then chew on it, stew on it, nurse it, feed it, foster it until it grew into a full-blown rage. There was never much chance of convincing him that what he'd perceived as a slight was not. As far as the towel went, I didn't even try. Considering how much I loved and doted on my Nelly, he should have been flattered. Considering how often he'd complained that I treated the pets better than I treated him, he should have been pleased.

HE STARTED TALKING ABOUT A WOMAN named Linda Porter, whom he'd met at the downtown Tim Hortons. With some pride, he said she'd come over to his apartment and taken all her clothes off. But he said nothing happened. He said he never touched her. He said he missed me so much, he wasn't interested. I found this hard to believe. I did not point out that this wasn't the "dating" arrangement we had talked about with Dr. Quinn. I was upset but did not say so. Maybe it was for the best if he found someone else. Or maybe he was just making it up to see how I would react, testing me as he often did. Maybe there was no such person as Linda Porter at all, with or without her clothes on.

WHEN WE LIVED TOGETHER, he never once took a book off the shelf. It was as if the wall of books in the living room that had once moved him to tears was now nothing more than wallpaper. But after he moved out, suddenly his interest in reading was revived. He started going to the library several times a week. He talked about all the books he was reading. When I asked him later why he didn't read when he lived with me, he said it was because he knew I wanted him to. He said he would read when *he* wanted to, not because *I* wanted him to.

HE SAID HE WENT DOWNTOWN TO THE ROYAL, a seedy tavern he'd frequented when he was young. He said he went there to "talk to his ghosts." He said he had one beer and left. He said no, he had a Coke and left. He said no, he never went there at all. He said he was just testing me to see what I'd say about him breaking his parole conditions. He was twisted about his conditions, even though they were the same as they'd always been. Why did he always have to answer to them? I pointed out that we all have someone to whom we must answer, that we all have conditions by which we must abide. Out here we call them "laws."

EVERY DAY THERE WERE MANY PHONE CALLS. His moods were erratic and unpredictable. Sometimes he wasn't making sense. I had no idea: Was he drinking? Was he doing drugs? Was he having some kind of mental breakdown? Was he trying to scare me? He could tell that sometimes I was afraid. He said he would never hurt me. He reminded me that his violent episodes were long in the past. By way of reassurance, he said that even then, they hadn't taken place after a long slow buildup of anger but because he'd snapped. I did not find this reassuring.

CHRISTMAS. AGAIN. Alex and I put up the small tree in the living room. I'd hoped one of Shane's relatives would invite him for dinner, but they didn't. I was worried about him being alone at Christmas, so

I suggested he join us for turkey. He had already admitted that he'd considered killing himself after he moved out. I was afraid spending Christmas alone might well push him over the edge.

Alex and I opened our presents in the morning. Shane came over in the early afternoon. He was cheerful and relaxed. Alex went to meet his friends at the only downtown bar open on Christmas afternoon. It was their tradition to gather there each year to celebrate the birthday of one of the girls, who was born on Christmas Day. His new girlfriend had gone home for the holidays. He'd be back in time for dinner.

After he left, Shane and I prepared the turkey and put it in the oven, peeled the carrots and potatoes. Then I got out the Scrabble game and set it up on the coffee table, thinking this would be a pleasant way to pass the rest of the afternoon. Shane sat on the couch beside me, but he wasn't interested in Scrabble. He tried to get romantic. He thought we should spend the afternoon in bed. I refused. He put on his coat and left.

Alex and I sat down to dinner just the two of us. For his sake, I tried not to let on how upset I was. I simply said Shane had decided not to stay after all. He didn't question this. After dinner he went out again, to the home of a friend who lived nearby. I couldn't blame him. If I'd had somewhere else to go, I would have gone there too.

Late in the evening, I heard the crunch of footsteps on the snow in the driveway, then Shane's characteristic pounding on the back door. I was afraid to answer it. I stood in the back porch listening at the door. Over the beating of my own heart, I could again hear footsteps in the driveway, receding. I pulled the curtain back an inch or two and could see him limping quickly away down the street. I could also see there was something on the back step. I opened the door a few inches and found two large garbage bags obviously filled with stuff.

I brought them into the kitchen, opened them warily. Inside the first bag were many things I'd given him over the past two years, clothing, knickknacks, books—including mine signed to him. The second bag contained all the cards and letters and photographs I'd ever sent him. Every single one of them had been ripped into little pieces.

EARLY THE NEXT MORNING, Boxing Day, I called Stuart and told him everything that had happened, including that Shane said he'd gone to the Royal, where he had or hadn't been drinking beer. Stuart said he was just trying to wind me up. I said it was working. I said he was crashing down a slippery slope and trying to take me with him. I wasn't exactly sure what I meant by this, but that was how it felt. I said I couldn't take it anymore and didn't want Shane coming onto my property ever again, and Stuart said he would make that clear to him. And he would advise Jerry Anderson of these developments as soon as he returned to work after the holidays.

I took down the little Christmas tree and put away the presents. With Alex's help, I moved my desk back into the living room in front of the wall of books, imagining that I would soon be able to pick up my life where I'd left off. A young man of few words, Alex didn't say much in this instance either, other than to note that this had been the worst Christmas ever.

Stuart called back later in the day. He said Shane had promised he'd stay away from me and my house, had said he didn't want to see me ever again either. Good. But what he did want, Stuart said, was to get his steaks back. What? It took me a minute to remember that some weeks earlier, when we were still living together, he'd bought three large sirloin steaks from a nearby butcher shop. I don't remember, if I ever knew, where he got the money. Not from me. We decided to save them for a special occasion. They were still in the freezer wrapped in brown butcher paper.

Stuart and I made an arrangement for the return of the steaks. I would meet him at my neighbourhood Tim Hortons the next morning at ten o'clock and give them to him. He in turn would give them to Shane.

When I pulled into the parking lot right on time, I could see Stuart's car with two people in it. Stuart got out, and when Shane opened the passenger door and made to get out too, Stuart hollered at him to stay in the car. I gave Stuart the bag of meat, got back in my car, and went home. Stranger things have no doubt happened in that Tim Hortons parking lot but not to me.

RIGHT AFTER NEW YEAR'S, I went out for lunch with Dorothy and Evelyn. They were beyond worried. They were nigh unto hysterical. Evelyn said she kept picturing me lying stabbed and bleeding to death on the kitchen floor. Perhaps she meant well, but this did not help. Dorothy said I should have the locks on my house changed. I'd already done that, because sometimes when I looked out the window at night, I thought I could see someone standing in the driveway of the house across the street. The end of a lit cigarette glowed orange in the darkness. Nobody who lived there smoked. Dorothy said I should buy some bear spray for protection.

After lunch I walked down the block to the Army Surplus Store. Having no idea where the bear spray might be located or what it might look like, I waited in line at the front counter. The young man at the cash register waited on two customers ahead of me, and then it was my turn. I made my request.

He said calmly, "You do realize bear spray will kill a person, don't you, ma'am?"

I guess I didn't look like someone who would be venturing into bear country at any time of the year, let alone in the dead of winter.

"No, I didn't realize that," I said, laughing nervously. "I don't actually want to kill him."

"Perhaps some dog spray would be a better choice then," he said cheerfully, turning to the display behind him, selecting several items, then spreading them on the counter for my examination. I chose a small canister that came with a handy Velcro wristband. He demonstrated how to use it.

I said, "Perfect, I'll take it," and got out my wallet.

Transaction completed, bag in hand, I turned to discover, standing right behind me, the owner of my favourite bookstore and his wife. Waving the bag in the air, I said, "Nasty dog in the neighbourhood," and fled.

Not many days later, I read in the newspaper of a woman who'd been charged and sent to jail for carrying a prohibited weapon: bear spray.

ONCE JERRY ANDERSON WAS BACK IN THE OFFICE, he called, and I confirmed the details of what Stuart had already told him. He shared my concern about Shane's erratic behaviour and said he'd see him as often as possible, every day if necessary, to keep an eye on things.

Shane continued to stay away, but he also continued calling constantly. I had not asked Jerry to tell him to stop phoning, because I felt that was the only means by which I could continue to monitor his frame of mind.

On the phone, he admitted that he'd wanted the steaks back because Brandy had come to visit him for five days right after Christmas. He said he was going to move to Windsor and live with her. Platonically, he said. As if I were likely to believe that. He was still talking about Linda Porter too, who was still coming over and taking her clothes off.

He said he'd been going to the house of a man we'd met at Vinnie's. Much as this man was a pleasant fellow, he also had serious problems with both drugs and alcohol, seemed more than likely involved in some kind of criminal activity. When I warned Shane that he shouldn't be going there, he said Stuart had warned him too, but he was so lonely, and what the fuck was he supposed to do since I kicked him out? Sit around in that horrible apartment all day and night by himself? I refrained from reminding him that I did not "kick him out"—that moving out was his idea in the first place, and I had simply agreed with him. I also refrained from suggesting that the Parole Board might not see loneliness as a good enough reason to be breaching his conditions. I said maybe he should call Lenny in Peterborough when he felt that way—maybe that would help.

Later he admitted that he didn't want anyone to know he was struggling—not even Lenny. Especially not Lenny. He'd always said Lenny was so institutionalized that he'd never make it out on the street. But Lenny, in fact, was doing just fine.

These phone calls were becoming more rambling, more disjointed, more disturbing. Sometimes he was crying, sometimes nasty and sarcastic. Sometimes he asked me for money or cigarettes. Sometimes I could hardly understand what he was saying. He said Dr. Chapman had put him on antidepressants, but they didn't work, so he'd stopped taking them after three days. I explained that this type of medication takes several weeks to take effect. No, no, he said, Dr. Chapman said these ones would work right away, but they didn't.

By the end of the third week of January, he said his welfare had been cut off; he'd lost his apartment and was going to stay at the homeless shelter until he could move to Windsor. When I pressed for details, he said he'd given his apartment to Linda Porter and now had nowhere to live. None of this made any sense at all. I knew that as a federal parolee, he was not allowed to stay at a shelter. Nor could he just pick up and move to Windsor. No, no, he said, Jerry Anderson was setting it all up now. I recognized this as his particular kind of magical thinking: that thinking, wanting, saying something out loud made it true. Then he said it was all my friends' fault that we broke up because they had turned me against him. He accused me of having sex with either or both of my neighbours, the two men who had taken him to the hockey game. He said he was coughing up blood and thought he was going to die.

I'd had enough with the bizarre phone calls. On Friday afternoon, I called Jerry Anderson and told him I was going to block Shane on my phone and wanted no more contact with him by that or any other means. Jerry said rather than tell Shane that day and risk having him enraged over the weekend when he, Jerry, wasn't around, he'd tell him on Monday morning. He said he had an appointment to see Shane early that day anyway and would call me afterwards to let me know how it had gone.

The weekend passed quietly. When I returned from driving Alex to work on Sunday evening, I found the folding table I'd given Shane when he moved out jammed into the snowbank at the end of my driveway. It was the one item I had said I'd like to have back eventually. In the snowbank, it was covered with the large white towel marked with Nelly's name.

ON MONDAY MORNING, I paced around waiting for Jerry to call. It was almost noon when I finally heard from him, and what he had to say was not at all what I'd been expecting.

Shane had been arrested. Not for committing any new crimes but for breaching his conditions and for something they called "deteriorating attitude." I'd often thought that if this were grounds for arrest for everyone, we would all be in prison. In this case, his erratic behaviour was deemed an indication that his risk level was no longer manageable.

His parole had been suspended, and he was now in a cell at the city jail, on his way back to prison. How was it that I could be so utterly shocked by this news? How was it that in the face of all evidence to the contrary, I had still believed Shane was going to pull himself together and become, as I'd described him to the Parole Board only three months ago, a success story?

Jerry laid out the scenario that had unfolded that morning. Shane had called him early, said he'd lost his apartment and now had to go to the homeless shelter. Their appointment was originally to take place at the apartment, but Jerry told Shane to walk over to his office instead.

When he arrived, he was met by several members of the ROPE Squad. I knew this acronym stood for Repeat Offender Parole Enforcement, a special police unit tasked with capturing parolees who had committed another crime or violated their conditions. I found it hard not to picture them on horses, with cowboy hats, spurs, and lassoes. When the armed officers surrounded him and asked if he had a weapon, Shane apparently said, "I've got a gun." Of course he didn't. Jerry was a bit vague about what happened next, but Shane ended up in handcuffs in a cruiser on his way to the police station. How was it that I hadn't once allowed myself to acknowledge that this was bound to be the ending of this part of the story?

There had also been, Jerry said, members of the ROPE Squad stationed in unmarked cars at both ends of my one-block street in case Shane decided to come to my house instead. When I asked Jerry why he didn't call and tell me they were out there, first he said it was policy, then he said he didn't want to scare me, then he said, what if Shane had an escape plan and I was in on it?

Shane had been a free man for a hundred and one days.

FOR FEDERAL PAROLEES, ESPECIALLY FOR LIFERS, there is no leeway if they are found to have breached their conditions. Following the standard protocol, Shane was held for two nights in the city jail, then moved to the provincial jail in Kenworth. After two nights there, he was transferred to the Temporary Detention Centre at Kingston Penitentiary. He would spend almost three weeks there, during which time he underwent a number of assessments of his psychological state and his risk level to determine which prison he should be sent to. Once this process was completed, he was transported to Bath Institution, a medium-security prison located about thirty kilometres west of Kingston. Originally opened as a minimum-security institution, Bath was the same prison from which Shane had escaped back in 1981, travelling to Toronto to meet up with Victor—the trip that had ended with the murder of Philip Bailey.

In the two weeks following Shane's arrest, I spoke to Jerry Anderson half a dozen times. Either he called me or I called him, most often the latter. He was gathering information for his report to the Parole Board, a report for the post-suspension hearing at which it would be decided whether Shane was to remain incarcerated or have his full parole reinstated and be released. I was completely honest with Jerry, telling him in great detail and sometimes with tears about the upsetting incidents of the past three months. As an example of Shane's escalating and unfounded jealousy, I told him about the bath incident, when he'd accused me of having been with another man. I told Jerry how he would push me until I lost my temper and yelled at him—or worse, in the case of the cutting board incident—and then he'd accuse me of being the mean one, the scary one, the crazy one. Jerry was kind and understanding, assuring me that none of it was my fault, that Shane could provoke Mother Teresa to lose her temper if he tried. He was a master of manipulation, Jerry said, and everything with him was all about power and control. I immediately recognized this as the truth.

Exactly two weeks after the arrest, I opened my mailbox to discover an envelope addressed to me in Shane's familiar handwriting, stamped front and back as having come from Kingston Penitentiary. My hands and legs were shaking as I sat down at the kitchen table and opened it.

Whatever I was afraid this letter might say, it was entirely innocuous. He began by asking me to please send his T4 slips to Roy. He said he wasn't going to Windsor after all, nor back to Peterborough, maybe to Ottawa or Toronto. He asked how the pets were doing. He wondered briefly about what went wrong between us: was it one thing or a multitude; was it his need to stay in his world versus my need to stay in mine? This surprised me. I hadn't understood that he wanted to stay in his world. I had thought he truly wanted to come into mine. He ended with a P.S. in which he asked if he could write to me again.

There was nothing in the contents of this letter to be upset about. What upset me was the fact that he had been allowed to send it to me at all. What about the no-contact order? Would this never end?

I called Jerry to complain. He said I didn't expect the KP staff to check every single outgoing letter, did I? Yes, as a matter of fact, I did. He told me to bring him the letter, and he would make sure it didn't happen again. I made copies for myself and took the original, still in its KP-stamped envelope, to his office. As it turned out, the ramifications of that simple one-page letter would go on for years.

When I called Jerry the next day, he said his report was already ten pages long, and he didn't want to write any more. It didn't occur to me to ask for a copy. I don't know if I had the right to do that or if he would have shown it to me if I had.

He told me to call the city police so I could then be registered with CSC Victim Services, who would keep me apprised of the situation. I didn't think of myself as a "victim," but I did want to be kept informed. The woman I spoke to at the police station was not much interested. Why was I calling them now, she wanted to know, if he was already back in prison? When I explained that his parole officer had told me to, she gave an exaggerated long-suffering sigh. But she took the information.

IT WAS ONLY AFTER I QUIT DRINKING back in 1992 that I began to understand some of the reasons why I'd been drinking in the first place. For one thing, when I was drinking, I was no longer anxious, afraid, shy, or self-conscious. When I was drinking, I no longer compared myself to others and found myself wanting. When I quit drinking, I thought all my problems would be solved, all my demons banished, if not overnight, then soon, very soon. This of course was not the case. All my demons were still there, but now they were sober too. In hindsight, I realize I was thinking much the same way when my relationship with Shane ended, and he was sent back to prison. I thought all my problems would be solved.

I had never wanted him to end up back in prison. I had just wanted him to go away and leave me alone, but not like this. In December and January, I'd been worried that he was having a mental breakdown. Now I was the one who was falling apart—broken perhaps by the stress of all that had come before, by trying to let go of the anxiety and adrenalin that had propelled me through the previous months. Whatever it was, I was incapacitated most of the time.

Each evening I sat on the couch staring at the TV until it was time to go to bed and stare at the ceiling. If I managed to sleep at all, even for an hour or two, I considered it a major accomplishment. When I did sleep, waking up in the morning gave me a few blessed empty-headed seconds, mere moments of peace and clarity, before everything came crashing down upon me, and I was stricken all over again.

I considered it a monumental triumph when I could get up, make coffee, have a bath, get dressed, tend to the pets. It felt like an exceptional achievement when I could eat something, even a chocolate bar, a bag of chips, a plate of cheese and crackers. It felt like a miraculous act of concentration when I could read the newspaper or a few pages of an actual book. It felt like a significant victory when I could drive Alex to work and get home again without wrecking the car. He was doing what he could to help me, but he was out of his depth. After all, I was his mother, and I was doing everything I could to hide how terrible I felt. I was scaring myself and didn't want to scare him too.

In pursuit of some semblance of normalcy, I continued making my daily trip to Tim Hortons, until the morning I ran into another inmate from Frontenac, now out on parole, who said he'd heard that Shane and I had split up and he was back inside. "Would you consider going out with another convict?" he asked—nudge nudge, wink wink.

"Not on your life!" I cried and fled.

I forced myself to leave the house several times a week. I went back to Vinnie's a few times, not to volunteer but just to visit, hoping that it would do for me again what it had before: lift me out of my misery, help me to heal and regain my strength. But this time it didn't work. This time it made me feel worse. There were too many questions about what had happened, too many rumours to be dispelled, too many other people's opinions to be deflected, and I didn't know how to be there without him.

Dreading the prospect of running into anyone I knew, I took to wearing my sunglasses wherever I went, sunny or not, inside or out, like some melodramatic movie star trying to avoid the paparazzi.

One afternoon, in the produce department at Loblaws, another woman in sunglasses pulled her cart up next to mine and said, "I really loved your new book." In itself, this was not an unusual encounter. Kingston is a small city, and I've lived here for decades, made many public appearances, frequently had my picture in the local paper. I get recognized fairly often, a phenomenon Alex and I refer to as me "being famous" at the drugstore, The Bay, or Canadian Tire. Once I was almost famous at the bank—a woman in line behind me tapped me on the shoulder and asked if I was "that writer Diane Schoemperlen," but when I said yes, I was, the woman said no, I wasn't, that writer was much younger.

That day I was famous at Loblaws. The voice of the woman also wearing sunglasses was familiar, but I didn't recognize her until she lowered them and said, "It's me, Marsha." I hadn't seen or heard from her since Vera's funeral almost a year ago. I resisted the urge to scream for help. Leaning on her cart, she said pleasant things about my new book and my writing in general, said nothing about Shane or Darlene or that day. Then she put her sunglasses back on, tapped them and said, "Hiding," as she pushed her cart towards the next aisle. I had only half the things I'd intended to buy, but I went directly to the cash and got the hell out of there. I drove around for an hour, afraid to go home in case she followed me, afraid that when I did get home, she would be there waiting for me. She wasn't.

Even doing basic chores and errands left me exhausted and whimpering, so I set myself a single goal for each day, one simple task I could do without thinking, then check off my list with some sense of accomplishment. Laundry, groceries, garbage, dust, vacuum, clean the bathroom, change the kitty litter box. At one chore per day, it took me all week. I made an occasional half-hearted attempt to do some creative work, but my thinking was so disordered, I'd lost the ability to string words together to form even the simplest coherent sentence. I had no inclination to take a drink, and I hadn't returned to AA, but I silently chanted their "One day at a time" mantra constantly. I found it much too vast in its ambition, so I began to break it down into smaller, more manageable increments as necessary: one hour at a time, half an hour, fifteen minutes, five minutes. One minute at a time.

Much as my friends tried to suppress their jubilance, I could see they were ecstatic with relief at our breakup and Shane's return to prison. Some were blatant in their "good riddance to bad rubbish" reaction. Walter, who had told me I was stupid, now said I was lucky. Utterly without irony, he said, "You really dodged a bullet this time." I resisted pointing out that Shane was under a lifetime weapons ban and that, as far as I knew, he had never shot anyone.

Others were more diplomatic, but still their sense of relief was palpable. I could hear them thinking, Thank God, now we can forget all about that spell of temporary insanity and get on with our lives.

If only it were that simple.

They tried to be patient with me, but I knew they didn't understand what I was going through. I didn't understand it myself, so how could I possibly explain it to them? They offered advice. Just give it time, they said. I kept counting the number of weeks since we broke up, the number of days since he was sent back. What was the magic number? You have to be strong, they said. Then I berated myself for being weak. Keep busy, they said. Clean out the kitchen cupboards, reorganize your books, get an early start on your spring cleaning. Get back to writing. Then I berated myself for not being able to keep up with the housework, let alone pile up the pages too.

Their patience soon began to wear thin. You're better off without him; you should be happy to be rid of him, they said. Chalk it up to experience and move on, they said. They seemed to be implying that I was wallowing in my misery. Maybe I was. Snap out of it, they said. I would have if I could have, and then I berated myself because I couldn't.

When I was still barely functioning by early March, I knew I had to find help. There had been other rough times in my life when I should have sought professional help but didn't, not because I was ashamed or embarrassed but because I was arrogant. I am an intelligent, educated woman: what could a therapist possibly tell me that I didn't already know? But this time I was on my knees, and I knew I couldn't get through it alone.

I called both Jerry Anderson and Dr. Quinn, but neither of them were willing or able to offer me any help. I couldn't really blame them: Shane was their responsibility, not me. The only other person I could think to call was Valerie, the community chaplain. The timing was fortuitous—the very next afternoon, she said, would be the second session of a new program being run for women whose partners were in prison. I was more than welcome to attend, she said, and she'd be happy to speak with me privately afterwards about Shane.

The program was held in the same building as her office, a three-storey ivy-covered red-brick Victorian house, where, for almost thirty years, dozens of community groups have been holding meetings, work-shops, and seminars. Officially called the Kingston Community House for Self-Reliance, it is more commonly known by its street address: 99 York. When I arrived that first afternoon, the other women had already gathered in the parlour, a large homey room with a fireplace and a cluster of comfortably used couches and chairs. On the round table in the centre was a box of doughnuts and a plate of cookies. I could smell coffee brewing in the kitchen. I took off my boots and helped myself to a pair of hand-knit slippers in the basket by the door. Valerie introduced me to the six or seven other women in the room including Rosemary, the facilitator.

Rosemary was with an organization called the Canadian Families and Corrections Network (CFCN), headquartered in Kingston but operating on a national level to help the families of federal prisoners with both incarceration and reintegration after release. She said she recognized me from Frontenac, where she'd had an office during the months I was visiting Shane. She said she'd often wanted to come over to our table and introduce herself, but since he'd never requested her assistance, she didn't know whether she should. I didn't understand why Shane had never once mentioned either CFCN or Rosemary, even though he knew I was sometimes struggling and would have jumped at the chance to have some support along the way. Nor did I understand why neither of the parole officers we were working with at the time had ever mentioned CFCN as an organization from whose help we might benefit.

Rosemary said they would be meeting every Thursday afternoon for another eight weeks and gave me a copy of the textbook for the program, *Be Your Best: Personal Effectiveness in Your Life and Your Relationships* by Linda Adams and Elinor Lenz.

I felt too shy and shaky to say much that first day, but those Thursday afternoons soon became the focal point of my week. No matter how difficult the other days might be, I could set my sights on Thursday as the beacon towards which I was navigating, those two or three hours during which I felt steadily stronger, saner, more like myself.

We made our way through the book week by week, covering topics like "Who Controls Your Life?," "What It Means to Be Assertive," "Learning to Say No," "Dealing with Anxiety," and "Who Owns the Problem?" Much as all of this was interesting and useful, it was being with the other women that mattered the most to me. However different we might be in some ways, the one thing we shared was prison. There I never had to justify having fallen in love with a murderer. There I never had to spell out the acronyms, describe the procedures, or explain the ever-changing

rules. There I could rant and rave about the endless frustrations of dealing with the Monty Pythonesque logic of the Correctional Service of
Canada. There I could laugh until my stomach hurt.

SHANE HAD ONCE JOKED that there were only two kinds of convict
thinking: "It wasn't me," or "It *was* me, but I couldn't help it." This put
me in mind of my son, these being two things I heard from him far too
often in his teenage years. Even into his twenties, whenever I was angry
with him, these were his default defence positions.

Rosemary and Valerie helped me understand that prison is not a
good place to grow up and mature, that long-term prisoners like Shane
get stuck emotionally and psychologically at the age they were when
they went in. They do not experience the same life events and challenges that help the rest of us grow and develop into mature adults.
The challenges of prolonged incarceration are entirely different but
no less transformative. These challenges are commonly referred to as
"the pains of imprisonment," a phrase originally used by the American
sociologist and criminologist Gresham M. Sykes in his 1958 book *The
Society of Captives*, a pioneering and now classic study of maximum-
security New Jersey State Prison. Sykes catalogued the primary pains
of imprisonment as being the deprivation of liberty, goods and services, heterosexual relationships, autonomy, and security. Adapting
over time to these pains of imprisonment, the prisoner develops habits
of thought and behaviour that become chronic and deeply internal-
ized. While these defensive techniques may ensure his survival inside,
they are entirely dysfunctional out here in the free world.

I finally began to understand what institutionalization really meant
and that much of what had gone wrong in our relationship was the
consequence of this pernicious process.

Much as the prisoner rebels at first against the structured carceral environment with all its rules and regulations and rigid routines, over time he becomes ever more dependent on it. In every aspect of his daily life, he is relegated to the powerless status of a child. Deprived of privacy, he is told when to go to bed and when to get up, when and what to eat, when he can move from one part of the prison to another, when he can go outside, when he can see or speak to his loved ones, and so on. In this extremely controlled environment, the prisoner becomes infantilized, losing both his autonomy and his sense of self-worth as a valuable functioning adult.

At the same time, the prison environment is also extremely hostile and dangerous. The prisoner must be hypervigilant around the other inmates, adopting a "tough guy" persona to protect himself. Deprived of security, his daily life in this dystopia is shaped by fear, distrust, suspicion, and paranoia. Not only must he abide by the rules of the institution that govern all aspects of his behaviour, but also he must constantly navigate the perilous twists and turns of the convict code of behaviour as well. Adding to this toxic and chaotic stew of power, control, and manipulation is the fact that those who are institutionalized have little or no insight into what imprisonment has actually done to them psychologically and even less idea of how to cope with or begin to reverse this damage after they are released.

I realized that if I had understood more of this when Shane and I were together, I would have been better equipped to deal with him. But the relationship had already felt like a full-time job, and I hadn't had time to include a research component too.

One day in one of our private conversations after the group, I admitted to Valerie, the chaplain, that I missed him, that I wished I could go and see him. She asked me what I really wanted from having contact with him. It took me some time to figure this out.

From the time we first met, I could always see the good in him. As time went on, I came to see his dark side too, what I thought of as "the other

Shane." But still I believed that the good Shane was the real Shane and would become *the only* Shane once he came home to stay. Instead, the other Shane had taken over, and the good Shane had disappeared altogether. What I wanted from having contact with him now was to see the good Shane again. I wanted to forgive him. I wanted him to forgive me.

AFTER I WAS OFFICIALLY REGISTERED with CSC Victim Services, I began to receive notifications by mail every time Shane was granted a pass to leave the institution. Because he was now in a medium-security prison, he would be escorted by two correctional officers and he would be "in restraints," meaning leg irons or handcuffs, or both. I did not let myself picture this. All the notifications I received were for medical appointments. The nature and exact location of these were not given, just the date and time of day, morning or afternoon.

After receiving three such notifications in one week, I called Jerry Anderson and asked him if Shane was sick. Was he seriously ill? Was he dying? Jerry assured me that no, he was not. I told him that if he was dying, I wanted to be there. Jerry said he could understand that, and he could make it happen. The being there, that is, not the dying. I began then to perfect what I thought of as my "deathbed fantasy"—his deathbed, that is, not mine.

There he was in the hospital bed hooked up to machines, and there I was in a chair beside him, as close to the bed as I could get, holding his hand, maybe both hands. There was his dark hair against the pillow, his tattoos stark against the white sheets. There was me in the beautiful jacket, having a good hair day, and, for once in my life, crying with just pretty tears sliding slowly down my cheeks. Except for the gentle humming of the machines, the room was utterly silent. I had said everything I needed to say. He was not talking either. His eyes were closed, and he was not snoring. He was quiet and peaceful, or at least as close to quiet and peaceful as he was ever going to get. Perhaps he was in a coma.

He'd told me often enough that one of his biggest fears was dying in prison, dying alone. He'd expressed this once in a program he was taking, and in the final report, the facilitator had noted this as an area of concern, an issue that Shane must find ways to deal with lest it prevent him from being able to live as a law-abiding citizen in the future. But wouldn't anybody be afraid of dying in prison, and aren't most people afraid of dying alone? Wasn't the fact that he shared this common fear proof of his humanity, rather than evidence of some insidious pathology that would eventually rear its ugly head in the form of some future violent criminal act? I would not let him die alone and afraid. I would be there beside him for as long as it took—until he stopped breathing, and the whole room went black. Perhaps then we would both be at peace—for once and for all.

THE WOMEN'S GROUP WOULD BE ENDING the first week of May. I was definitely in much better shape than I'd been when I began attending. I could now get through whole days without falling into despair, sometimes two or three days in a row. I could now, on a good day, be awake in the morning for an hour or more before I even thought about Shane.

Most important, I was working. I was not actually writing, was still not piling up the pages, but yes, I was working. Well known for my love of lists, I'd been invited to be Guest Editor of a special Lists issue of *The*

New Quarterly, a respected literary journal published at the University of Waterloo. Sitting down each morning to the growing stack of manuscripts we had received in response to our call for submissions, I was in my glory. I was also nudging ever closer to writing a list story of my own for the issue.

But I was still prone to unexpected eruptions of anger, anxiety, grief; could still find myself paralyzed on the couch for hours, either obsessively replaying one unpleasant incident after another or trying to understand why, after everything that had happened, I missed him. I was, to say the very least, conflicted. Regardless of what anyone else thought of him or me or our relationship, I loved him—in my way—and he loved me—in his. We didn't either one of us know how to do it any differently than we had. We didn't either one of us know how to have a healthy relationship. I was still talking to him in my head, sometimes out loud too. When I noticed people giving me a wide berth as they passed me on the sidewalk, I realized I was muttering to him as I walked down the street.

With the women's group winding down, there was some talk of continuing to meet informally for coffee every couple of weeks. I didn't think that would work for me. I knew I still needed help but felt it should be of a more structured and therapeutic variety. Besides, I was beginning to feel that being part of a group of women dedicated to making their marriages to inmates work, while I was trying to get over my relationship with Shane, had become counterproductive, keeping me engaged with the carceral life rather than helping me put my prison years behind me.

So once again I was left wondering where to turn. One evening while flipping through the weekly newspaper, I spotted a small ad for a therapy centre specializing in issues of trauma and abuse. It was the word *trauma* that caught my attention. My friend Evelyn, a retired nurse, had suggested several times that I might be suffering from post-traumatic stress disorder. All I knew of PTSD had to do with soldiers returning from horrific war zones like Afghanistan and Iraq. I thought Evelyn was exaggerating—surely my struggles with Shane weren't on the same level as what soldiers had experienced in these deadly conflicts. But I knew there were other kinds of trauma too, so I cut out the ad and stuck it on the side of the fridge. It included a phone number and an email address. At the bottom it said, *New clients welcome.* I studied the ad every day for two weeks, and then I sent an email.

I received a prompt reply from a woman named Louise, who suggested we set up an intake appointment. The address she gave, just a few blocks from my house, was familiar, but I couldn't place it. When I got there a week later, I found that her office was on the second floor of the same building as the Parole Office. Thankfully my appointment was at five o'clock, when the Parole Office was already closed for the day. Just walking past it was hard enough, never mind having to worry that I might run into someone I knew.

Having never been for therapy before, I was nervous and didn't know what to expect. In my first email, I'd told her only that I needed help getting over a broken relationship. I hadn't mentioned prison. What would she ask me? What would I say? Would I cry? I hate crying. How much would I cry? Would she mind if I cried? What if she said she couldn't help me? What if she said I was a hopeless case?

We sat in two chairs facing each other with a small round table between us. There was a loveseat with several cushions against the wall. She said I was welcome to sit there, but I chose the chair. Within ten minutes, I was entirely comfortable with Louise. Within fifteen minutes, I'd launched into the abridged version of the last three years. She listened attentively. I cried. There was a box of Kleenex on the table. I took several. I cried some more. She listened some more. By now I wanted to throw myself at her feet, cling to her ankles, and cry, "Help me! Help me!"

As we neared the end of our appointment, and I began trying to pull myself together enough to leave her office and go back out into the world, I could see she was smiling. I was still helping myself to the Kleenex and wiping my wet face.

"I know I can help you," she said.

Thank God. My whole body went weak with relief. Now she was grinning. She explained that not only had she worked in the prisons for years as a facilitator of the Alternatives to Violence Program, but some time ago, one of her close family members had spent several years in prison. We agreed that I would continue seeing her every Tuesday at five o'clock.

Week after week, I got comfortable on the loveseat and told her everything. I soon realized that despite all the pain and destruction of my relationship with Shane, there was one thing I had to thank him for. It had all screwed me up so badly that finally I'd been desperate enough to get therapy. I should have done it decades ago.

IN AN UNSUCCESSFUL ATTEMPT to cleanse the ghost of Shane from my house and my head, I had already ripped the smoke bush out by the roots and thrown it in the compost pile. I had already disposed of most of the things he'd given me—but not the beautiful jacket—as well as most of what was in the garbage bags he'd dumped on the back step at Christmas—but not my own books signed to him. And perhaps because I am of such an archival bent that I was reluctant to destroy the evidence even of my own misery, I had also kept all the cards and letters he'd torn to pieces.

One afternoon in June, after I'd been seeing Louise for about a month, I decided I had to do something more to erase him. It was one of those days when I was feeling so angry at him that I'd spent the entire morning pacing around the house talking out loud to him and accomplishing exactly nothing. Alex was working the day shift, because someone had called in sick. I went to Canadian Tire and bought a bag of briquettes. I hauled the bag of torn-up cards and letters out of the basement. I moved the barbecue to the far end of the backyard. When I bought it two summers ago, I'd thought of it as a nod to the future. This was not the future I'd had in mind. I spread a layer of briquettes in the bottom and lit them. While the charcoal turned from cold black to hot grey, I dumped the contents of the bag on the grass. I flipped through the torn pages and ripped them into even smaller pieces.

In both my real life and my fiction, I had considered performing this exorcism-by-fire before, after the dissolution of other rotten relationships. But I'd never actually done it, had convinced myself it was too immature, too melodramatic, too made-for-TV-movie even for me. Besides, I had reasoned when talking myself out of it in the past, with my luck, one of my neighbours would see the smoke and call 911. Either that or I'd burn my house down in the process and end up on the evening news.

Not this time. I unrolled the garden hose and placed it near the barbecue just in case. When the charcoal looked to have reached the proper heat, I neatly placed a layer of the scraps of paper on top and watched, mesmerized, as they browned, curled, smoked, then burst into flames. I fed paper into the conflagration a few bits at a time. Occasionally I stepped back and clapped my hands in delight. Then I stopped being careful and started chucking in the pieces of paper by the handful. The cards burned the most dramatically, their dyes and glitter crackling and popping in the fire, sending up sparks and pretty purple smoke. Over and over, I watched the words *I love you, Shane* in my own neat handwriting being gobbled up and swallowed by the flames. When I got to the end of them, I ran back into the house and rummaged through the linen closet to find the box in which I'd kept all the cards and letters he'd sent me. Back outside at the barbecue, I tore each of them into tidy pieces and tossed them in.

By the time the last *I love you, Diane* in his scrawling handwriting had been reduced to ashes along with the rest, the entire immolation ceremony had taken almost two hours. I turned on the hose and, while filling the barbecue with water, giddily contemplated the similarity between the words *incinerate* and *incarcerate*.

For a few hours that evening, I felt exuberant and unburdened. But when I got up the next morning, I was disappointed to discover that he was still there, sitting at the kitchen table as he always had, not scowling now but smirking with triumph.

"Good morning, asshole," I said into the empty kitchen and made myself a pot of coffee.

∞

SHANE'S POST-SUSPENSION HEARING was scheduled to take place at Bath in late August, by which time he would have been there for seven months. After some discussion with both Jerry Anderson and Louise, I submitted my Request to Observe a Parole Hearing. This time, in the box "Reason for Wanting to Attend," I wrote that I believed it would help me in my recovery from this traumatic relationship.

I was still so angry, hurt, and confused that I couldn't seem to go forward with my life. I still had so many unanswered questions. I wanted to hear what Shane had to say for himself. Yet, after everything that had happened, how could I believe anything he said now? I didn't write that there was also a part of me that wanted to see him because I missed him. I still could not reasonably explain this, not even to myself.

My application was quickly approved. I knew that, according to CSC and Parole Board policies of "sharing," the fact that I'd be attending would be passed on to Shane. There were to be no secrets or surprises, at least not for him. I enjoyed imagining his reaction. I hoped he was upset and anxious. I hoped he was afraid.

Because I was registered with Victim Services, I would be escorted to the hearing by a Parole Board staff person, a young woman named Angela. I still didn't think of myself as a victim but was just as glad I'd have someone with me. Angela sent me an information sheet titled "What an Observer Should Know" with subheadings on various topics including "Entering an Institution" and "What Happens at a Hearing." Being a veteran of both entering an institution and attending a hearing, I knew more or less what to expect. But still, I read this sheet over so many times I practically had it memorized. Each time I read it, I was mildly amused by the cautionary note at the end: *If the hearing extends into the lunch period, no food or cafeteria will be available.* It seemed to me that the regrettable absence of lunch would be the very least of my worries that day. Angela assured me that although there would be no food, there would be water and also Kleenex if I needed it.

She asked me where I would like to sit in the hearing room. I could either be directly behind Shane, where he couldn't see me once the proceedings began, or I could sit to the side in full view of everyone in the room. I chose the second option. I wanted to see his face as the hearing unfolded, and I wanted him to see me. I especially wanted him to see exactly what he had lost.

ꝏ

ON THE LAST WEEKEND OF JULY, I was giving a reading at the Leacock Summer Festival in Orillia, a hundred and fifty kilometres north of Toronto. This was one of the several literary festivals Shane and I had been to together last year. The day before I was to take the train to Toronto, where I'd be picked up and then driven to Orillia with two other writers, the VIA Rail engineers went on strike. I took the bus instead.

This was the first public reading I'd given since everything fell apart. I was relieved that it went well, that I felt comfortable and confident being back on the stage, proving, if only to myself, that I was on my way to a full recovery from the train wreck.

The festival housed all participating writers in a small luxury boutique hotel in downtown Orillia. Staying there again, alone now in a room identical to the one Shane and I had shared last summer, was much harder than giving the reading—not because we'd had a difficult time there, but because it had been especially pleasant. In fact, it wasn't just a room—it was a suite with a fully equipped kitchen and a sitting room. Behind a pair of French doors was the bedroom, decorated in elegant shades of cream and grey, featuring a large flat-screen TV and a king-size bed.

Getting into the enormous bed alone that night, I tried not to think about how dazzled Shane had been by the sheer size of it, how at three in the morning I awoke to the feel of him patting the expanse of mattress between us, whispering, "Where are you?"

In the morning, I made coffee and tried not to think about how Shane, still in his pyjama bottoms, had gone outside to have a smoke and then returned with a tray of breakfast from the restaurant downstairs.

I took my coffee into the sitting room. Last year we'd sat on the sofa together to have our breakfast, and then I'd read aloud to him from *Donald Barthelme: The Genesis of a Cool Sound*, the biography of one of my favourite writers written by his former wife, Helen Moore Barthelme. I read from the chapter called "The Creation of a Strange Object," in which Helen describes the strict discipline of Donald's daily morning writing routine, how everything else in their lives was planned around that, how he'd adopted this custom when he was only twenty-nine and stuck to it, even on weekends, until his death. We had a lot in common, me and Donald Barthelme. He too read every sentence he wrote out loud. He too was a slow writer who might have only one or two pages to show for four or five hours' work. He too used canary yellow newsprint for his drafts, as I'd done until it was no longer sold in stationery stores (a development so distressing at the time that I was afraid it might well mark the end of my writing life). He too was afraid of fire and at the end of each writing session took his ashtray into the kitchen and emptied it. On this safety issue, I did Donald Barthelme one better—I didn't empty my ashtray in the kitchen but put it on the counter and covered it with a pot lid, for fear a smouldering butt would start a fire in the garbage can.

Shane quickly got the point of this impromptu reading. "So," he said, "you're trying to tell me you're not the only one who has all these weird habits."

Now I repacked my overnight bag and checked out of the hotel with relief. The good news was that the rail strike had been settled. The bad news was that train service wouldn't resume until late that evening. So I would take the bus home. I was given a ride directly to the Toronto bus station.

The bus pulled out of the station right on time. Traffic heading out of the city on a Sunday afternoon was light. On the other side of the median, traffic coming into the city was much heavier. I tried to read, but my eyelids were too heavy, also my heart. I dozed briefly, opened my eyes again when I felt the bus slowing down. We crawled along for some time, then came to a complete stop. There were sirens coming from all directions, it seemed, and no oncoming traffic now across the median. A collective sigh rippled through the bus. There must have been an accident. How long were we going to be stuck here?

We sat for several minutes, and then the driver opened the door to admit a police officer, who came halfway up the steps. I was sitting near the front but not quite close enough to hear what he was saying. He got off the bus and began directing the driver to move into the outside lane, which had somehow been cleared. The rest of our side of the highway looked like a parking lot. There were other officers on the highway too, motioning a number of transport trucks into the lane ahead of us. We were nearing an overpass on top of which I could see more officers, more police cars. What the hell was going on?

When we reached the overpass, we could see that the officers had cleared all the lanes directly below it on both sides of the median and were now directing transport trucks—and us on the bus—into the space. Finally the bus driver made an announcement. There was a man up there, a distraught man threatening to jump off the overpass. "And we," he said, "are going to do whatever we can to save him."

He manoeuvred the bus to within inches of the transport truck on our left, which was itself positioned tight up against another truck pulled up against the concrete pillar supporting the overpass. Another truck slid into place on our right and another on its right. Within minutes, all lanes below the overpass in both directions were blocked solid by transport trucks just inches apart. We were the only bus. If the man jumped, he could not fall all the way to the ground. He could fall only as far as the top of one of those trucks—or the top of the bus.

Directly below the overpass now, we could not see what was happening above. A line of officers stood in front of the line of trucks, all of them looking up. On the bus, we held our collective breath. After several minutes, the officer in front of our bus nodded, grinned, and threw both hands in the air with his thumbs up. They had talked the man into a police car. He had not jumped. He was safe.

The bus filled with cheering and applause, the truckers leaned on their horns, the officers on the highway shook hands and slapped each other on the back. Then they got on with the matter at hand: unravelling the arrangement of trucks and getting the traffic moving again.

Like me, everyone else on the bus seemed awestruck at having witnessed this event, elated at having played some small indirect part in saving a desperate stranger's life. Half the passengers were on their phones now, telling the whole story to whoever would listen on the other end. Except for the man sitting right behind me, who said to his seatmate, in a deep gravelly voice much like Shane's, "He won't thank them for saving him. If he's in that much pain, he'll just find another way to do it next time."

The rest of the way home I thought about pain. That invisible cargo we are all carrying, every single one of us. Perhaps this is the one thing we all have in common: pain of one sort or another, the burden we are all labouring under, the ball and chain we are all dragging along behind us, the weight we are all bearing until maybe one day we cannot bear it anymore. Then we have to either make a change or line up on the overpass. I thought about how sometimes we hold so tightly to that pain because we have come to believe it makes us who we are. It has become our anchor in the world, the way we recognize ourselves, that which sets us apart from the madding crowd, that which makes us special and unique. Who would we be without the pain we so desperately cling to?

AS THE HEARING DREW CLOSER, my anxiety level was increasing daily. Angela assured me that I always had the option of changing my mind. Even right up to the moment of standing at the gate, I could still opt out, get back in my car, and go home. Knowing this made my anxiety even worse. I didn't want to have the option of losing my nerve at the last minute.

I saw my doctor and begged her for some Ativan. Being well aware of what she called my "addictive personality," she was reluctant. But she was also well aware of my situation with Shane. In the end, she wrote me a prescription for six—and only six—with no refills. I promised her I would take one the night before, one the morning of, one the afternoon following, and the remaining three pills one at a time as necessary in the immediate aftermath.

I thanked her profusely and went home and took one. Just one.

HAVING NEVER PUT MUCH STOCK in that old warning to beware of any enterprise requiring new clothes, I went to the mall to look for my parole hearing outfit. I wandered through the ladies' department of The Bay, amusing myself by thinking that in my world when someone said they were going to The Bay, they didn't mean the department store. They meant Collins Bay, the prison. It was Saturday afternoon, and the store (as opposed to the prison) was crowded with shoppers. I deflected the solicitous attention of three different sales clerks asking, "May I help you?" I could not imagine saying, "Yes, please, I'm looking for something special for a parole hearing."

As an observer, I would not be allowed to speak at the hearing. I would have to say everything I wanted to say with my appearance alone. After trying on at least a dozen disappointing outfits, I was ready to abandon the mission and try again another day. On my way out of the store, I gave a few racks one more half-hearted look-through—and there it was.

There was only one, a single dress hanging on the end of a rack with many other dresses entirely unlike it, probably placed there by accident. It was a little black dress, Jones New York, with a shirt collar, cap sleeves, fitted waist, slightly flared silk-lined skirt, black-on-black embroidered eyelet designs at the bodice, the waist, and the scalloped hem, which fell just below the knee. A little black dress is often said to be the all-purpose perfect choice for any special occasion. Perhaps that included parole hearings too.

I went back to the dressing room and slipped it on. It fit like the proverbial glove. It said everything a dress could possibly say and then some. It cost three times as much as I had intended to spend. At the cash register, I whipped out my credit card with barely a quiver of misgiving.

With renewed determination, I embarked on the second stage of my shopping expedition: the shoes. On a tiered stand at the front of the very first shoe store I came to, I spotted a dressy black sandal with a three-inch wedge heel. It was simple and stylish, with two thick bands across the top of the foot and a subtle silver embellishment between. What set it apart was the light blue inner sole.

I took the single sandal to the salesclerk. Yes, they had my size. Yes, she'd be happy to bring me a pair to try on. Yes, they fit me just fine. They were comfortable enough, and I could walk fairly well in them, well enough that I figured, with some practice at home beforehand, I'd be able to manage them without walking like a stork, twisting an ankle, or falling flat on my face in front of Shane and the Parole Board.

Like the dress, the shoes were priced well beyond my budget. Again, I handed over my credit card with barely a qualm and was soon on my way home grinning.

I did a brief modelling session in front of the full-length mirror on the back of the bathroom door. Maggie and Nelly jumped around joy-fully, expressing their exuberant doggy approval. The cats ignored me, as cats will do. In recent years, Alex had grown accustomed to being asked for his opinion on my wardrobe choices, and he was hardly sur-prised when I came out of the bathroom and pirouetted around the kitchen in my new finery. He nodded his approval and said with a grin, "Don't worry, Ma. You'll be the prettiest girl in the prison!"

I hung the dress in my closet and tucked the sandals back into their box, pleased to discover that the tiny gold lettering stamped into the blue inner sole just below the brand name said DYNAMIC SUSPENSION. This was, after all, Shane's post-*suspension* hearing, and I was indeed feeling quite *dynamic*.

I have frequently been guilty of this in my life—guilty of searching for and finding signs, portents, connections, and significance where, in fact, there are none.

THE FOLLOWING TUESDAY was my regular weekly appointment with Louise. The hearing would take place on Friday. I'd been count-ing the days for weeks, and now it was down to a rather alarming three. Just before leaving the house, on impulse I packed up the dress and the shoes and took them with me. When I came barging into her office with my shopping bags in hand, Louise raised her eyebrows in surprise. I spread everything on the conference table in the middle of the room. Short of staging a full-scale modelling session, I put on the fancy sandals, held up the dress, and struck what I hoped was a fetching but serious pose. Louise agreed that the outfit was perfect.

We spent the rest of the hour going over the details of preparation for the hearing. Again. If Louise was ever bored or impatient with my incessant and obsessive need to keep going over things, she humoured me kindly and never once let it show. For that I was grateful.

She warned me that because Bath was a medium-security prison, there would be many fences topped with razor wire, as well as a series of large metal gates slamming shut behind me as I went in. She said I might find this unnerving. I said yes, I probably would. She cautioned me to be careful with the Ativan, suggesting I take only half a pill beforehand, for fear I might fall asleep at the hearing. I laughed out loud. I'd taken Ativan before. In this case, I figured there wasn't even a remote chance that taking a whole one might cause me to nod off.

She worried about me driving home alone afterwards. Angela had offered to pick me up and drive me back, but I had politely declined. I preferred to be alone. Louise said two or three times, as she'd said during other appointments about other issues, "Let yourself feel what you're feeling." In this case, however, she added a cautionary codicil: "But not until you're safely home."

All too soon, our hour together was over, and I was packing up my shopping bags and heading for the door.

Louise asked, "Are you ready?"

I said, "Yes, I'm ready."

"Are you sure?"

"Yes," I said. "I'm as ready as I'll ever be."

And I truly thought I was. I thought I was ready for anything.

I HAVE ALWAYS BEEN AFRAID OF THUNDERSTORMS. I've never understood those people (like Dorothy) who actually enjoy them, greet them with delight and revel in the spectacle, standing at the window or going out on the front porch to get a better look. I've never quite believed those people (like Shane) who, after a dramatic crashing storm in the middle of the night, insist they slept right through it, never heard a thing. I'm quite sure I have never slept through a thunderstorm in my entire life, not even when I was wearing earplugs to try to block out Shane's relentless high-decibel snoring.

I know I'm not the only person who has carried this fear forward from childhood. I heard recently on the radio that 10 per cent of the adult population has a fear of storms, yet I've never met anyone else willing to admit it. I tell myself my fear is childish, silly, probably neurotic, but calling it names doesn't make it go away. Even calling it by its scientific name doesn't help, the fear of thunder and lightning being *astraphobia*, not to be confused with *astrophobia*, the fear of stars. I am not afraid of stars.

I blame this fear on the fact that I grew up in Thunder Bay, a city that lives up to its name. It seems to me now that throughout my childhood, violent thunderstorms were always rolling in over Lake Superior; the power was always going out; lawn furniture, garbage cans, and shingles were always being scooped up by the wind and deposited three blocks over; and houses all around ours were always being hit by lightning.

We took thunderstorms seriously in my family, and from an early age, I was taught to take precautions. Unplug the TV. Get out the flashlight and the candles. Turn off the lights in case there is a surge when the power comes back on. Don't talk on the phone during a storm.

Stay away from the windows. Also stay away from water, including the kitchen sink, the bathtub, and the toilet. All these years later, taking these precautions (with the additional step now of unplugging the computer) is a reflexive ritual I've often been teased about. Sometimes I make fun of myself too, so nobody will think I take it all seriously. But in fact, I do.

Thunderstorms were in the forecast the day before the hearing. As if my anxiety level wasn't already high enough, by noon we were under a severe thunderstorm watch. By mid-afternoon the watch in our area had been upgraded to a warning. Having been plagued by persistent weather anxiety for so long, I was well aware of the difference between a watch and a warning. A watch means conditions in your area are favourable for the development of a severe storm, and you should be paying attention. A warning means severe thunderstorms are imminent or occurring in your immediate area, and you should take cover if you see the storm approaching.

As the day wore on, I wasn't accomplishing much of anything. Mostly I was indulging in a time-honoured anxiety-discharging activity, the propensity for which I inherited from my father: I was pacing. My father's pacing annoyed my mother mightily, but Alex wasn't home to be bothered by it, and while the dogs paced with me, the cats slept on. Sometimes I paced in my new sandals, practising my walk in those three-inch-high wedge heels. My circuit included stops at every window to check on the darkening sky.

When I did sit down, it was in the living room in front of the TV, torn between unplugging it and torturing myself by watching the progress of the storm front on the Weather Channel. They were doing their usual "Storm Watch" coverage featuring an ominous throbbing soundtrack and full-screen red warnings. An attractive woman in a pretty sleeveless summer dress gesticulated vigorously in front of several different radar maps as she tracked the storms raging across the province. Large blobs that were yellow on the edges, then orange, then deep red in the middle changed shape like malignant amoebas as they moved across the screen, each one of them heading directly towards Kingston.

The weather woman became increasingly animated. I couldn't tell if she was alarmed or excited, and I could no longer distinguish between my parole hearing anxiety and my storm anxiety. They had leaked all over each other and mutated into a solid front, much like those blobs on the radar maps.

Just after four o'clock, the first tornado touched down in Durham, about four hundred kilometres due west of Kingston. An eleven-year-old boy was killed. For the next two hours, tornadoes ravaged through towns and cities to the west of us. I was well beyond pacing now and could do nothing but sit in front of the TV. By six o'clock, there was thunder and lightning in the near west, and it had started to rain. The severe thunderstorm warning was changed to a tornado watch, then abruptly upgraded to a tornado warning. The screen was now showing the list of what to do in the event of a tornado. *Take shelter in the basement or an interior room. Stay away from windows. Get as close to the ground as possible. If driving, don't try to outrun it. If outside, take shelter in a ditch.*

An instruction I'd never seen before appeared at the bottom of the list: *Avoid the instinct to help.* Even at the time, it occurred to me that I could have used this sage piece of advice three years ago when I first met Shane.

A new weather woman took over, her demeanour grim as she narrated the footage of the destruction that had already occurred. She sounded genuinely shocked as she announced that ten million people were now under a tornado watch or warning as the storms continued to roll through. Over and over again, she said, "Go to the basement."

I don't know why I didn't go to the basement. Even without her repeated admonitions, I already knew that would have been the best thing to do. But the idea of being down there by myself and not being able to see what was happening was more frightening than the prospect of sitting on the couch while the roof blew off and the walls collapsed around me. Whatever was coming to get me, I wanted to see it first. Fear, like love, is not famous for its rationality. Nor am I.

Instead of going to the basement, I went to the kitchen, fed the animals, took an Ativan. Then I returned to my post on the couch, where I remained planted for the rest of the evening, watching the coverage, waiting, praying, smoking, and clutching my flashlight.

I kept thinking that if a tornado did hit us, then maybe the hearing would be cancelled. That at least was something to hope for. Then I realized that probably one of the safest places to be during a tornado would be a prison. The rest of the city might well be flattened, but the prisons, I imagined, would be left standing stalwart and unscathed.

Alex was at work, serving up pasta, pizza, and prime rib for those intrepid diners who weren't about to let a little thing like a province-wide tornado warning ruin their evening. He called several times to check on me and to assure me that he was okay. For him, I gladly disobeyed the injunction against telephone-talking during a storm.

By late evening, all watches and warnings for Kingston were finally dropped. We had been spared.

I was so exhausted from my own anxiety that after one more phone call from Alex, I went to bed and fell asleep quickly, without any of my usual prolonged insomniac flopping around.

THE NEXT MORNING, I WOKE UP MUCH TOO EARLY, drank coffee, and looked at the pictures of the tornado damage in the newspaper. Nineteen twisters had touched down across the province, making it the largest single-day tornado outbreak in Ontario history. How was it that I did not take this as a sign of what lay ahead?

I had a bath, fussed with my hair, and put on my new outfit. I took an Ativan, got in the car, and drove to the prison. I hadn't seen Shane in eight months, hadn't spoken to him in just over seven. I had counted this out on my fingers many times.

Angela was waiting for me in the parking lot, and as we walked across the road to the gate, she admired my outfit, especially my shoes (which were giving me some trouble on the uneven gravel), and commented on the morning's clear sunny skies, such a contrast to yesterday's drama. She didn't ask me if I was okay or if I was sure about going in. I was glad of that, because I was not okay and I was not sure. But I was determined to do it anyway.

We stood in silence at the gate. As Louise had predicted, I found the sight of all the fences topped with razor wire unnerving. Apparently of its own volition, the twelve-foot-high chain-link gate began to grind open before us, slowly and noisily, with much clanking of its metal parts. We stepped through the opening into the sally port and stood facing a second identical gate as the first one slid closed and clanged locked behind us. Then the second gate opened, and we walked out on the other side. Or rather, we walked out on the *inside*. Now there was no way out.

Angela led the way to the building through which we would enter the prison. If I'd thought it was appropriate, I would have held her hand. Once we were at the door, I could see inside to the control centre, where a guard pushed a button to unlock the door. After the first door, we were faced with a second. We waited in the small compartment between while the first door locked behind us, then the second clicked open, and we could proceed. This entry area was small and quiet, not at all like the open horseshoe and bustling entry area at Frontenac. There was a bank of small metal lockers against one wall. Angela and I put our car keys in one of them. We showed our ID and paperwork at the desk. We walked through the metal detector. A guard led us down a hallway to an empty room, where we waited for a few minutes, me pacing anxiously, Angela sitting quietly.

The guard returned and took us to the hearing room. We sat in two chairs against the left wall as he indicated, then he took the seat beside me. The two Board members, one male and one female, were already seated at their table and the hearing officer at hers beside them.

Everyone else came into the room through a different door. A pinched pounding started up in my heart. I hardly recognized Shane. I was shocked by how much older he looked, how broken and sad and defeated he seemed. He was pale and walking with a cane, had grown a moustache and shaved his head. He was wearing the bright pink striped polo shirt I'd given him for Christmas, not last year, but the year before. He sat at the far end of the long table facing the Board. From where I was sitting, I could only see the side of his face. He did not look at me. He was joined by Jerry Anderson; his Bath parole officer, Deirdre Lang; and his lawyer, serving today as his assistant. Stuart from LifeLine was there too, sitting in a chair behind them. There were two more Parole Board staff members in chairs beside him. This made thirteen people in a small windowless room.

No one looked in my direction. For a moment, I thought I must be invisible. Angela was the only person in the room who seemed able to see me. Maybe I wasn't there after all. Maybe I'd chickened out at the gate and gone home. Or maybe there *was* a tornado last night, and it had picked me up and carried me away. Maybe I wished it had. Mostly I wished I had another Ativan.

After the hearing officer went through the preliminaries, Jerry

Anderson described the situation briefly, referring the Board to his lengthy report for the details. He said he was recommending revocation. Deirdre Lang gave a positive report on Shane's behaviour since he'd arrived at Bath in February. She said his tendency to become tearful during interviews led her to refer him to Psychology to determine the level of his emotional stability. They reported no concerns. In summation, she said he had been "a model inmate." That term again.

Noting that Shane had appeared before him several times over the years, the lead Board member began his questions. He referred back to the October hearing, at which the Board had put great weight on our relationship and on me as Shane's primary prosocial support. But, he said, our relationship was not as solid and stable as we had portrayed it. If the Board had been aware of the true situation, he said, they would not have granted full parole. This was contrary to what Dr. Quinn had said when he tried to dispel our belief that Shane's chances of getting full parole were contingent upon our relationship. As I heard it, the lead Board member was now confirming that this was indeed the case.

He went on to discuss Shane's lack of honesty with Jerry Anderson about Brandy coming to stay after Christmas. Shane admitted that yes, he had invited her to come, and no, he didn't tell Jerry until later. He still maintained he didn't have sex with her. He said he was going crazy in that awful apartment all by himself, that he just needed someone to talk to, that he was a basket case at the time. That term again. I wondered if the Board members knew about those limbless First World War soldiers.

The lead Board member reviewed the details of Shane's arrest by the ROPE Squad and asked him why he would have told them he had a gun unless he wanted them to shoot him. Shane said it was just a stupid sarcastic remark.

As the interview continued, the lead Board member pointed out several times that Shane was an emotional wreck, and the hearing officer passed him the Kleenex. Shane said he was the Rock of Gibraltar now compared to how he was when everything fell apart.

They discussed Linda Porter, the woman he said he had given his apartment to, the one he had also insisted he never had sex with. He now admitted that he'd had sex with her on New Year's Eve, but that was the only time. He did not tell Jerry this either.

The discussion meandered around for a while, then got back to our relationship. Shane said he'd been accused of controlling me through housework. After saying that I was the first woman he'd ever truly loved, he then said I wouldn't let him do the laundry because I said he might shrink my pants. It was all I could do not to jump up and shout, "You *did* shrink my pants!" I wondered how many times laundry had been raised as an issue at a parole hearing.

He said he was flabbergasted when the relationship ended, that he had thought we could work things out. He made it sound as if breaking up was all my idea and didn't mention that he was the one who'd said he wanted to move out. He said he'd never seen a good relationship in his life except at a distance, that he couldn't build one in prison and didn't get enough time to build one out there.

The female Board member pointed out that Shane had to take responsibility for his own behaviour and must develop tools to ensure he didn't make the same mistakes again in the future. He agreed. She said he needed to regroup and get a better picture of his own needs and expectations. He struggled to reply that he'd thought he could overcome everything by himself, that he knew now that he should have asked for help.

Shane's lawyer spoke next, agreeing that he needed to regroup and achieve a level of emotional independence. He pointed out that love is always stressful and emotionally risky, and that for Shane, the failure of our relationship had been devastating. He said Shane had always been sincere and thoughtful, never hostile, when he talked about me, had only been appropriately sad and regretful in response to having his heart broken.

The lawyer's voice hardened as he went on to say that the Board should carefully consider my credibility, given that at the previous hearing, I had represented everything as being fine between us when it was not. He said it was now in the record that I had alleged that Shane broke into my house and confronted me when I was naked in the bathtub. If this was true, why were no charges laid?

Given his final chance to speak, Shane said he was thankful for having had at least a taste of a true loving relationship and bore no ill will towards me. He said maybe neither of us had the right tools to handle the situation in a prosocial manner. That word again.

We were all asked to leave the room. Angela and I were escorted out first, led by the guard back to the empty room where we'd waited beforehand. As soon as we were alone, I told her that the whole bathtub story was incorrect. He did not break into my house. He still lived there at the time. He did not confront me naked in the bathtub. The argument took place in the kitchen. Angela asked me if I wanted her to return to the Board and tell them. I said yes, and she did.

When we were called back in to hear the decision, the lead Board member began by stating that he'd like to clarify that there had been no allegation of Shane breaking into my house as was previously stated. Then he said they had decided to revoke his parole and that he needed to have a period of stability before being considered for release again. He noted that Shane was clearly comfortable within the confines of a federal institution and maybe that was one of his problems. He said he might well be institutionalized and could face additional difficulties when back in the community in the future. He made it sound like this was the first time anybody had considered this possibility.

No one was surprised by the revocation, not even Shane. He asked if he could say one more thing. The lead Board member smiled and nodded. Shane said, "When I didn't show any feelings, they called me a psychopath. Now I'm crying all the time, and you keep calling me an emotional wreck."

The lead Board member said gently, "Or else you're somewhere in between. Just like the rest of us."

PART FOUR

September 2009 to November 2011

I will generally fight the urge to cry as vigorously as I fight the urge to vomit. In both instances, I am successful 99 per cent of the time. Many times Louise and I had discussed my aversion to crying and why I feel ashamed of myself when I give in to the impulse. Crying is not a sign of weakness, she said, but a healthy way of releasing pain. We worked on trying to ferret out the reasons why I am so afraid to cry. Part of it, I suppose, might be because when I was young, my mother often told me I sounded like a stuck moose when I cried. I didn't know then and don't know now exactly what she meant by that. A moose that was stuck somewhere, like between a rock and a hard place? Or a moose that had been stuck somewhere, like with a dagger in the heart? Either way, this wasn't something I wanted to look or sound like.

Over time I was able to explain to Louise that I'm afraid that if I start crying, I will never be able to stop. That if I let loose that vast Pandora's box of unshed tears I've been sucking back for decades, I'm sure I will drown in them and die. It is one thing to die trying, quite another to die crying. This epiphany also helped me understand why

I am especially afraid to cry when alone, am more likely to do it when I'm with someone else, someone who surely wouldn't let me die but would administer mouth-to-mouth while calling for an ambulance.

Although I had told Louise just three days before the revocation hearing that I was ready, in fact, once again I was not. In the aftermath, I cried for the rest of the day and most of the next—quietly in the backyard or in the bathroom when Alex was home, loudly all over the house when he was not. Alex was not in the category of "someone else" I wanted to cry in front of. Louise was on holidays, and I wasn't scheduled to see her again for three weeks.

At home alone, I was crying with abandon and didn't much care whether I died or not. I was either letting out great gulping heaving sobs while clutching a cushion to my chest on the couch or wandering from room to room weeping into my hands. For once in my life, I didn't care how I looked or sounded, stuck moose or worse. I could not have specifically named the source of my tears: grief, anger, guilt, sorrow, regret, frustration, all of the above. At first, my rampant crying alarmed the little dogs, but soon enough they got used to it, accepting it as simply a new part of the daily routine. The cats, as always, were unfazed by the incomprehensible habits of humans.

I was also talking to Shane again—in my head when Alex was home and out loud when he wasn't. By Sunday morning, I had started writing it all down. By Sunday evening, I was writing him a letter. I didn't intend to send him the letter, but trusting in the therapeutic value of writing, I thought it might help. By Monday afternoon, I was making phone calls to have the no-contact order lifted so I could send him the letter and he could write back if he chose to. By Tuesday the letter was ten typewritten pages. By Wednesday I had talked to Stuart, Jerry Anderson, Deirdre Lang at Bath, and the lead Board member. They all agreed, with lesser or greater degrees of reservation, that it was okay for me to send him the letter. By Thursday it was fourteen pages long.

On Friday I read the letter over one more time and went to the post office.

∞

Dear Shane,

I came to your hearing for two reasons: because I wanted to see you and hear what you had to say, and because I thought some of my questions would be answered. But they weren't. I was anxious about attending, of course. I was worried that you would say horrible things about me and blame me for everything that happened. I was also worried that I'd be completely overwhelmed by memories of all the bad times. I didn't expect that I would be completely overwhelmed by memories of all the good times instead.

Dear Shane,

For a person my age, I am far too trusting. Because I'm a lousy liar and generally don't tell lies myself, it seldom occurs to me that other people often do. The last time I checked, being naive, even at my age, was neither a sin nor a crime. But I certainly won't be so foolish in the future. The bottom line is this: I'm asking you to come clean. Please tell me the truth. You have no reason to lie to me now. I am so frustrated by still not getting the whole story from anyone.

Dear Shane,
Sometimes I get so angry it feels like the top of my head is going
to blow off.

Dear Shane,
We were BOTH damn fools to be arguing about things like
laundry.

Dear Shane,
I want to be sure you understand this is NOT me saying: I still
love you and I want to get back together. This is me saying: I do
still love you, and I want to open this communication between
us in the hope that we can figure out what the hell happened
and why, and that by doing so, maybe we can find some peace.
Whatever happens further down the road is not something I can
think about now.

FOUR DAYS LATER, WHEN THE PHONE RANG in the middle of the
afternoon, the words "Government of Canada" in the call display were fairly
glowing with radioactive energy. The male voice on the other end identified
himself as the chaplain at Bath and said Shane would like to speak to me.

He tried to say hello, but he was crying. I don't remember what I said. He said over and over again how much he missed me, how much he loved me, how sorry he was for everything that had happened. He told me that when they took him to the Temporary Detention Centre at KP, the intake nurse asked him if he wanted to see Psychology—and was he feeling suicidal? Yes, he said, he needed help. They stripped him naked, took away his clothes, gave him a set of fire-retardant pyjamas he called "baby dolls," and put him in a cell with only a sleeping mat, a hole in the floor for a toilet, and a camera in the ceiling so they could watch him. They kept him there on suicide watch for ten days. Now I was crying on the phone too.

We couldn't talk long. This was not strictly an approved call. I'd have to be officially put back on his phone list. In the meantime, we agreed that over the weekend he would answer my letter in detail, and I would write more to him too.

BY THE TIME I SAW LOUISE AGAIN in mid-September, I had written four more long letters to Shane and received ten from him in reply. His handwritten letters filling up my mailbox were more in quantity, but mine, typewritten and double-spaced, were definitely more in number of words. I held nothing back in those pages. I spent hours writing and rewriting them as carefully as if they were my next manuscript about to be submitted to my editor. As clearly as I possibly could, I articulated every detail of my anger, my pain, my disappointment, my regrets, and my questions, so many questions. His letters too were filled with questions. But even more, they were filled with apologies for the damage he'd done to our relationship, with declarations of how he had always loved me, still loved me, would never stop loving me no matter what. His letters were also filled with hope. Despite my insistence in the first letter that I was not saying I wanted to get back together and that I was not ready to think about the future, we had already slipped into talking about exactly that, about what we had learned from our mistakes and how we might do things differently this time.

Although his parole officer Deirdre Lang had been reluctant to give her approval, I was back on his phone list. Calls to cell phones were now permitted, so that number went on his list too. Deirdre had insisted that as long as I was still registered with Victim Services, I couldn't possibly be on his phone list. When I called Victim Services to check, they said this was not the case. There was no policy to prohibit me being both with Victim Services and on his phone list. After some back-and-forthing, however, to avoid a stretch of bureaucratic wrangling that might well take months while they figured out their own rules, I decided to deactivate my Victim Services registration with the understanding that I could reactivate it at any time and that I would remain on the Parole Board's Registry of Decisions.

When I told Alex that Shane and I were talking about giving our relationship another try, he was ambivalent, hovering between skepticism and relief. In the end, his desire to see me happy again was enough to outweigh his doubts. If Louise was alarmed when I told her the news, she, ever the consummate professional, did not shriek, gasp, or rend her garments. She did, however, send me an email early the next morning in which she reiterated some of the suggestions she'd made during our appointment and listed a number of questions I should ask myself.

Be cautious. Be aware of all that was happening. Think about everything very carefully and rationally, taking out the emotions. Reread my letters to him and his to me.

Was he showing the same type of behaviour he'd shown when we first became involved? Was he manipulating me? Was he just telling me what I wanted to hear?

Was this the real Shane?

How had he changed?

Had he asked me to come and visit him?

Yes, he had.

Five days after that appointment with Louise, I submitted my visiting application form. This time I didn't care what the men at the camera store did or did not think. This time I understood about *extenuating* circumstances. Rather than try to explain it all in the single allotted line, I typed up a *Reader's Digest* version of our story and attached it on a separate sheet. Again I went to the post office. This time it took a month for my application to be approved, but finally it was. Visits to Bath could be made by appointment only, and they must be booked by telephone no less than forty-eight hours and no more than seven days in advance.

On a Thursday, exactly one year since Shane had been granted full parole, I called and booked my first visit for Sunday, exactly one year and one day since he'd come home to stay.

WHAT WAS I THINKING?

I was thinking that I loved him. I was thinking that he had touched a part of me no one else ever had. I was thinking that if we had the proper support, we could make our relationship work. I was thinking that I knew more now than I'd known then. I was thinking that now I understood that rarely does somebody spend thirty years in prison and come out a better person. Joan Didion, in her memoir *The Year of Magical Thinking*, wrote: "Time is the school in which we learn." True. Also true that for Shane, *doing* time was the school in which he'd learned. I was thinking that by loving him and helping him, I could show him there was another way to be, another way besides angry, miserable, malevolent, and full of hate. I was still thinking I could shine my light and lead him out of the darkness.

I believed in the redemptive power of love—for both of us. I was thinking that together we could rewrite both our lives. I was thinking our story could still have a happy ending after all.

WHAT WAS I THINKING?

Louise said that only 5 per cent of relationships that begin while the man is incarcerated are successful after he gets out. I was thinking we could be part of that 5 per cent. Who doesn't want to believe they can be the exception to the rule? She also said it takes a long-term prisoner at least three to five years to adjust to life in the community, even if he has all the support in the world. I was thinking we had given up too easily.

WHAT WAS I THINKING?

I was not thinking. I was feeling. I did not know how to follow Louise's advice and consider the situation rationally while removing my emotions.

I was feeling intoxicated, exhilarated, defiant. Throw caution to the wind! To hell with trying to be smart, reasonable, wise! Follow your heart! Love conquers all!

I was feeling that in my heart of hearts I knew I hadn't been 100 per cent committed to him the first time. This time I would be ALL IN. Maybe this is the feeling people have when parachuting out of an airplane, diving off a cliff, bungee-jumping off a bridge—if not the overpass. Here there were no transport trucks and buses lined up on the highway to break my fall.

I HADN'T EXPECTED THAT MY FRIENDS would jump for joy about my relationship with Shane in the first place, and they didn't. Now here we were in the second place, getting back together.

Months earlier I'd once hazarded to admit to Valerie, the community chaplain, that sometimes I thought about getting back together but I was afraid that if I did, I would lose my friends. Predictably she said, "Then you'll know who your friends are." What this really means, of course, is "You'll know who your friends *aren't*." I didn't see it that way. I just knew some people would be able to handle it and some wouldn't. I wasn't sure ahead of time who would fall into which category.

When it came to the actual telling, I didn't handle it well. I didn't tell them all at once, and I didn't tell them in the right order. As if we were back in high school, I told one friend I thought would understand and then asked her not to tell another I thought wouldn't. Some people

I didn't consider close friends I didn't tell at all, assuming the gossip would find its way to them soon enough. It did.

Much upset and outrage ensued all around.

Only my friend Lily remained neutral about it. She'd been cautiously optimistic when we got together in the first place and now again seemed willing to give this unexpected development the benefit of the doubt. For that I was grateful. Some of my friendships were severely strained but recovered. Others were damaged beyond repair and ended. In a couple of cases, it seemed that the amount of work it would take to preserve the friendship coupled with the amount of work I knew it would take to make things right with Shane was just too much. There wasn't enough of me to go around. Nor was I prepared to go forward with Shane while always having to justify or defend our relationship to other people. There was no comment at all from Walter, who had called me first "stupid" and then "lucky." Perhaps there was simply no word in the entire English language to describe this mind-boggling turn of events.

After some stumbling, Dorothy and I came to the conclusion that while it is easy enough to be friends when your friend is doing something you agree with, the hard part comes when they're not—when they've chosen to follow a path you don't approve of and are behaving in a manner you find pretty much incomprehensible. She seemed to understand that I was still the same person I'd always been for the twenty years we'd known each other. We agreed that we weren't about to stop being friends over this. Without actually laying out a new set of guidelines, we managed to maintain our friendship over the coming years. She never said anything negative about Shane, but she never asked about him either. With him being back in prison, it wasn't as if she ever had to see him. For my part, I tried not to mention him too often, and I didn't go into much detail when I did.

If we were having problems, I discussed them only with my therapist Louise. I was, after all, an old hand at hiding parts of myself, even from my closest friends.

THE DAY BEFORE I MADE MY FIRST VISIT to Shane at Bath, I drove one hundred kilometres east to give a reading at the Thousand Islands Writers Festival, held in the grand and impressive Brockville Courthouse, a designated National Historic Site, to which is attached the city jail. The readings took place in one of the actual courtrooms. I sat in the judge's chair and then in the prisoner's box to see what it felt like. My life has never been short on irony.

The next morning, I pulled into the Bath parking lot promptly at eight-thirty. I waited at the gate just as I had with Angela two months before. Today there were two other women also waiting. They were chatting, but I was too anxious and excited to make small talk. We waited some more, and then I spotted something I hadn't noticed when I went in for the hearing: a buzzer on the fence to the right.

As I eyed it, my hand moved involuntarily towards it, and one of the women shrieked, "Don't do it!"

"It just pisses them off, and then they'll make us wait even longer," said the other.

Together they laughed the knowing cackle of experience.

Finally the first gate groaned and began to grind slowly open. We entered, and it ground closed behind us. Then the second gate opened, closed. We walked along the sidewalk to the building. The first door clicked open, then shut. Second door, open, shut. We were in. This was all much more disconcerting than going into Frontenac had ever been, and much more unnerving without Angela beside me.

Angela and I had only had to show our ID and walk through the metal detector. I knew that entering now as a visitor, there would be more to it than that. This was not camp, this was medium security. This was *serious*. There were more rules. I must bring my change for the vending machines in a Ziploc bag rather than the leather change purse I'd used at Frontenac. I must leave my cigarettes in my purse in the trunk of the car. In May 2008, smoking had been banned anywhere on prison property inside and out, for inmates and staff alike. Tobacco had thus become contraband, elevated now to the same level as drugs inside. Shane had warned me that there might or might not be a drug dog on duty. There had been no dogs at Frontenac.

I put my car keys in a locker and carefully watched the other two women go through security ahead of me, so I could see what was involved. There was no drug dog today. While I waited, I spied something else in the glassed-in control room that I hadn't noticed when I went in with Angela. Mounted on the back wall was a collection of at least two dozen pairs of handcuffs, tidily arranged in order from the smallest, which would fit around my skinny wrists, to the largest, which would surely fit around my thighs.

The other two women passed through the security steps and were then let out of the entry area through two more locked doors to cross over to the building where the visiting room was located. Now it was my turn.

I put my driver's licence, my bag of change, my locker key, and an unopened pocket pack of Kleenex on the counter. I'd brought this last as a bit of a joke, because on the phone the night before, we'd agreed there was bound to be some crying at this first visit. The female officer nudged the Kleenex pack with one finger as if it might detonate and looked at me over her glasses. I blathered on, trying to explain, but she was not amused. Her already pinched-looking face curled up even tighter. She picked up the phone, punched in a few numbers, and said into the receiver without preamble, "So, are we letting Kleenex in now?" No, apparently they were not. Kleenex was contraband. She pointed a long finger at the lockers, as pleased with herself as if she'd caught me trying to bring in a gun in a cake. I put the Kleenex in the locker with my car keys. She studied my driver's licence and my bag of change for what seemed like a very long time. She turned to the ion scanner and snapped on a pair of black latex gloves, not at all, I noted, like the pretty blue ones they used at Frontenac. She plucked the little square cloth from the box beside the machine, then rubbed it on the buttons down the front of my suede jacket. She inserted the cloth into the mouth of the machine and waited, staring at the screen. I couldn't see it from my vantage point. The machine was silent. Thank God.

But wait. Now she was writing in a large ledger, checking the screen again, then typing rapidly on the computer keyboard.

I asked, "Is there something wrong?"

She ignored me and kept typing. Other visitors were coming in now, crowding into the small entry area. She ignored them too. She did another test, this time rubbing the cloth down the right sleeve of my jacket. With her back to me, she studied the screen of the ion scanner, wrote in the ledger, then picked up the phone again. This time I couldn't hear what she was saying. She hung up, typed some more, then finally deigned to look at me.

"Take a seat," she said, pointing at the single chair in the small space. I sat.

I sat and watched the clock on the wall for twenty-five minutes while she processed more visitors and didn't once look in my direction or offer anything by way of explanation.

Then two male officers, one in the light blue shirt of a keeper, appeared and took me to another room to be interviewed. As it turned out, the ion scanner at Bath was not set to sound an alarm when it detected the presence of drugs. Here it delivered its verdict silently. And I, the keeper said, had hit positive for morphine. As it also turned out, the word *interview* was a euphemism for *interrogation*, also known in CSC language as a Threat Risk Assessment (TRA). The keeper proceeded to pepper me with questions about my drug use as the other officer looked on silently. I said I didn't use drugs. I said it many times. I did not yet understand that in prison the fundamental principle of "innocent until proven guilty" does not apply. Now I was guilty until proven innocent. Now I was in the land of "We think, we feel, we believe"—a land where I could be declared guilty on the basis of suspicion alone. I could not prove my innocence, and they didn't have to prove anything to declare me guilty. I could not give a reasonable explanation as to why I might have morphine on my jacket. I could not do anything. So I cried and hated myself for it.

Eventually the keeper decided he'd let me in to see Shane despite my now-questionable character. He would not send me home. He would not order a strip search. He would not call the police. He would not put us on a closed visit, which would have meant the two of us seated across from each other in a tiny booth with a sheet of Plexiglas between us, just like on TV. He would allow us to visit today on "designated seating," which meant that I must be escorted to and from V&C by an officer, that Shane and I must sit at a table right beside the bubble, that we couldn't go outside to the visiting yard, that we couldn't leave the table at the same time to go to the vending machines or the washrooms. He said my case would be put before the Visitor Review Board (VRB), which would determine what risk I might present "for the security of the penitentiary or the safety of any individual" and what would happen next.

The young female guard who escorted me to V&C was a petite pretty blonde who didn't speak to or look at me. As she led me to the designated table, the other visitors and inmates already in the room, including the two women I'd met at the gate, took a quick look at me, then turned their heads. Whether this was because they were obeying the "mind your own business" visiting room rule or because they wanted nothing to do with me for fear of tarnishing their own visiting status, I had no way of knowing.

When Shane got to the table and hugged me, I cried on his chest and wished for my pocket pack of Kleenex, now safely stowed in the locker out front.

"Never mind, never mind, never mind," he said, stroking my hair. "I love you, I love you, I love you."

When I went to the ladies' bathroom to wipe away my tears, I found myself facing yet another locked door with another buzzer. Throwing caution to the wind—I was already in trouble, so what difference did it make?—I pressed the buzzer. And found it didn't work. So I waited at the bathroom door until someone inside the bubble finally noticed me and unlocked it from there. So far this place was nothing like Frontenac. Only the toilet paper, single ply so thin it was almost transparent, and the paper towels, stiff, brown, and scratchy as sandpaper, were the same.

The paperwork from my encounter with the ion scanner was brought to our table by another female guard, this one much kinder than any of the others I'd met so far. She set down two pages titled "Positive Indication Using Non-Intrusive Search Tools" with a big X beside the word *Morphine* on the long list of drugs the ion scanner had to choose from.

The officer patted me on the shoulder and said, "Don't worry. This happens all the time. Everything will be fine."

I was desperate to believe her. She flipped to the second page, where it explained that I now had five working days to send a letter on my own behalf that would be considered by the VRB in their decision. It gave the name of the person I should write to: Brian Shepherd, Corrections Manager, V&C.

Once we had recovered from the shock of this inauspicious beginning, Shane and I could get down to the business at hand: our happy reunion. Other than at the hearing in August, we had not seen each other in ten months. There were more tears, happy tears this time, first him, then me, then him again. The stress of our separation and all that had preceded it had visibly affected us both. He was still pale and walking with a cane. I had lost twenty pounds; he had gained that much or more. We both looked much older. My hair was greyer. His was still gone. I didn't mind the shaved head, but I was just as happy when he let his hair grow back in the coming months. Holding hands across the table that day, we couldn't stop smiling. The rules about physical contact being much stricter here, there could be no kissing. But there were no rules about talking, and it seemed we couldn't stop. Even after all the letters and phone calls of the past six weeks, there was still so much to say.

Joyful as I was to be getting back together, I also felt that I was re-entering this relationship with my eyes wide open and a firm resolve to get it right this time. I had shed my naïveté and replaced it with knowledge and determination. On that very first day, I warned him, as I already had in my recent letters, that I was not the same as I had been—that this time we were going to do things differently. This time we were both going to learn how to have a healthy and happy relationship.

He said he couldn't believe how lucky he was that I had come back to him. He said he'd hoped, dreamed, prayed that we would be together again someday but had never really believed it would happen. And now here we were.

He said, "I will do anything—absolutely anything—to make this work."

I said, "Yes, you will."

He said, "I will be a better man."

I said, laughing, "Oh yes, you will, my love."

THE NEXT DAY, WITH MUCH ASSISTANCE from Shane by phone, I composed my letter to Mr. Shepherd. I explained what had happened with the ion scanner, noting that the day before I'd given a reading at the Brockville Courthouse, wearing the same jacket. Many of the people who attended were elderly. Many of them had hugged me and shook my hand afterwards. Perhaps I'd come into contact with something there? At Shane's suggestion, I included the information that in visiting him at Frontenac well over a hundred times, the only time the ion scanner went off was when Lorne Matheson set it to do so for a joke. Shane said this would let Brian Shepherd know this was not my first rodeo and that I knew the machine could be tampered with by staff to achieve the desired result. Shane was convinced this was what had happened in this case—to cause problems for him. "Mr. Paranoid Pants," I teased, but I put it in the letter.

I concluded with an extremely officious paragraph in which I explained my position as a writer well known and respected not only in Kingston but nationally and internationally as well. I listed a number of my accomplishments and noted that I had been commended by and socialized with many top-level politicians including Governor General Roméo LeBlanc, Speaker of the House of Commons Peter Milliken, and James Bartleman, former Lieutenant Governor of Ontario. Henceforth, Shane and I referred to this as my "Do you know who I am?" letter, harking back to that much-coveted T-shirt at Vinnie's.

Whether this letter had any effect on the outcome or not, the VRB decided we must remain on designated seating for thirty days, at which point my visiting status was reviewed, and we were allowed to have regular visits.

~~

BECAUSE SHANE WAS NOW in a medium-security institution, he had no passes out, no work releases, no weekends home. The only time he was allowed to leave the prison was for medical appointments. We would be able to see each other only when I visited. Almost every weekend, I went on both Saturday and Sunday, arriving at 8:30 a.m. and staying until the end of visiting hours at 3:30 p.m. I soon saw how prison could come to feel, even for a visitor, more real than the real world. Now I understood why for some of the women in the prison group, it seemed to be all prison all the time. I noticed how often I too now said, "When *we* were at Frontenac . . ." or "Now that *we're* at Bath . . ." We were now faced with the challenge of rebuilding our relationship here and only here in this locked room, with no opportunity ever to interact anywhere else except on the phone.

I had since reconnected with Rosemary from CFCN, and Brenda and Tammy from the prison group. They were the only people I knew who were genuinely happy to hear that Shane and I were back together. We began meeting informally once a month for lunch at a Chinese place that featured an unlimited and delicious buffet for under ten dollars. Sometimes we ended up sitting there all afternoon talking about our prison experiences. They'd been doing this a lot longer than I had, and I knew that this time around, I needed them for support, both emotional and practical.

After my first ill-fated experience of trying to get into Bath, they gave me detailed advice on how to prepare properly for going inside. This involved an increasingly complicated cleaning routine. Prior to that first visit, I had done nothing but wash my driver's licence as I always had before going to Frontenac.

Now I began washing my glasses and my earrings too. Better to keep the jewellery to a minimum, Brenda and Tammy advised, and leave your watch at home unless it is waterproof and can also be washed thoroughly. Leave the suede jacket in the closet. Buy a washable jacket for visiting. Wash it every Friday night, then hang it somewhere where it doesn't touch anything else—not a bad idea to wash it again on Saturday night in preparation for the Sunday visit. In fact, wear all freshly laundered clothes for every visit. (Better not to wear an underwire bra.) Upon leaving the house in the morning, drive directly to the prison with no stops lest you become contaminated somewhere along the way. Carry hand sanitizer in the glove compartment for last-minute touch-ups before going in.

So habituated did I become to performing the cleaning routine over the next thirteen months that I often caught myself putting my earrings and my driver's licence into the sink full of soapy water even when I was getting ready to go for groceries or lunch with my friends. The inmates are not the only ones who become institutionalized.

Brenda and Tammy also coached me on how to deal with the drug dog. Face the wall and cross your hands on your chest. Assume the position, breathe calmly and deeply, and wait for the dog to be brought in. Do not flinch when he sniffs your behind. Turn around when the handler tells you to. Do not talk to or make eye contact with the dog. Do not recoil when he sniffs your crotch. If the dog sits down beside you, do not say, "Oh look, he likes me." Sitting down is how the dog indicates to his handler that he has detected drugs on your person.

Despite my best cleaning efforts, I hit positive on the ion scanner twice more in the coming months—once more for morphine and then, after a problem-free stretch in which it looked like I'd finally kicked that pesky morphine habit, for LSD. Every time a visitor sets off the ion scanner, it is recorded on the inmate's permanent record. This information can and will be used against him.

After each of these incidents, I ramped up my cleaning routine, until I was a frenzied Lady Macbeth muttering, "Out, damn spot! Out, I say!" while trying to eradicate not blood but microscopic drug residue that might or might not be there anyway. Deep down I knew it was futile, that even if I dipped my entire body in bleach and went in stark naked, that damn machine would find something. I much preferred the dog, a large brown lab named Charlie, who proved over time to be far more reliable and intelligent, so much more human after all. In fact, my favourite officer at Bath was the dog handler, who was always respectful, professional, and loved to talk about books. Charlie was also respectful and professional and extremely well trained, although not much of a reader. I always thought Charlie liked me as much as I liked him, but not, fortunately, well enough ever to sit down beside me.

AT BATH THE VISITING ROOM was much bigger and brighter, with a wall of windows and a glass door leading directly to the outside visiting yard, which was encircled by a twelve-foot-high chain-link fence topped with coils of razor wire and, at regular intervals, cameras. Several feet beyond this fence was another exactly the same with a grassy berm between. As at Frontenac, both the visiting room and the visiting yard were entirely removed from the actual working parts of the prison, well out of sight of any bars or cells or other inmates not receiving visits, but here it was impossible ever to forget that we were in a prison.

Once we were taken off designated seating, we sat at the same table each time, the one in the corner close to the vending machines, from where we could see the whole rest of the room and the yard too. There were a few more guards in the bubble watching the room here, but, as at Frontenac, they were neither menacing nor armed. The population of Bath was almost triple that of Frontenac, but here it was also the same two dozen or so men who got visits each weekend. They looked just like the Frontenac inmates: men of all ages, shapes, sizes, and colours, dressed not in orange jumpsuits but in ordinary clothes of varying styles and quality, most of them not likely recognizable as criminals if you were to someday meet them on the street.

The rest of the inmates, hundreds in this case, received no visits at all. Shane said he met one man in his late seventies who'd had no contact with the outside world—no visits, no phone calls, no mail—for over five years. This man was one of several who died of cancer or other medical issues during the time Shane was there. Just as prison is not a good place to grow up, it is also not a good place to grow old. One in five federal inmates is now over the age of fifty and facing all the same problems of aging as the rest of us, problems that cannot adequately be addressed or accommodated within the institutional setting. No country for old men indeed. Each of these deaths amplified Shane's fear of dying in prison alone. He often said sadly, "Live by the sword, die of cancer like everybody else." Later, on a form provided by the prison, he would draw up a living will naming me as the person to ensure that his wish not to be kept alive by any artificial means was carried out. He also specified that after his death, his body should be released to me, and I would take care of the arrangements as he had instructed. This eased his anxiety somewhat.

In the Bath visiting room, there were no large wooden tables with comfortable chairs. Here the tables were round white laminated particleboard, and the chairs were hard purple plastic. Here the rules about how we must sit were clearly outlined in the information sheet I had received when my visiting application was approved. *Visitors and inmates must sit up on the chairs and must remain in the chairs turned towards the table with their feet on the floor. The chairs are not to be used as footstools. Sitting with legs wrapped around the torso, limbs, or lap of the other person is prohibited, also hands inside the clothing. Lying on the floor is not permitted.*

I could not imagine anyone actually lying on the floor in V&C, but sometimes there were couples who had trouble restraining their amorous activities, resulting in a stern reprimand, not from a guard coming discreetly to their table but by a blast from the loudspeaker for everyone to hear. Although I often slid my chair closer to Shane's than I was supposed to, so I could rest my hand on his leg or his back, he knew better than to suggest I do anything more risqué than that.

As we worked on rebuilding intimacy, removing sex from the equation for the time being was a positive thing from my point of view—not so much from his. I was glad we did not have the option of jumping into bed together, hoping that sex would somehow solve all our problems. Based on my experience prior to falling in love with Shane, this never works, and it tends to cloud the issues rather than resolve them. In the first part of our relationship, sex had become a battlefield, and now I felt that being forced to discuss and consider it all theoretically without the pressure of actually having to test out our new understanding of our former difficulties was an advantage.

A great many other issues needed to be sorted through first, not the least of which were jealousy and trust. I forgave him for having sex with Linda Porter on New Year's Eve. I forgave him for wanting to run back to Brandy. I also forgave him for frightening me.

Repeatedly he said, sometimes with tears, "I'm so sorry. I never meant to scare you. I was out of my mind. I'm so sorry. You are the last person in the world I would ever hurt."

I said, "I believe you. But whether you meant to scare me or not, you did." On this issue I added another condition. "If you ever frighten me like that again, I will leave you."

I forgave him for not knowing how to love me in the way I deserved to be loved. I forgave myself for not knowing how to love him either.

He said he wanted to learn how to think about love differently so he didn't make the same mistakes again.

"Love is a verb," I said, quoting something I'd read in a self-help book years ago. "It means we should be treating each other in a loving manner, not like enemies."

He said, "I get it."

But it is always much harder to forge new good habits, remains all too easy to slide headfirst back into the old bad ones. Each time he did, I called him on it. When he questioned *my* fidelity, wondering what I'd been up to for all those months we were apart, I reminded him that *he* was the one who had slept with someone else, that just because *he* had done it didn't mean I would too. Now I understood that his mistrust of me was a matter of projection, that because other women, including Brandy, had been unfaithful to him, he assumed I would be too—and that because he obviously couldn't trust himself very much, he didn't know how to trust me either.

There was also the matter of testing. Now I understood that this too was part of being institutionalized, that every single day in prison was a long and unrelenting series of tests of one sort or another. I worked on convincing him that life out in the free world is challenging enough without the addition of all these tests from the person who loved me.

"But how can I know that you really love me?" he asked.

I said, "Here I am back again. How can you not?"

When we decided to get back together, I had not been deluded enough to think it would be easy. Yes, he was my person. But he was a difficult person. He would always be a difficult person. And I can be more than a little difficult myself. Perhaps this was another way in which we were a lot alike. But those first few months were not all relationship boot camp. We were back on familiar ground now—in a different prison, yes, but the basics were the same. We had hours to be together, hours and hours to talk about anything and everything that came to mind, past, present, and future. And every day I was hopeful and happy as we set about starting over.

∞

I BEGAN THE NEW YEAR OF 2010 as I always do, putting up my new calendars around the house. Regardless of how difficult the previous year has been—and certainly 2009 had been one of the worst—I always draw hope and optimism from this small ritual of ringing in the new. I took extra care in choosing this year's kitchen calendar, the main one that hangs above the telephone stand and on which I record important events and upcoming appointments. It was called *Mindful Living: The Words of Thich Nhat Hanh*, Vietnamese Zen Buddhist master, poet, and peace activist, one of the world's foremost spiritual leaders.

I chose this calendar because on the front, with a photograph of white lotus blossoms in a terracotta bowl, it said: *In TRUE dialogue, both sides are willing to CHANGE.* The January photograph was another lotus blossom, deep pink, resting on a bed of crystalline snow. The message for the month read: *I am DETERMINED to CULTIVATE only thoughts that increase* TRUST *and* LOVE. As Shane and I continued to work on rebuilding our relationship, I thought bearing these wise messages in mind was bound to help.

I bought him a calendar too: twelve months of photographs of Ché Guevara, Ché being one of his heroes. But I was never able to get permission to bring or send it to him. Was this because it was Ché, or because it was a calendar, a device for marking out time perhaps not welcome in a place where time is truly of the essence—treacherous, torturous, and weighted with tension, but essential nonetheless? I was disappointed, but Shane said it didn't matter: he already knew what day it was and how many had passed since he got sent back.

He said, "I don't need a constant reminder of the days spooling out in front of me for God knows how long before they let me out again."

Not surprisingly Shane and I had completely opposite relationships with time. For me, and for everyone else I knew, there was never enough of it. I was always trying to figure out how to make more time in the day: get up earlier, stay up later, no more naps. For Shane, naturally enough, there was always too much of it. He was constantly trying to find ways to pass it, fill it, get through it. For him, time was something to be endured. For me, it was something to be made the most of. In his world, time was a punishment. In mine, it was a precious commodity.

Despite what he'd said about the calendar and not wanting to be reminded of the days ahead, in fact, Shane was always preoccupied with the future. He suffered from a kind of chronic hopeful looking-forward that seemed both to indemnify the past and countermand the present. Always, always the next thing would be better. This was aided and abetted, I felt, by the whole concept of gradual release: having finally managed to take one step forward, he must then immediately focus on the next step. He could never be satisfied with where he was or what he had achieved. He could only be hungering for the next thing.

When he was at Frontenac, he could think only of making day parole and getting to the halfway house in Peterborough—then everything would be better. When he got to the halfway house, he could think only of making full parole and getting home to stay—then everything would be better. Home was the ultimate goal, the final frontier, the brass ring, the pot of gold at the end of the rainbow—at the end of the six rainbows we'd seen right before he was granted full parole. And that was where it all broke down. Everything was not better. Everything was worse. He had nothing left to look forward to. There were no more steps.

After our brief disastrous attempt at living together, I realized that he didn't know how to settle in and accept, how to relax and just go along, how to let go of the anger and the hate and be happy. He did not know how to stop *doing* life and start living it. He also did not know how to stop thinking of himself as a convict, as Janice Mackie at Frontenac had long ago advised. On the inside, he'd been a *somebody*, murderers being at or near the top of the prison hierarchy, a rigid ladder of crimes, with sex offenders, especially those whose offences had involved children, being at the absolute bottom. But on the outside, he felt like a nobody, or, as he sometimes said, just another loser and an old one at that.

When he was still in Peterborough, I'd once said that if we didn't get the present working better, we weren't going to make it to the future, at least not together. He didn't ever seem to see the present as entirely real. For him it was just a shadowy way station between the past (which had been unmitigatedly miserable) and the future (which, in its as-yet-unlived brilliance, was bound to be perfect).

As the months at Bath passed, he sometimes lapsed back into this kind of thinking. If only we could get Private Family Visits, then everything would be better. If only he could get transferred back to Frontenac, back to camp, then everything would be better. I reminded him that this time at Bath was not wasted, that this was our chance to work on our problems and make our relationship healthier and stronger.

By the time we'd been back together for six months, he had twice taken a program about boundaries given by the Bath chaplain, and I had enlisted Louise's help too. She was providing a kind of couples counselling customized to accommodate the fact that one member of the couple couldn't come to her office. She gave me worksheets and exercises that I would then copy and mail to Shane, so we could work on them together when I went to visit. I wasn't permitted to bring these in myself, but he could bring them from his cell to V&C. They covered topics like empathy and sympathy, guilt and shame, cognitive distortions, core beliefs, problem solving, and boundaries and expectations. On a good day, we could work on these together and learn something.

On a bad day, they just caused more problems, especially when they focused on expectations for the future when we hoped to be living together again someday in the free world. In response to one of these exercises, he wrote out a detailed plan for managing our future daily lives, including when and for how long I would work each day. He presented this to me proudly. I appreciated the effort he was making, but I disagreed with some of what he'd outlined and suggested that the decisions regarding my work should be made by me, not him.

He said grimly, "You like it better when I'm in prison, don't you?"

I said, "No, I don't. Of course I don't."

But in retrospect, I can see that in some ways perhaps I did. Considering my own problems with relationships, perhaps with him in prison I felt I could have a partner but maintain my independence too. I did not have to figure out how to find a healthy balance in the real world. I did not have to deal with him all the time, and I did not have to have him in my house. Perhaps with him in prison, I thought I had more control.

That day I could see he was working himself into a big bad mood, so I tried to jolly him out of it. I said, "Of course I don't like it better when you're in prison, you silly duck."

Like all couples, we had pet names for each other. His for me included "pixie," "munchkin," and "Charles in Charge," because, he said, I was bossy and liked to be in control of everything. I called him "silly duck" because I liked the sound of it as a variation on the more common "silly goose" and because it made me think of the ducks we'd so enjoyed feeding in Peterborough. I've always liked ducks.

But that day he said, "When you call me that, do you really mean 'stupid fuck'?"

I was annoyed and I said, "Yes." Sometimes we were both guilty of "deteriorating attitude."

But it was never that. It was only ever a term of endearment. Now it was ruined, and I never said it again. Perhaps I should have told him that Shakespeare used it in *A Midsummer Night's Dream* to mean "dear" or "darling." But what did Shakespeare know? In his day, the word *bully* was a term of endearment too.

AT BATH VISITORS WERE NOT ALLOWED to bring in food or beverages of any kind. Here there would be no home-cooked healthy meals, no pretty placemats, no real plates or cutlery. Here we could eat only what was available in the vending machines: sandwiches, hamburgers, bagels, and sometimes, on a good day, wraps and the odd hot entrée. Shane could bring in certain items he'd bought from the canteen: pop, chocolate bars, microwave popcorn, and large bags of potato chips. I was hardly surprised when, at my next physical, not only had I gained weight but my cholesterol level was up too.

Here books and newspapers were contraband. This meant the inmates could not help their children with their homework, and Shane's reading was once again limited to what he could find in the prison library. It also meant that we could not do crossword puzzles anymore. Here I was not allowed to bring my crib board or my Scrabble game from home. Here a small stack of battered board games for use by inmates and their visitors was kept on a shelf beside the door.

It was not unusual for us to play five or six games of Scrabble in a day, and now it was no longer unusual for me to win. Shane was as bad a loser as he'd ever been, possibly worse, and might sulk for an hour or more if I beat him badly. I was all out of patience with this routine. One day after I trounced him thoroughly two games in a row and then laughed about it, his sulking went all the way to nastiness. In my work on boundaries with Louise, we'd talked about this sort of thing. I decided to put into practice some of what I'd been learning. I told him calmly and firmly that his nasty sulkiness was not okay with me, especially over something as trivial as a Scrabble game. He continued. I warned him that if he didn't stop, I would go home, even though it was early yet, with two hours still remaining in the visit. He continued. I tried one more time. I stood up and said, still calmly, "I didn't come all the way out here to sit and be treated badly by you. I'm going to the bathroom now, and if you're still acting like this when I come back, I'm leaving."

Shane didn't seem to understand one of the fundamentals of human nature—if you treat someone badly, they are not then likely to want to do things for you, to help you, or, in this case, to spend the day with you. Was this another part of institutionalization? After all, as long as he didn't cross the line too far, the prison staff was paid to put up with him whether they liked it or not, and the other guys were hardly in a position to break up with him.

When I came back to the table, still he showed no sign of stopping. Although we'd talked many times about his bad habit of testing me, I knew that was exactly what he was doing—testing me to see if I would really do what I'd said I would. In the first part of our relationship I wouldn't have.

I cleaned off the table, put the Scrabble game back on the shelf, went to the exit door, and waited for them to let me out. Shane was obviously surprised.

"And now you're just going to leave?" he said incredulously, as if I hadn't warned him at all.

"Yes, I am."

"Easy for you," he snarled. "You've got a home to go to."

Louise had warned me that when trying to implement boundaries now, I should not imagine that he would be happy about it.

"Yes, I do," I said, "and I'd much rather be there alone than here with you." The door clicked open and I was gone.

I signed out on the clipboard, stomped down the hallway, grabbed my jacket off the rack, stomped across to the other building, waited for the two doors there to be unlocked, stomped to the lockers, got my car keys, waited for the next two doors to be unlocked, stomped down the sidewalk to the gate, waited again for the two gates to be unlocked, then stomped out to the road. Even with a superlative stomping technique, it was difficult to make a dramatic exit with so much stopping and starting, locking and unlocking along the way. But I knew that in the prison world, making an unplanned early exit from a visit was dramatic enough.

As I headed, still stomping, for the parking lot, I could see one of the scout trucks coming towards me. These were blue and white pickup trucks that constantly patrolled the prison property. Shane had been amused by my naïveté, when, after watching them drive around for weeks, wondering why and commenting that that must be the most boring job in the world, it finally dawned on me that the scout truck drivers were armed and watching for someone trying to escape. Now the truck pulled up beside me. Surely they weren't going to shoot me for leaving a visit early. Surely as a visitor I was free to leave the property whenever I wanted to.

The driver rolled down the window and stuck his head out. It was Arthur, one of the pleasant guards with whom we'd become friendly over the past few months, the one with whom I'd once shared one of my nicknames for Shane—"Mr. Grumpy Pants"—another term of endearment that Arthur now also used liberally.

"Going home early?" he asked.

"You bet," I replied. "He's throwing a fit because I beat him at Scrabble. I've had more than enough of Mr. Grumpy Pants for today."

"Don't blame you," he said, laughing and continuing on his way. My angry early exit would no doubt be noted on Shane's record, and I didn't care.

As I got into the car, I could hear gunshots coming from the firing range farther on down the road, around the corner, and out of sight, where the officers gathered to practise their shooting acumen. Not armed as they went about their daily duties, they nevertheless had ready access to firearms in case of an emergency.

On a normal day, our visit ended as it began, with a quick kiss and a rib-crushing hug. Then Shane left the room through the inmates' door, while I went out through the visitors' door. Usually I took my time signing out and going back to my car. He was often, but not always, searched after a visit. This search could be of the "bend over and cough" variety, what he called a "skin fan." With any luck, by the time I was driving out of the parking lot, he'd be done with this and standing out on the hill behind the fences with three or four other inmates, all of them waving as their visitors drove away. As he advised, I would wave back with my window closed for fear of being accused of trying to throw him something from the moving car. I'd wait until I was out of sight before lighting my first cigarette for the drive home.

But today I lit up as soon as I got in the car and drove away immediately, waving at Arthur in the scout truck as I passed him on my way out to the highway.

From that day forward, win or lose, there were no further Scrabble problems.

ONCE THE WEATHER HAD WARMED UP, we could go outside and sit at one of the picnic tables. We usually chose a table to the left, overlooking the parking lot and the forested area behind the prison, hoping to catch a glimpse of the wildlife. At Frontenac there were always the groundhogs to keep us entertained and the ungainly geese waddling around the grounds; here there were prehistoric-looking wild turkeys and three or four elegant white-tailed deer. Here the squirrels were not fat glossy pets like they were at Frontenac, but death-defying tightrope artists scampering fearlessly through the razor wire. As the months passed, I began to identify more and more with those squirrels. Much as Shane liked to think of himself as a wolf longing for the wild, perhaps I was a squirrel dancing on a wire.

In the yard, there were more rules as to how we must sit. *Visitors and inmates must remain seated on the bench of the picnic tables. Straddling the bench or sitting on top of the picnic table is not permitted. Lying on the grass is not permitted.* Although I was not any more likely to stretch out on the grass outside than I was to lie on the floor inside, I did have trouble sitting on the benches properly. To alleviate the discomfort of sitting too long, some couples walked laps around the yard, around and around for hours, the perfect synchronization of their steps a testament to how long they'd been doing this in one prison visiting yard or another. We seldom walked the yard because of Shane's bad leg. But the benches were so uncomfortable that often, without thinking, I would lean sideways up against him with my legs stretched out on the seat in front of me. With little physical contact allowed in the visiting room, it was comforting to feel his body against mine. Several times when Stanley, the head V&C officer, was taking his regular stroll through the yard to keep a closer eye on things, he shook his head and pointed at my feet. I quickly put them down. But somehow they always crept back up again. Until finally one day Stanley, in relatively good-natured exasperation, said, "Do you think you're at the fucking beach?"

Teasing back, I said, "What? You mean this *isn't* the beach? No wonder I couldn't find the fucking lake." He guffawed, and I put my feet down and kept them there.

THE RULES FOR WHAT AN INMATE COULD WEAR to the visiting room were stated clearly enough: no kitchen whites, no track pants, no cut-offs, no muscle shirts, no jackets, coats, or bulky sweaters, no workboots or any other kind of steel-toed footwear. The rules for what a visitor could wear, however, were unwritten, unclear, and unpredictable. How these rules were interpreted or enforced seemed to depend on who was on duty and what mood they were in.

Despite the several large fans installed around the room in the summer, V&C became extremely warm, and I often wore a sleeveless shirt.

Not a tank top, not a halter top, just a loose-fitting buttoned cotton shirt with no sleeves. But then one Saturday afternoon, Stanley came to our table and told me I had to cover up my arms. I thought he was joking.

"You mean this?" I said, grabbing the flabby underside of my right arm and shaking it at him. "I call them my flappers." When brushing my teeth before bed, I tend to avert my eyes or gaze up at the ceiling so I don't have to watch my arm jiggling in the mirror.

"Yes," he said, laughing. "We've got all kinds in here. You never know what'll turn them on."

It had been cool enough that morning that I'd worn an overshirt too, so now I put it back on to conceal my aphrodisiac arms and sweated through the rest of the visit.

The next day, Sunday, there was a different set of guards on duty, and the dress code for female visitors had apparently changed overnight. There I was with my arms now carefully covered, lest they incite who knows what manner of mayhem among the men. And there all around me were see-through blouses, skin-tight tank tops, crotch-length skirts, a pair of white pants so tight you could see the colour of the thong beneath. But no one said a word to these young women about their wardrobe choices. Clearly their voluptuous and amply displayed assets didn't hold a candle to my flappers in their ability to drive a roomful of locked-up sex-starved men right round the bend.

"Of course they don't," Shane teased. "You are the sexiest woman in the room, no matter what you're wearing."

AMONG THE MOST ANTICIPATED EVENTS in prison life are the socials. Frontenac didn't have them at all, but Bath, like most prisons, had two a year: one in early December and another in mid-July, held in the visiting room and attended by inmates and their visitors. Due to my unfortunate encounter with the ion scanner in the fall, we hadn't been allowed to attend the Christmas social, but Shane bought our ten-dollar tickets for the July party as soon as they became available. The ticket money was collected by the Inmate Committee and used to buy food for the party, this year's menu featuring jumbo buckets of Kentucky Fried Chicken and vats of pasta salad and coleslaw from Loblaws, along with cake, ice cream, and Popsicles for dessert.

As is customary for attendance at any party anywhere, everyone got dressed up, especially the women, most buying new outfits and taking extra care with their makeup and hair. I bought a floaty new summer blouse in various shades of blue and a pair of dangly turquoise earrings to match. I even wore the fancy sandals I'd bought for the revocation hearing and hadn't worn since, because I never did get used to those three-inch-high wedge heels.

Behind the festive atmosphere, though, there was also an increase in security. There would be a much higher number of visitors than usual that day, many of whom didn't otherwise visit and who would come from out of town for the party. Prison socials were notorious as occasions on which visitors attempted to smuggle drugs inside. This meant, Shane warned me, that for sure there would be a car sweep that morning. These were staged at random on other days throughout the year as well, so I'd already been through a few and knew what to expect. Just to be on the safe side for the social, the evening before, I spent an hour in the driveway, washing and vacuuming the car thoroughly. I cleaned out the glove compartment and the trunk, polished the windows inside and out, and wiped down the entire interior including the ceiling.

The next morning, when I turned off the highway and headed in, yes, there they were: trucks, police cars, officers, and dogs, all set up strategically at the T-intersection where the road to the left went to Bath, the road to the right to maximum-security Millhaven. All cars heading to both prisons were being checked. There were already five or six cars in line, and I pulled in behind them. An officer I didn't recognize came to my window, asked which prison I was going to, and checked my ID against a list on his clipboard. He told me to unlock all the doors and the trunk, and he handed me a pamphlet called "Keeping Drugs Out: A Visitor's Guide." I thanked him and put it in the glove compartment from which just yesterday I had removed several copies of the same pamphlet.

One by one, the cars were directed to the left or the right, and then, in an orderly fashion, the drivers and their passengers were instructed to get out, leave all belongings inside, and put the keys on the hood. We were then lined up in small groups to be sniffed by the dogs. We remained in our lineup while the dogs were put inside the cars to continue searching. I managed not to laugh at the sight of a large German shepherd trying to get into the trunk of my little Echo. Fortunately, clumsy though he was, he wasn't interested in either me or my car.

Not everyone was so lucky. The car that came in right behind me had now been moved to an adjacent parking area for further inspection. The young driver and her two passengers were wobbling across the gravel in their high heels towards a picnic table where several guards and a police officer were waiting.

When I finally pulled into the Bath parking lot, there was still the rest of the usual security procedure to get through. But finally I was in, sitting at our usual table in my pretty outfit, and there was Shane coming across the visiting room towards me. He was grinning and so handsome in his best clothes, black dress jeans and a short-sleeved white shirt I'd bought him in Peterborough.

"Hello, darling," he said, putting his arms around me. "May I have this dance?"

There was no music, but we took a few quick twirls beside our table before heading to the coffee machine.

By noon the room was crowded, and the party was in full swing. Mostly that meant being able to eat food that didn't come from the vending machines and being allowed to mingle more freely with the other inmates and their visitors. The guards came out of the bubble and mingled from table to table too. This was all enough of a change from the normal routine to make it feel like a celebration.

In fact, we did have something to celebrate. A week before, on my fifty-sixth birthday, Shane's security classification had been lowered back to minimum, and his application for a transfer back to Frontenac finally had been approved. He'd now been at Bath for seventeen months. The transfer was such good news that we could hardly stop grinning. But after being reminded by one of the V&C officers that envy and jealousy run rampant in prison and it was not inconceivable that one of the other guys might try to sabotage the move, we were keeping the good news to ourselves.

The prison photographer was at the social all day. Shane had paid for three pictures at a dollar each. We took our turn posing outside in a shady corner beside the building, three more photographs to add to my growing collection of prison shots. There we were, just another happy couple smiling for the camera on a bright summer afternoon, squinting into the sun, our arms around each other's waists. If you look closely, you can see my turquoise earrings and my fancy shoes. If you look closely, you can see the ghostly reflection of the razor wire in the window behind us.

∽

BECAUSE THERE WAS NO SPACE available at Frontenac, Shane wasn't moved until four months after his transfer was approved. Having never been long on patience, he did not handle this wait well, becoming ever more irritable, quarrelsome, and twisted as the months passed. Finally one morning at the beginning of November, he was told it was time to pack his stuff. He'd been packed for weeks. He was back at Frontenac by noon.

It was immediately apparent that there had been many changes there since we'd left three years before.

Despite much public protest, the prison farm had been closed. A money-saving measure, the Harper government said, completely discounting all evidence to the contrary. Not only did the six farms at various Canadian prisons have multiple proven rehabilitative, therapeutic, and environmental advantages, but also all the food produced on the farms had gone to feed inmates throughout the federal system, making them economically advantageous as well. The government had also outraged all farmers everywhere by saying that the skills the inmates learned on the farms were no longer important in modern society.

For fear of repercussions that might directly affect my security clearance, I was reluctant to participate in the protests, much as I believed strongly in the cause. Shane said they were pointless anyway, would make no difference in the end. I tried to explain to him about the importance of civil disobedience regardless of the outcome. He was not convinced.

I attended only one large rally, held on a Sunday afternoon in early June 2010, a protest that began at a downtown church with music and several speakers, including farmers, environmental activists, the General Superior of the convent, the current Liberal Member of Parliament, Stuart from LifeLine, and Margaret Atwood, all on stage in their SAVE OUR PRISON FARMS T-shirts. By bringing her international reputation to the fight to save the farms, Margaret had helped raise the campaign to a new level. It was, after all, not just a local issue but one that affected all Canadians and regularly made the national news. I'd met Margaret many times over the years, and after her address, we had a brief chat. Then we all marched several kilometres from the church to CSC Regional Headquarters, where signs were posted on the door and more speeches were made. We numbered in the hundreds, led by a large red tractor bearing a sign at the front that said HARPER ASLEEP AT THE WHEEL, and pulling a hay wagon carrying Margaret and the other speakers and more signs, including PRISON FARMS MAKE OUR COMMUNITIES SAFER. The most popular member of the protest was a donkey also bearing a sign: CONSERVATIVE PRISON FARMS CONSULTANT.

Throughout the summer, several more demonstrations had been staged at the entrance to Frontenac. All I could do was honk wildly and wave helplessly as I drove past on my way to and from visiting Shane at Bath. The largest blockades were held at the beginning of August—a hundred and fifty protestors, and an equal number of police officers in neon vests lined up across the entrance. Two dozen protestors were arrested and two hundred and fifty cattle removed from the farm to be sold at auction elsewhere. The youngest calf was bought by a Kingston area farmer and named "Hope." All the farms were closed.

Sometimes public protest does work. After many years of it, the only halfway house in Kingston had also been closed. Housing mostly sex offenders, it was located in a residential neighbourhood near schools and playgrounds. CSC had finally closed it and moved the residents into Frontenac. The Phoenix living units where Shane had been previously were renovated and turned into an on-site halfway house. This was to be a temporary measure until a new facility could be built elsewhere on the sprawling prison property. There had been no progress yet on that front. In the private sector a building intended to house forty or fifty people could be completed in a matter of months, but with CSC at the helm, it appeared it would take years. When it was eventually completed, it would be named the Henry Traill Community Correctional Centre, in honour of the first Kingston prison guard killed in the line of duty back in 1870, the son of Catharine Parr Traill, the nephew of Susanna Moodie, the man whose grave Shane and I had passed by many times at the Cataraqui Cemetery.

MUCH AS I'D BECOME COMFORTABLE AT BATH and friendly with many of the officers, I was happy to be going back to where we started, back to the familiar and more predictable minimum-security prison, where the general atmosphere was more relaxed, and the living, if not exactly easy, was somewhat less stressful for both of us. I'd had a pleasant enough rapport with most of the guards at Frontenac the first time. Shane was ambivalent about the fact that I got along so well with them—alternating between resenting it because he said it was an ideological betrayal of him, the convict, and appreciating it because them liking me might be an advantage for him.

The truth was, I had more in common with most of them than I did with him. Going in, I'd often chatted with whoever was on duty about mortgage rates, the price of gas, gardening, car troubles, home renovations, vacation plans, children, pets, aging parents, that week's great deals at Loblaws or Costco, and once at length about acid reflux. The truth was, given a different set of circumstances, I could easily have become good friends with several of the guards I got to know at both Bath and Frontenac. I intentionally never adopted the adversarial stance with them that many of the other visitors seemed to take. I had come to the conclusion that just as the only thing all prisoners truly have in common is that they're in prison, so the only thing all prison guards truly have in common is that they work in a prison. The guards, like the visitors, seldom fit the stereotypes featured in movies and on TV. When interacting with the few who remained consistently surly, imperious, and uncommunicative, I tried not to take it personally and assumed they would have been like that no matter where they worked.

Three days after Shane was moved back to Frontenac, I made my first visit. There were several familiar faces around the horseshoe that Sunday morning and much laughter when I slapped my driver's licence down on the counter and announced, "We're ba-a-a-ack!"

WHEN AN INMATE IS TRANSFERRED to a different institution, there is a thirty-day window in which he can receive clothing and other personal items up to a certain dollar value. I offered to go shopping and deliver the box to Frontenac. Shane was initially resistant to this idea because of the cost. I promised not to spend more than two hundred dollars, but still he was reluctant.

"No, no, save your money," he said. "My clothes are fine. It's not like I'm going to a fashion show or anything."

Finally I said, "Listen, honey, I'm not doing this for you. If I have to look at you in those crappy old T-shirts and bleach-spotted sweatpants very much longer, I'm going to scream."

He got me a copy of the list of what he could have: "National List of Personal Property of Men Inmates."

Most of the clothing items on this detailed list were unremarkable, if, in my opinion, a bit excessive. I could understand the need for ten pairs of socks and ten pairs of underwear. But did he really need twelve

T-shirts, six pairs of jeans, four pairs of sweatpants, and a bathing suit? Where was the fucking beach anyway?

Neck chains were allowed but only with no heavy pendants and links no larger than six millimetres. An inmate could have one musical instrument, stringed, wind, or keyboard—however, in maximum security, stringed instruments were allowed only at the discretion of the warden. A reading lamp was allowed provided it didn't have a gooseneck or a weighted base. Boots and shoes must have no steel inserts; belts must have no oversized buckles; sunglasses must be non-mirrored only; bandanas (up to four) must bear no gang-related insignia. Among the permitted miscellaneous items were one coffee mug (maximum twelve ounces, non-ceramic only), one stapler, one jump rope, one pair of scissors (six inches maximum, blunt-ended only), one geometry set, and two prayer mats (no larger than eighteen by thirty inches). It was that geometry set that worried me. When was the last time CSC had checked out the contents of a standard geometry set?

In the box of new clothes, I also included the T-shirt I'd brought back for Shane from California. In mid-October I'd attended a symposium there, a three-day event called "Mary in the Modern World" that took place at Saint Mary's College of California, a small private Catholic school located in the town of Moraga, a half-hour drive east of San Francisco. I was invited to speak about and read from my novel *Our Lady of the Lost and Found,* which had been put on the curriculum there. I was picked up at the San Francisco airport by one of the De La Salle Christian Brothers who lived and worked at the college. As we drove across the Golden Gate Bridge, I had a good view of Alcatraz out on the rock in the bay. I wouldn't have time to visit the prison while I was there. I found myself telling Brother Charles all about Shane.

As it happened, not only was Brother Charles an expert on Vatican art, he was also a professor of medieval history, very knowledgeable about the development of the penitentiary system and the history of prison reform. He noted that most people don't consider the fact that the penitentiary system was originally based on the monastic model and that the term itself comes from the root word *penitence.* That it was intended to be about penance, not just punishment. Contrition, not just conviction and containment. Repentance and redemption, not retribution and revenge. He said he would pray for us both.

The next day, when I met the Brothers and Fathers in the college dining room for lunch, Brother Charles arrived a little late with a plastic bag in his hand. He had a gift for me—two gifts, in fact. He spread them on the table: two Alcatraz T-shirts, a small one for me and an extra-large for Shane.

THERE WERE NO LONGER FRIDAY EVENING VISITS at Frontenac, but I was going for the whole day on both Saturdays and Sundays, as well as on Tuesday evenings after my appointment with Louise. Going directly from her office to the prison meant that I couldn't perform my full pre-visit cleaning routine. This made me uneasy— as did the fact that once I got there, Shane usually spent half the evening wanting to know what Louise and I had talked about. Since most of what we talked about was him, I preferred to keep it to myself. He was not happy when I soon stopped coming to see him on Tuesdays.

There were many other things to be unhappy about, some big, some small. Because of the Harper government's Tough on Crime measures, Frontenac had become more like Bath and less like camp.

Such privileges as ETAs, UTAs, and work releases were now at a pre-mium, and Shane, it seemed, was no longer entitled to any of them. From his first week back at Frontenac, he had problems with his new parole officer, Dennis Walker. Each encounter was a battle, often sev-eral a day. Dennis would not let him apply for anything, Shane said, not even for ETAs, so he could start going to Sunday mass at the con-vent again. Shane had been attending a weekly Buddhist group in the prison, and Dennis said he couldn't be a Buddhist and a Catholic too. As the months passed and Dennis would still not recommend him for passes of any kind, Shane repeatedly asked to be assigned to another parole officer. Their personality conflict seemed so irremediable that I wrote letters to the warden about this situation as well. Shane's requests were denied, and my letters, as usual, were ignored. Shane was told that he and Dennis Walker would just have to learn to get along. This was never going to happen.

Now at Frontenac, as at Bath, we would only be able to spend time together in the visiting room, with no opportunities to interact outside the prison. Visits to Frontenac must now be booked in advance, news-papers and books were now considered contraband, smoking was now prohibited anywhere on the property, and both home-cooked meals and kissing were now forbidden in the visiting room. After a visit, the inmate must now return immediately to his cell—no more waving and blowing kisses in the parking lot. All security procedures for visitors had been increased. Rumour had it that by January, there would be drug dogs there too. Given all the problems I'd had getting into Bath, Alex had not visited Shane there, and he decided not to resume visiting him again at Frontenac either.

Despite the enhanced security measures, and despite the millions of dollars spent by CSC each year trying to keep them out, it still seemed there were more drugs inside than out on the street. There was frequent cynical grumbling among the visitors, because although

CSC professed to recognize that inmates who received visits and had prosocial family support did better both while they were incarcerated and after release, the new security measures made it increasingly hard and more stressful for us to get in. We all resented the fact that while there were more and more hoops we must jump through to see our loved ones, none of the prison staff was ever checked for anything.

Now, on the wall beside the door to the women's bathroom at Frontenac, there was a new sign, a single Xeroxed sheet of paper taped to the concrete block wall. It was titled SAFER NEEDLE CLEANING. Beginning with the general instruction CLEANING OF YOUR NEEDLE & SYRINGE SHOULD BE DONE TWICE—JUST BEFORE YOU USE THE NEEDLE AND IMMEDIATELY AFTER, it went on to explain the four steps of cleaning your needle with bleach, each illustrated with a line drawing. The instructions concluded with the general warning that THE ABOVE PROCEDURE WILL NOT GUARANTEE THAT THE HIV IS INACTIVATED—ONLY THAT YOU HAVE REDUCED YOUR RISK. YOU COULD BE PLAYING RUSSIAN ROULETTE!

At the bottom it said in capital letters: DON'T SHARE YOUR NEEDLES WITH ANYONE! The exclamation mark was surely intended to emphasize the gravity of the advisory, but somehow it made this command sound cheerful, as if they were saying in closing, HAVE A NICE DAY! followed by a yellow smiley face.

Peculiar though it struck me to find this sign posted in a prison, at least they were being realistic.

Conditions for the inmates had changed dramatically. Through no fault of their own, the men who'd earned their way to living in the Phoenix units had now been moved back into ordinary cells on the range. This, plus the Harper government's increased implementation of double-bunking meant that Frontenac was now seriously overcrowded, with nearly twice as many inmates as it was designed for. Contravening both the United Nations minimum standards regarding the humane accommodation of prisoners and their own stated policy that single-cell occupancy was the most desirable and effective means of housing inmates and that double-bunking should be used only as an exceptional and temporary measure, CSC was now packing them in two to a cell. This was happening not just at Frontenac and other minimum-security prisons, but also at medium- and maximum-security institutions across the country, including in some segregation units.

The cells now housing two inmates were not larger cells meant for double occupancy. They were former single cells of approximately sixty square feet, about the same size as my small bathroom at home, retrofitted with two narrow metal bunks screwed into the wall one above the other, so close together, Shane said, there was hardly room enough to roll over, let alone swing a cat. Because of his bad leg and other health issues, he was allowed to have the bottom bunk. He said the man on the top bunk weighed at least three hundred pounds. There was no air-conditioning in any of the cells. As the population continued to grow, there were no commensurate increases in programming, medical and mental health resources, or basic services like bathrooms, showers, telephones, or laundry facilities. Nor had the number of correctional officers yet been increased.

Shane said, "You don't need to be a sociologist, a psychologist, or a criminologist to know what happens when you put too many rats in a cage."

As numerous studies have indicated, prison overcrowding adversely affects inmate health, morale, and behaviour. Increased frustration, tension, and conflict leads directly to increased disruptive and aggressive behaviour including more violent assaults of all kinds requiring more use-of-force interventions by staff. There are also more incidents of inmate self-harm and suicide as well as an increase in the spread of infectious diseases.

The implementation of all these changes did, as intended, make prison life harsher and more punitive, but it also made it more volatile and dangerous for everyone, including the staff. Their union president was frequently on the evening news expressing concerns about double-bunking as an unsafe and ineffective practice that put not only offenders and correctional staff at higher risk but ultimately the public as well. For once, it seemed that the guards and the inmates were on the same side.

WHEN I ARRIVED FOR MY USUAL VISIT on the first Saturday of December, I could see before I even turned onto the prison property that something was going on. Shane had now been back at Frontenac for exactly one month. A cold and snowy morning, it was not yet eight-thirty. Usually at this hour, the parking lot closest to the road was still empty, save for a scout truck or two. This morning it was crowded with guards, dogs, vans, and police cars from the OPP and City of Kingston forces. For a brief moment, I thought something terrible had happened inside. But as an unfamiliar guard waved me into line behind the three or four other cars ahead, I realized it was a car sweep. Much as I'd been through several of these at Bath, there had never been one when we were here before.

Although Frontenac itself didn't have socials, Collins Bay, the adjacent larger medium-security prison, did, and today was the day, three weeks before Christmas. When I told the guard I was going to Frontenac, I hoped he'd wave me on through. But no. They were searching everyone. I waited my turn, then got out of my car and lined up with three or four other visitors I didn't recognize, all of them, I assumed, going to the social. By now it was snowing heavily.

One of the handlers from Collins Bay, a large man who looked angry even from a distance, brought over his dog, a muscular mixed-breed with a broad chest and a stumpy tail who also looked mean. The dog sniffed first our backs and then our fronts. He was disturbingly interested in me but did not sit. I made the mistake of looking him in the eye, even though I knew better. He jumped at my face and nearly knocked me over, but still he did not sit. The handler brought him down the line again. This time the dog liked me even more, nuzzled up and down my left side, then stuck his nose into my jacket pocket. Again he did not sit.

The handler pulled me out of the lineup. The dog circled around me wagging his stumpy tail. The handler leaned his angry face close to mine and yelled, "What have you got in your pocket? What kind of drugs are you carrying? What are you trying to hide? What are you trying to pull here?" I was stunned and shaking. In all my prison years, I had never before been yelled at by any guard, anywhere, at any time.

He led me to a CSC van and ordered me to sit in the front seat, while his dog searched my car. The van driver drummed his fingers on the steering wheel and did not look at me. At least he had the heater on. After rummaging around in my car for a few minutes, the dog sat on the console between the front seats and looked proudly up at the handler.

I was then put into the back seat of an OPP cruiser. The female OPP officer behind the wheel was pleasant enough. The male City of Kingston police officer in the passenger seat was not. He interrogated me angrily for fifteen minutes or more. No matter what I said, I could not defend myself. When I said I didn't know why the dog had stuck his nose in my pocket, that in fact, I'd washed my jacket just yesterday, he said, "Why did you wash your jacket? What were you trying to hide?" When I said I'd taken my own dog to the vet also just yesterday, that she was given a flea treatment and a veterinary steroid, that she had sat in the front passenger seat and was possibly in heat, he ignored me. When he asked who else had been in my car, I said my son. While running his name through the computer, he interrogated me about Alex: where did he work, who did he associate with, was he involved in the drug trade? Alex's name did not come up on his computer.

I was taken out of the police car and put back in the CSC van to wait for the keeper from Frontenac to come down. I was relieved to see it was John Logan, an older man with whom I'd always had a good rapport when we were here the first time. Surely John would bring some sanity to this situation. I started to cry when he said he couldn't let me in, he had to send me home. For a person who doesn't like crying, I seemed to be doing a lot of it. John handed me the paperwork. Visit denied.

I could see he wasn't enjoying this any more than I was. "But John," I cried, "you know I have nothing to do with drugs!"

"I have to do my job," he said.

"But can't you use your own judgment here?"

"No," he said sadly. "I can't."

WHEN I GOT IN THE DOOR, IT WAS STILL SNOWING, I was still crying, and the phone was ringing. For the rest of the day, Shane kept calling, ranting and raving, going further and further off the deep end each time, accusing everyone of having set him up. When I told him to get a grip and calm down, he said, "So I guess I'm just not supposed to get upset about anything ever again."

"Oh, come on!" I cried. "Nobody's saying you should never get upset again. Everybody gets upset sometimes. The important thing is how you handle it, how you deal with conflict, problems, disappointments. Haven't you learned anything from all those bloody programs you've taken?"

John Logan called too. He said he was sorry about all this, but I wouldn't be allowed to visit again until the VRB had reviewed the incident. In the meantime, I should write a letter to the warden and bring it to him, John, on Monday afternoon. He would see that the warden and the VRB got it immediately, so they could do their review when they met on Wednesday afternoon.

On Monday morning, I delivered my letter to John Logan—yet another "Do you know who I am?" letter, even though they already knew full well who I was. You could just never get any traction with these people. John shook my hand and thanked me for handling this in a "mature and reasonable manner"—unlike some people, neither of us said. Unlike Shane.

We were put on designated seating for our next three visits. Just a week after we'd completed these, I was in trouble again. For a month and a half now, I'd been bringing my car keys into V&C just as I had when we were there before. No one had said anything about it. But one day right before Christmas, the guard on duty objected when she saw the keys in my hand. It wasn't as if I'd tried to hide them before, but now I was breaking the rules. This involved an unpleasant few minutes at the X-ray machine and me then being sent back out to the lobby to put the keys in a locker before I was allowed to proceed to V&C.

Shane spent the entire visit making a ruckus, sure once again that this was somehow directed at him, even though I was the one who had been reprimanded and embarrassed. He was upset with me too. When I pointed out that it was an honest mistake on my part, he said bitterly, "There's no such thing as an honest mistake in prison."

So much for being happy to have returned to a more relaxed routine in which the rules were clear and consistent. For the next year and a half, each time I went to visit, I put my car keys in a locker and watched all the other visitors going in with their keys in their hands.

∽

I WAS VISITING ONLY ON WEEKENDS, and while that should have made it easier to keep up with the other parts of my life, still I was constantly juggling to get everything done: writing, housework, errands, spending time with Alex and my friends. Although I was only actually at the prison two days a week, still it was the focal point around which everything else must be arranged. Much as the other parts of my life had been somewhat neglected the first time around, in this second incarnation of our relationship, they seemed to be in danger of falling away altogether.

There was also still the matter of the phone calls. I could only call the prison in the event of an emergency, but there was no limit to the number of calls an inmate could make in a day. They had now implemented a phone card system. As long as Shane had put money on his card, the calls were cheaper, but once that money was used up, we were back to collect, at a dollar a call. With almost fifteen thousand inmates in federal institutions across Canada, I cannot imagine how much money Bell Canada and other phone companies make on inmate phone calls on any given day.

It was still not unusual for him to call me several times a day, delivering a play-by-play account of all that was happening there. I understood by now that in his circumscribed world, small things took on an exaggerated importance all out of proportion to their actual significance. It seemed that everything on his end was urgent, while everything on my end was, in his opinion, infinitely interruptible. This was a problem I still had not solved.

After a hundred or more phone calls a month for all these years, I had become an expert at gauging Shane's mood just by the way he said hello. One afternoon in early January 2011, he sounded excited in the way I knew meant something out of the ordinary was happening there—a kind of negative excitement generated by prison drama to which I knew I too had become somewhat addicted.

The city police had come in, he said, and hauled one of the guys right out of his cell, put him in handcuffs, and took him away. The inmate in question, Richard Joyce, was someone I knew too, in that way I knew the other inmates who were often in the visiting room. Almost every weekend, an older man I assumed to be his father brought his two young daughters to see him. I'd never actually spoken to him, but they were a familiar family in the room, and I'd noticed how good he was with his little girls. He was a lifer too, and now in his early forties, he had already been in for almost twenty years on a first-degree murder charge. Clearly his daughters had been born while he was incarcerated. Their mother never came, so I assumed that relationship had ended but that he was doing his best to be a good parent. Pleasant, polite, and congenial, he got along well with the guards. He was always smiling.

But the murder he had committed back in 1991 was especially horrific, well-known, and still remembered around Kingston, a crime that was said to have changed the entire city, the kind of crime that had been given a name: the Nozzles Gas Bar Murder. Early on the morning of May 6, 1991, Richard Joyce and his friend Terry Kennedy had killed a young wife and mother of three named Margaret Yvonne Rouleau in the kiosk of the Nozzles Gas Bar in downtown Kingston. Yvonne ran the gas station, and Terry Kennedy had been working there. The two young men left her dead on the floor and made off with seven thousand dollars, money they later said they intended to use to finance their dream bicycle trip to the southern United States and Mexico. After they killed her, they went home and got cleaned up, then went back downtown for breakfast at a restaurant right across the street from the gas bar. They got there just as Yvonne Rouleau's sister discovered her body in the kiosk. She ran to them for help.

Richard Joyce and Terry Kennedy were arrested nine days later and charged with first-degree murder. In the trial the following year, it became clear that the murder had not been a robbery gone wrong, as they maintained, but a thrill killing of stabbing and torture with sexual overtones. Both men were sentenced to life with no eligibility for parole for twenty-five years.

After the murder, the gas bar was closed and then demolished. It is now the parking lot of a Shoppers Drug Mart. Some Kingstonians, including me, still find it difficult to drive past without remembering what happened there to Yvonne Rouleau.

I could not reconcile what I knew of the murder with the man I saw regularly in V&C. It was one of those cases where I wished I knew nothing about his crime. When Shane was at Bath, he would sometimes ask me to look up one of the other inmates on the computer to find out what he'd done. Not all of them, particularly the sex offenders, were as open about their crimes as he was. I did it a few times but then refused to continue. My natural curiosity was knocked right out of me. It was much too disturbing to know the truth about some of the men I was sitting beside in V&C, sometimes chatting and joking with them, getting to know their wives and children. I preferred to think they were all just drug dealers, which, on the spectrum of possible offences, had come to seem the least of it. This was a kind of denial, I suppose, but I was there to see Shane, not them, and I had no control over who else happened to be in the room.

Now Shane said the rumour around the prison was that Richard Joyce's arrest had something to do with the DNA testing recently conducted on all federal inmates. At the time, I'd asked Shane if this was something he was worried about, something I should be worried about. "No, definitely not," he'd said, and he was right.

The rumours about Richard Joyce were right too. Based on the new DNA testing, he was charged with the kidnapping and savage sexual assault of a nine-year-old girl on February 20, 1990, fifteen months prior to the Nozzles Gas Bar Murder. A week later, he pled guilty to the new charges even before the full DNA analysis had been completed.

The crime had taken place early on a Tuesday evening. The girl and her mother were planning to watch *The Wizard of Oz* on TV that night, and around six o'clock, the girl walked alone to the corner store to buy a bag of chips to have during the movie. It was a good neighbourhood. The store was three short blocks from her house, barely a five-minute walk in the early dark.

On her way back from the store, passing the public school she attended, almost home, she was grabbed by a man and forced screaming into his vehicle. He beat her into silence and drove her to a remote location northwest of the city, where he brutally assaulted her several times in several ways. By seven o'clock, her mother had called the police and reported her missing. By eight o'clock, the man had returned her to her neighbourhood and released her, threatening to kill both her and her mother if they told the police. He had never been caught. Until now. Richard Joyce was that man.

The street where that little girl and her mother lived is one block south of mine. The corner store to which she walked is my corner store. The public school she attended and near which she was abducted is the public school my son began attending six months later, when he started kindergarten.

It was because of what had happened to that little girl that I walked Alex to school and back every single day until he was twelve years old and in Grade 6. Even then, for the first two weeks, I hid behind a bush so I could see he'd reached the school safely. I only stopped because he caught me and was mortified. It was all because of Richard Joyce.

I could not believe that I had been sitting in the same room as the man who tortured that child and left all of us in my neighbourhood terrified for years. I could not believe that I'd admired him for being so good with his two young daughters. Richard Joyce went on to plead guilty to two other brutal sexual attacks on young girls, one with Down's Syndrome.

I had often reflected on and tried to explain to my friends how becoming part of the prison community had stretched my mind, had forced me to see criminals as people who were also in need of compassion and understanding. But whatever arrangement I had made in my head to try to make sense of the fact that some of the men I saw regularly in the visiting room had committed horrific crimes, it could not be adjusted to accommodate this.

I was thankful that Alex was not coming to visit anymore.

Shane repeatedly apologized for being the one who'd put me in the position of having to be anywhere near such people. But I don't think he ever fully understood either the impact the abduction of that little girl had had on me then or the impact the identification of Richard Joyce as her attacker was having on me now.

For him, this case served mainly to confirm three things he already believed.

Never trust anyone.

Never trust anyone in prison.

Never trust anyone in prison who is always smiling.

DESPITE HOW HARD SHANE HAD PUSHED, and despite the fact that I'd had a second positive Community Assessment, we had never been allowed to have Private Family Visits at Bath. The Bath Visitor Review Board had said we did not qualify because of the previous problems in our relationship, our eight-month separation, and the fact that they considered us a couple only since I'd started visiting him in October 2009. But at Frontenac, because now we had been together for another eighteen months with no serious problems, we were approved for PFVs, and I was given a new acronym: CLS. Common-Law Spouse. The standard PFV lasted seventy-two hours, but we would move up to that gradually: first we would have three twenty-four-hour PFVs, then three forty-eight-hour ones, and then, if and when they approved it, we could go all the way to seventy-two. These would take place once every month or six weeks.

Given the fact that we had not been entirely alone and unobserved for one minute since getting back together a year and a half ago, this development had us both beside ourselves with anticipation, more than ready to quit talking about sex and actually have some.

I reported to Frontenac that Monday morning in early March at ten o'clock carrying a small blue bag Brenda from the prison group had given me. With her gift had also come detailed instructions on how to prepare and pack for the occasion. Before the usual cleaning routine, there was now another whole series of steps to be taken. I was happy to do whatever it took to get myself in there. Mostly this involved laundry and plastic bags.

The first principle was to take in as little as possible, thus lowering the number of items that could set off either the ion scanner or the dog. Wash and dry all clothing to be worn or taken in, hoping that neither the laundry soap nor the dryer sheets contain any chemicals the ion scanner could mistake for heroin, morphine, LSD, or anything else in its repertoire. Upon removing each item from the dryer, drop it directly into a large clear plastic bag hung on the clothesline in the laundry room. Also wash and dry the little blue bag, which is never to be used for any other purpose besides PFVs, and put it into another large clear plastic bag on the clothesline.

Everything else must be wiped down and placed directly into appropriately sized Ziploc bags. This included all makeup and hair products, all personal hygiene items, all books, papers, and so on. I wondered if the plastic bag manufacturers, especially Ziploc, had any idea how important their products were in the carceral world. I imagined a TV commercial demonstrating their extensive use in this context.

Once everything has been washed and bagged, with the little blue bag open inside its large clear plastic bag, carefully transfer all other items into it. When the bag is packed, zip it closed and leave it inside the clear plastic bag. Put this directly into the trunk of the car and leave it there. Do not open the trunk again for any reason.

On the morning of the PFV, after performing the usual cleaning routine, get into the car and drive directly to the prison. Open the trunk. Remove the blue bag from the clear plastic bag. Leave the clear plastic bag in the trunk, nonchalantly sling the blue bag over your shoulder, and stride confidently from the parking lot to the main building. Once inside, open a locker, put your car keys inside it, insert a quarter, remove the locker key, close the locker, tuck the key into your pants pocket. Do all this without putting the blue bag down on the floor or letting it touch anything around you. Wish you had three hands.

Do not sign in at the main desk as usual, but stand there until someone waves you down the hallway to V&C. Put your bag on a table and sign in on the clipboard beside the bubble. Prepare to be searched.

That Monday, the regular V&C officer, Grant, went through the contents of my bag, tsk-tsking at my Nicorette gum, making no comment on my granny panties or my KISS MY BASS nightshirt. Then he called for the dog handler. I was relieved to be spared the ion scanner this time but dismayed to see that the dog handler was Dwayne, the same angry man who'd yelled at me on the day of the car sweep. We moved to the children's play area, where Dwayne spread my bag open on one of the low benches, so his dog could reach it. After snuffling through the bag, the dog then sniffed me front and back. He did not even wag his stumpy tail. Dwayne was not angry. The dog was not interested. All was well. Grant called Shane over the intercom and searched his backpack when he arrived.

We loaded up a metal wagon with our bags, a plastic laundry basket of towels and bedding, and a cardboard box marked with Shane's last name and filled with the food we'd ordered for the visit. We'd spent one Saturday afternoon filling out the food order, choosing from the limited list of items that would then be purchased for us at the Food Basics store right across the road from Frontenac. Cheese, bread, margarine, milk, a can of coffee, two small striploin steaks, mushrooms, broccoli, potatoes, a frozen apple pie. The cost of the food, plus the ten-dollar delivery fee charged by the store to drive the food across the street, would be deducted from Shane's inmate account. Today the food box was topped with a bouquet of fresh flowers he'd secretly ordered to surprise me. Try as we might to be economical in the months to come, even without splurging on steaks and flowers, the cost for a twenty-four-hour PFV was always at least fifty dollars, more than Shane cleared at his prison job in two weeks.

With Shane now towing the wagon behind him, we followed Grant to the trailers. There were three of them, each in their own small yard behind an eight-foot chain-link fence with a locked gate. In fact, only one of them was actually a trailer, very similar to one I'd lived in briefly in the trailer park in Canmore. The other two were both sides of a small prefab duplex, each with its own yard, entrance, fence, and gate. These two faced away from the prison, overlooking the fields and gardens to the south. Grant led us to the first one, closest to the visiting room, facing the stone wall and the guard tower of Collins Bay. He unlocked the gate, then the door. Shane and I unloaded the wagon and took everything inside. Grant took the wagon away, locking the gate behind him. I was too excited about the prospect of a whole twenty-four hours alone together to be bothered about being locked in. It was almost eleven o'clock. Grant would be back for the four-thirty count.

In what became our usual PFV routine, first we put away the groceries and made a pot of coffee. I arranged the flowers in a plastic water jug and set them on the kitchen table. Then we hung the towels in the bathroom and made the bed. Much as I had been eagerly looking forward to this moment, suddenly I felt a little shy. While clearly not feeling shy himself, Shane was uncharacteristically patient and said, "Maybe we should have something to eat first." So while he put together a plate of cheese and toast, I snooped.

It was indeed a trailer, long and narrow like a train car, one room after another strung from front to back with a narrow hallway running down the right side. The kitchen was the first room, equipped like an ordinary slightly rundown kitchen anywhere with a double sink below one window that looked onto V&C and the cell area of Frontenac, and a small table and three chairs below a second window looking out at Collins Bay.

Between the fridge and stove was a stack of drawers: cutlery in the first, cooking utensils and many wooden spoons in the second. I laughed out loud when I opened the third drawer to find a collection of knives of all sizes—from a pair of humble paring knives to a set of gleaming black-handled butcher knives with blades two inches wide and nearly a foot long. The logic of the Correctional Service of Canada could always be counted on to boggle the mind. For all their endless fussing around about safety and security, did they not see anything peculiar about locking up inmates and their families with a dazzling and deadly array of knives?

"Good point," Shane said, laughing. "But don't mention it to anybody else."

Beyond the kitchen, in an open concept layout, was the living room, furnished with a large couch and matching loveseat, a coffee table, two end tables with lamps, and a large television set. There was a phone on the wall in the hallway, a direct line inside to be used in case of emergency. The first room down the hallway was a child's bedroom with a small bed, a crib, an overflowing box of toys. Next was the bathroom, with a toilet, a sink, a full-sized tub and shower. On the door of the bathroom storage cabinet was the same sign posted in V&C: SAFER NEEDLE CLEANING. I couldn't resist poking around in the cabinet. In addition to cleaning supplies and extra toilet paper, there was an impressive selection of condoms in various sizes and colours and many shiny packages of lubricant. There were also three or four of the tiny bottles of bleach to be used for needle cleaning. They were all empty.

The last room was the bedroom, *our* bedroom for the next twenty-four hours: double bed, dresser, closet, two bedside tables, a second smaller TV. There were no security cameras or listening devices anywhere in the trailer, and the privacy their absence afforded us was palpable. My shyness disappeared as quickly as it had appeared, and we spent the rest of the afternoon in bed.

The phone rang shortly before four-thirty, Grant calling to tell us they were on their way. Stand up and be counted. Both inmate and visitor must be on their feet at the open door. The guards didn't come into the trailer but chatted for a few minutes at the doorway, then inserted an electronic stick-like device called a "Deister" into the punch station on the outside door frame, and we were officially counted. They would return again at eight-thirty, then not again until eight-thirty tomorrow morning. Because this was only a twenty-four-hour PFV, they would return in mid-morning to bring us out. We would be interviewed by the keeper as to how the visit had gone, and then I would be on my way home.

We made supper, then lay around in the living room snuggling and watching TV in our pyjamas. Shane said he thought he might just have a shower. I said I thought I might just join him.

An hour later, while he was drying off and I was singing and doing a naked happy dance around the little bathroom, there was a sharp rapping at the bathroom door, which was then flung open to reveal Grant and a female officer. I grabbed for a towel, so embarrassed that I didn't know whether to cover my face or my body. It was just after eight-thirty. We had not heard the phone ringing when they called to let us know they were on their way. We had not heard them knocking on the outside door. We had not heard them coming down the hallway.

Grinning, Shane said, "Oh shit."

Grant said, "Well, at least you're standing up," and they left laughing.

Back in the bedroom later, we settled in for the night. I was beginning to twitch some for want of a cigarette, and my jaws ached from chewing all that Nicorette gum. Being without my computer, my iPad, and my iPhone all day had been something of a digital relief, but now I caught myself wishing I could check my email and call Alex to see how everything was at home. But the sex and the novelty of having a sleepover at the prison more than made up for these deprivations.

I could not sleep. The spotlight on the twenty-foot-high stone wall of Collins Bay bore directly down on the bedroom window. The slats of the blinds were broken and bent. The room was filled with horizontal bands of white light—across the walls, the floor, the bed, and our bodies. Even with my eyes shut tight, I could still see them, like the black and white stripes on an old-fashioned prison uniform. Shane snored on beside me, oblivious.

AFTER MUCH LOBBYING ON SHANE'S PART, we received permission to have counselling together inside Frontenac with the new community chaplain. Valerie, the previous chaplain, had left Kingston to become the minister of a church in a small town out west. Her replacement, Edward Blake, had been a prison chaplain in various institutions for almost thirty years. Now as community chaplain, he would continue going inside to meet with individual inmates while also working with the recently released and their families outside. While Shane was still at Bath, I had started seeing Edward myself once a month, meeting at my neighbourhood Tim Hortons for lunch. I also saw him at the monthly potluck dinners now being held at 99 York, the building where I had attended the women's group. For ex-offenders and their families, as well as the loved ones of those still in prison, these were congenial social gatherings with no agenda other than sharing food, stories, and many boisterous games of dominoes.

Shane had also been seeing the chaplain once a month at Frontenac. We were both benefiting from our separate sessions with Edward, a wise and compassionate man well-educated in the psychology of both prison and relationships. In theory, being able to see him together would multiply the benefits for both of us. In reality, through no fault of Edward's, it only created more problems.

First there were security issues. We were meeting one afternoon a month in an office in the chapel. This meant I had to park my car in the visitors' lot, walk to the main building to sign in, walk to the chapel to meet Edward and Shane, then do it all again in reverse when we were done. At first this was simple enough. The parking lot and the chapel were both clearly visible from the main building: the guards could see where I was and what I was doing at all times. Then it was decided I must be escorted for all this walking back and forth. For a month or two, my escort was the prison chaplain—not Edward, but the full-time on-site chaplain. Then it was decided I must be escorted by a guard, then by a keeper. Each time I went for counselling, the rules had been changed, causing more and more disruption for more and more people.

Then there were issues with the counselling itself. Edward had devised a plan for us, a sequence of topics to discuss with him and a series of assignments for Shane and me to think and talk about between sessions. But more often than not, whatever we had intended to work on at any given session was derailed—usually by something else that Shane was angry and upset about. Often this involved some part of the daily prison drama: an argument at breakfast with a guard or a guy, or perhaps the disgusting quality of breakfast itself.

Sometimes it was problems with his parole officer. His constant conflicts with Dennis Walker meant there was always something to be upset about: Dennis wouldn't see him, Dennis wouldn't do his paperwork, Dennis was always accusing him of something, Dennis still wouldn't let him apply for passes.

Sometimes it was problems with his cellmate. He could not cope with being double-bunked. Each cellmate was worse than the last, it seemed. The first one never showered. The second was a thief. The third was dealing drugs. The fourth was a schizophrenic off his meds. The fifth was always trying to get into his pants. He repeatedly requested to be moved to a single cell. But each time one became available, it was given to someone else, and he became more and more enraged.

Sometimes the problems were political. Just three weeks after we began our counselling with Edward, Stephen Harper was re-elected—with a majority government this time. We spent our next two sessions being collectively upset about that.

Whatever we might have been learning from Edward was mostly lost in the commotion. And yet we persisted for seven or eight months. It would look bad if we quit, Shane said, they would use it against him. I wondered if he'd only pushed so hard for this counselling because he thought it would make him look good—not because he really wanted help. It seemed he was no more willing or able to accept help than he'd ever been.

∽

THERE WAS ME SAYING, "I've always wanted people to like me."

We were in the visiting room on a Sunday morning, and I was upset because I hadn't been invited to a party everyone else I knew had gone to the night before. The truth was, I didn't much like parties anyway, but still I felt hurt, left out, excluded, shunned. All my old fears that I didn't belong, that nobody liked me, that nobody wanted me around, that nobody loved me except him, had gone into overdrive. I wasn't exactly crying, was stuck somewhere between whimpering and snivelling—which made me feel even more pathetic.

There was me saying, "I've always just wanted to be liked."

There was him saying, "Me too."

I couldn't for the life of me see how this was true. Was he being sarcastic? Or maybe he was imitating Alex, who had a habit of saying, "Me too," whenever I complained of a headache, an upset stomach, a sore throat. I found this endearing, took it as his own brand of shorthand empathy.

But no, Shane was being sincere. In all the years I'd known him, it seemed he'd been inclined to go out of his way to make people dislike him, then to complain bitterly when they did. Maybe now he was referring back to some much earlier time, long before I knew him, when he really did want people to like him, a time before he decided it wasn't worth trying to please anyone, that it was much easier and possibly more enjoyable to piss them off instead. I'd seen him do it often enough. And once he'd succeeded in pissing someone off, he'd then flash a sneer of triumph, followed by a surge of anger at them for being pissed off at him. Surely it was even harder *being* Shane than it was trying to understand him.

I could never figure out how much of the way he behaved was the result of his having been in prison for so long and how much of it was just him being him. How could I possibly separate the two? Perhaps still not comprehending the full implications of institutionalization, I did now understand, at least superficially, the damage thirty years in prison was likely to do to a person. I kept thinking he didn't know any better— how could he? I was in love with the wonderful person I had seen flashes of from the very beginning, the person he could be, would be someday as long as I stood strong beside him. I knew other people thought this was impossible, but I was determined to prove they were mistaken.

I have always been reluctant to abandon a project—or a person— despite all evidence pointing to the fact that I should. Was this pride— me being so unwilling to admit I was wrong, to just cut my losses and give up? Was this chronic contrariness on my part? Was I all the way to perverse in responding to phrases like "You can't do that" or "That will never work" the way a bull responds to a red flag? Perhaps I was so busy reacting to those red flags that I missed all the more important ones I should have been paying attention to. I still cannot fully explain why I continued to remain loyal to Shane for all those difficult years. I still cannot make sense of it in a way that sticks. Perhaps the bottom line is that like many things we humans do, especially in the name of love, it doesn't make sense.

I am stubborn, and I am not a quitter. I am not one to back down from a challenge. I am also a hoper. These are qualities that have served me well in many areas of my life, especially in my writing. In retrospect, I can see they didn't serve me well in my relationship with Shane. I am such a hoper that sometimes I can't see what's right in front of my face.

Sometimes it seemed that Shane wanted to prove the naysayers right: "So you think I'm a miserable bastard? I'll show you. I'll show you just how much of a miserable bastard I can be. You ain't seen nothing yet." Perhaps it was the "yaysayers," including me, that he most wanted to prove wrong. I thought my love could fix him, and he seemed determined to show me that it could not. Did he hate me for loving him? Did he want to prove that he could not and should not be loved?

I ARRIVED AT THE PRISON ON A FRIDAY MORNING in early June with my little blue bag in hand. We had now completed our three twenty-four-hour PFVs as required, and this was to be our first forty-eight. At the horseshoe, they waved me down to V&C as usual. Passing the offices in the hallway, I could see John Logan was on duty, so I stopped and briefly chatted with him. His wife had died two months ago, and I'd sent him a sympathy card. To me this was a simple gesture of condolence and respect. Shane wasn't sure the card was a good idea, worried that it would somehow come back on him, but it didn't. Today John told me about a vacation he was planning to take next month with his son and his family. Then I went on down the hall to V&C.

As usual, Grant went through the contents of my bag and then called for the dog handler, Dwayne. Although we'd never talked directly about the car sweep incident, he had one day said, "I have to do what my dog says," and I had replied, "I know." So we were over it now and got along well enough. The dog sniffed the contents of my bag. Dwayne looked at the books I'd brought. He said he didn't read much, but his wife did. I still tended to hold my breath while the dog gave me the once-over, but I was almost used to all this by now, no longer much bothered by having first a man and then a dog checking out my underwear, no longer struck by the incongruity of the search being conducted in the children's play area in front of a pink plastic stove and two Fisher-Price high chairs, all under the watchful eye of Talking Elmo. I was hardly even rattled anymore by the cognitive dissonance of the prison world. Even at the time, I realized this was not necessarily a good thing.

Dwayne and his dog left, Grant went back into the bubble, and I gathered up my bag and sat at a table to wait for Shane to be called down. An inmate came in and sat down with a man in a suit—his lawyer, no doubt. Another inmate with a noisy bucket of water on wheels and a disgusting string mop proceeded to swab out the bathrooms. There was a great deal of activity in the hallway between V&C and the horseshoe, but from where I sat, I couldn't see what was happening. Being well inured by now to the "mind your own business" rule, I didn't think it would be wise to move to another table for a better look. I waited. I stared at the clock. I sat there for over half an hour. It shouldn't be taking this long. Grant came out of the bubble, went down the hallway, returned after a few minutes, and went back into the bubble, all without looking at me. This couldn't be good. I waited some more.

Grant came out of the bubble again, directly to my table this time. Apologizing for the delay, he said there was a problem, but they'd get it sorted out shortly. Like the rest of the staff, he had an excellent poker face. He asked me if there had been any trouble between Shane and me lately. I knew better than to ask what kind of trouble.

"No," I said.

"Okay, good, I didn't think so," he said and went back down the hallway.

More time passed. Grant returned and told me I would have to be interviewed by the acting MAI—the Manager of Assessments and Interventions—a new acronym to me, not to be confused with MIA, Missing in Action. Grant led me down the hallway to a small conference room on the left. The person waiting for me there was none other than Jerry Anderson.

Momentarily flushed with relief at seeing a familiar face, I asked, "What the hell is going on?" I knew Jerry was working at Frontenac now, but this was the first time I'd seen him since the revocation hearing at Bath two years ago. He said they'd received a "kite," an unsigned note, indicating that Shane was planning to harm me during this PFV. I reminded Jerry that he had been there with us through the worst of it, before Shane got sent back, and that difficult though it had been, there had never been any actual or threatened physical violence. Yes, I had been briefly fearful in that circumstance because of Shane's erratic behaviour, but I was not fearful now. Jerry assured me that he didn't believe Shane would ever hurt me and that this sort of thing happened all the time, one inmate waging a vendetta against another who had somehow offended, insulted, or otherwise rubbed him the wrong way. But still, he said, according to policy, they must investigate further.

The interview went on for fifteen or twenty minutes. Several times Jerry referred to "a member of the public."

Finally I asked, "Who? Who are you talking about?"

"You!" he said. "You are a member of the public, and we must ensure your safety and security."

Even at the time, this struck me as funny. I had, after all, been deemed "a threat to the institution" by both the ion scanner and the dog. In my experience so far, "security" was only about keeping drugs, weapons, and other contraband out while also keeping the inmates in and safe from each other. But now I was "a member of the public" who needed their protection.

Finally Jerry said our PFV would have to be cancelled until he could get to the bottom of this. We would be allowed a few minutes together before I went home, and I'd be permitted to take the perishable food items with me. He led me back to V&C. Shane and Jimmy, the chair of the Inmate Committee, were brought in by John Logan. As I had expected, Shane was apopleptic. I wasn't sure if Jimmy was there to advise him of his rights in this situation or to keep him from losing control completely. Before leaving us to our brief discussion, John Logan said we should remain calm; it would all be figured out quickly, and we could probably have our PFV next weekend instead. This was reassuring. But I was hardly surprised when it didn't happen that way.

THE DISTRESS OF LOSING OUR PFV was mitigated somewhat by the fact that on the same day Shane was finally approved for a work release. He would have a *real* job this time, a paying job not in the prison but in the community. He and several other inmates had been hired by the local call centre of an organization raising money in support of youth safety charities, drug awareness groups, and teen suicide prevention programs. Shane would be a telemarketer, soliciting donations for these worthy causes from people not only in the Kingston area, but also across Canada and the United States. Other than the fact that he loved talking on the phone, with no office experience and only minimal computer skills, Shane had no qualifications whatsoever for this type of work.

The best thing about this job was that he would be paid the current Ontario minimum wage of almost nine dollars an hour. Although the United Nations standards state that prisoners shall not be used as labourers without equitable pay, the wage for jobs inside the prisons was between five and seven dollars a day. Even after CSC took their 25 per cent off the top for room and board, in an eight-hour shift at the call centre, Shane would make more money in one day than he'd been making at his prison job in two weeks.

As the partner of a prisoner, the prospect of this job made me happy. Not only would Shane have enough to buy whatever he needed at the canteen and keep his phone card topped up, but also he would send the rest of the money to me to help with the household expenses.

As a "member of the public," however, I had some reservations. Irritated as people already are by the incessant calling of telemarketers, how would they feel if they knew that the person calling and asking for their credit card number just as they were sitting down to dinner was a federal inmate—a convicted bank robber and murderer no less?

Shane had some reservations about the job too. The call centre was located on the second floor of a small office building just four short blocks from my house. Situated on the southeast corner of the main intersection leading into and out of my neighbourhood, it was across the street on one side from the apartment building where he had briefly lived and, on the other, from the Tim Hortons where I went every day. With no sign anywhere to indicate its existence, I'd had no idea it was even there. Shane said they were testing him by placing him so close to my house, putting us both squarely in the path of temptation, hoping

THIS IS NOT MY LIFE

he'd sneak away for an afternoon quickie or maybe I'd slide over to see him at work, to bring him some lunch or a coffee or something more sinister. He was sure they were setting him up. At an earlier stage in our relationship, this would have had me calling him "Mr. Paranoid Pants," but now I thought he might well be right. We agreed that to be on the safe side, we would be extremely careful. Whenever possible I would avoid that intersection and take another route, even though it meant driving ten blocks out of my way. I would go to a different Tim Hortons for my daily French Vanilla, even though it meant changing my routine of a dozen years. If I did happen to be driving by and saw him on the street, I would just wave and keep going—even if, I teased, he was stark naked, crying his eyes out, and throwing himself on the hood of my car.

Only three days into the job, Shane was having reservations of another sort. For one thing, he'd been told by the boss not to use his real name when making calls. He did anyway. For another thing, it bothered him that many of the people he was calling and asking for donations were elderly, some of whom, he said, were so lonely they kept him on the line just to have someone to talk to. He felt like he was being paid to prey on these vulnerable and defenceless people. He was beginning to feel suspicious about the whole operation. There were so many things that just didn't feel right, just didn't add up. He gave me the website address and asked me to have a look. What I saw appeared to be professional and legitimate, but all the links were dead.

When the phone rang just before noon on Friday, Shane's eighth day on the job, I could see by the call display that it was him, calling from Frontenac at a time when he should have been at work.

In his sheepish little-boy voice, he said, "Don't be mad at me."

In my cranky big-mommy voice, I said, "What did you do?"

He said, "I got fired."

During yesterday's lunch break, he said, he was standing outside the front of the building with two or three other non-inmate employees. They were all smoking. A Frontenac staff member happened to be driving by at that very moment.

This morning, Shane said, he'd been taken to work with the other inmates as usual, but within an hour, he was picked up and returned to the prison. He'd lost his job for smoking. He admitted that yes, he was smoking, but no, he said he didn't know he was no longer allowed to smoke while away from the institution on a work release. Maybe he knew, maybe he didn't. That was never quite clear to me. But I certainly hadn't imagined that CSC's no-smoking policy now extended beyond the boundaries of prison property. Did they actually have the power to prohibit an inmate from smoking anywhere in the free world? Did this mean that if Shane had been coming to my house on UTAs the way he used to, he wouldn't have been allowed to smoke in my car, my house, or my backyard? Apparently it did. Just as he wasn't allowed to drink or do drugs anywhere at any time, now he was also not allowed to smoke—ever.

Of course I understood the need for conditions prohibiting the use of drugs and alcohol that were imposed on most prisoners and parolees. For most of them, including Shane, drinking and drugs were significant factors in their offences and might well trigger the commission of more crimes if they started using again. But smoking? As a smoker myself, it seems to me that more crimes are likely to be committed for the lack of nicotine than for having freedom of access to it.

Upset as we both were about the loss of this job for such a flimsy reason, within four months it turned out to have been a blessing in disguise—as blessings so often tend to be.

ON THE LAST FRIDAY OF JULY, it was raining lightly when I got up. The previous afternoon I'd been to the dentist for my regular check up, and we bemoaned the fact that we'd had no rain to speak of for weeks. In my yard, the grass was dying, the ground beneath so hard and dry, it was cracking like a desert. An avid and award-winning gardener, my dentist said he didn't know how much longer his plants could bear up under these drought conditions. As I was leaving, he joked that he was going to do a rain dance when he got home from work. Maybe that would do the trick.

Apparently it had. I happily settled in at my desk that morning, looking forward to a full day of work and to the particular comfort a quiet rainy day can bring. Shane had changed jobs again, was now working on the prison loading dock, and he'd been doing a good job of not calling until either right before or right after the four o'clock count.

As was my custom when hunkering down to work for an extended stretch, I didn't open the drapes. I find a window as distracting as a TV set, a riveting rectangle demanding to be gazed out of, even if all it revealed was my little street deserted as usual on a weekday morning. With my desk in the living room, I worked facing the wall of books. By the sound of the rain pounding on the roof, I could hear that the light showers of early morning had turned into an all-out downpour—no thunder, no lightning, just heavy rain. I hoped my dentist was happy.

Time passed unnoticed and unchecked, just as it always does when I'm deeply immersed in my writing. When I finally looked at the clock, it was nearly noon. I could hear that it was still pouring, and the sump pump in the basement had been coming on frequently. I pushed my chair back from the desk, stood up, and took a step towards the window. My bare foot landed on something wet. Having lived in a house full of pets for so long, my first thought was, Who peed on the rug? I may well have said it out loud. But the wet spot I was standing in was very cold.

I went to the window and pulled back the drapes. It was raining so hard, I could barely see across the street. Turning back towards the desk, I stepped in the wet spot again. I looked up. There was water dripping from the ceiling light. This could not be good. With the drops being silently swallowed up by the carpet, I had been completely unaware of what was going on right behind my back.

I ran to the basement and turned off the power. There was water on the floor down there—not an unusual occurrence in itself as the basement tended to leak. Although this was aggravating, it had never presented a big problem. The basement was only partially finished, divided into three rooms but used only for storage, laundry, and a place to put the kitty litter box—not as a living space.

For the moment, I was far more alarmed about the roof leaking, something that had never happened before. I grabbed a bucket from the laundry room and headed back upstairs, only to meet Alex just coming out of his bedroom with the news that there was a leak in his ceiling too. And, I discovered, another in the back room as well. I ran outside to get more buckets from the tool shed. It was still raining so hard that even with my jacket on, I was instantly soaked to the skin. Overwhelmed, I started to cry as I ran back into the house with the buckets. I had never had to deal with anything like this before.

I didn't know what else to do so, for the first time in my life, I called 911. The dispatcher answered immediately and asked the nature of my emergency. In the background, I could hear what sounded like utter bedlam. I pulled myself together enough to explain about the leaking ceilings and that I'd turned off the power. After she assured me that I'd done the right thing, and after I assured her that for the moment we were okay, she said, "Now I'm going to have to put you on hold, dear, just for a minute. All hell is breaking loose here. But don't hang up. I'll be right back."

I clung to the receiver with one hand and held my head in the other. Alex was monitoring the buckets and the pets, and patrolling the rest of the house to be sure we weren't springing any more leaks. When the dispatcher came back on, I clung to her voice as hard as I'd been clinging to the phone. I told her I could now hear what sounded like a waterfall running into the basement. She said not to go down there, but if I could see from the top of the stairs that the water was reaching the level of the electrical outlets, I should call the fire department. Then she said, "Whatever you do, dear, don't go out. Don't go on the roads. Half the city is flooded." I loved her calling me "dear" and took some fleeting consolation in the knowledge that Alex and I weren't the only ones in trouble.

By mid-afternoon the rain had ended, the ceilings had stopped dripping, and from the top of the stairs, I could see with my flashlight that although there was now six or seven inches of water in the basement, it had stopped rising and hadn't reached the electrical outlets. But there was a terrible smell wafting up the stairs that I knew was more than water.

This definitely qualified as an emergency at home, so I called the prison. The officer who answered was Graham, with whom we were quite friendly, and he was suitably concerned and sympathetic. He said he'd go and get Shane and have him call me right away. When Shane phoned back, it took him a few minutes to grasp the gravity of the situation. He didn't know what to do any more than I did and was certainly not in a position to come home and help me, but he was reassuring, and just hearing his voice calmed me down considerably.

Alex was due to work at five o'clock. By then the flash flooding on the streets had subsided, and it was safe to go out. Much as I wanted him to stay home, there seemed no point in that—I didn't know what I was supposed to do now, let alone what he could do—so off he went, promising to call during the evening. Even with the power off, the phone was working, and luckily I'd charged my cell phone the night before.

I don't know why it didn't occur to me to call any of my friends for help that day or in the difficult days ahead. I don't know what this said about me or them or what was wrong with my life.

I did know the deep smelly water in the basement was not something I could just mop up myself the way I had on previous leaky occasions. I also knew I wasn't about to go down there and turn the power back on while standing in it. I recalled seeing a number of company trucks around the city proclaiming FIRE AND FLOOD RESTORATION and 24-HOUR EMERGENCY SERVICE. I got out the phone book and started making calls. All lines were busy. I went down the list until finally someone at a company called Winmar answered. She was kind and calm, and my eyes pricked with tears when she said, "Don't worry, we can help you." She also said the same thing the 911 dispatcher had said earlier: "All hell is breaking loose here." After I gave her my details, she asked, "Is this an insurance claim?" If she didn't already know that I had no idea how to handle this, she knew it for sure when I burst into tears and said, "I don't know." In an even kinder, calmer voice, she said I should call my insurance company and then call her back.

I had never had to call my insurance company before, had simply paid my premiums year after year for twenty-four years, seldom giving it another thought except to note it was awfully expensive. I wasn't even sure where my insurance documents were. If I'd ever imagined that I was prepared and knew what to do in the event of an emergency, I had been kidding myself.

By the time I found my documents, it was after six o'clock, so I called the toll-free after-hours number. When I told the young man who answered that I was calling from Kingston, he said pleasantly, "My God, we've had a hundred calls from Kingston in the last half hour!" He was in Vancouver. He took down the details and gave me the claim number I needed to proceed. I called the Winmar woman back, and the process was set in motion.

The rest of the evening in the steadily darkening house was filled with phone calls on both the land line and the cell phone. With Shane and Alex periodically calling to check on me, sometimes I was talking on both phones at once while taking notes by flashlight at the kitchen table. By ten o'clock that night, after many calls from a man named Frank at Winmar, arrangements had been made for the next day.

The electrician was here by eight o'clock in the morning, wearing a pair of hip waders. He removed the ceiling light, turned the power back on, and checked the water heater and the sump pump, which, he said, should now be able to take away most of the water. It ran for four hours straight. Frank from Winmar arrived with his camera to take pictures of the damage both upstairs and down. He said the furnace and the washer and dryer would also have to be checked by professionals. As it turned out, the furnace was fine; the washer and dryer were not. Because this was also a sewer backup, Frank said everything that wasn't well up off the floor or stored in plastic tubs was now contaminated and would have to be destroyed. Including the walls. In the afternoon, he returned and set up four gigantic fans and two even larger dehumidifiers in the basement. With all six of them running at once, even upstairs it was like being inside an airplane.

Frank left me with a dozen cardboard boxes, into which I was to put the undamaged items. I went to Canadian Tire and bought a pair of rubber boots and a mop. The store was crowded with other people doing the same. With the power back on, I now had more information. Kingston, it was said, had received over a hundred millimetres of rain in less than four hours. Hundreds, possibly over a thousand, homes and businesses had been flooded. For the next few days, the television news and the local paper were filled with pictures of cars submerged in parking lots and on downtown streets, of damaged homes now sprouting in their driveways ever-growing piles of soggy smelly furniture, drywall, clothing, and children's toys. As was mine.

On Sunday morning, I visited Shane, crying off and on at the table, feeling comforted not only by him but also by the guards, all of them offering sympathy, suggestions, and some flood stories of their own. Then I came home and got back to the task at hand. Alex and I, with help from some neighbours, spent the next three days hauling stuff out of the basement and piling it in the driveway. We were also packing up all that could be salvaged and moving it upstairs. Soon the kitchen, the hallway, and the back room were filled with boxes.

I have always been something of a pack rat, and for years, I'd been guilty of stashing things in the basement—things that were broken, worn out, or just no longer of any use to us, things about which I invariably said, "I'll just put this here for now." I called this "storage," but in fact, it was just me not being very good at letting things go. As a friend had once said of herself, I was about three boxes away from an episode of *Hoarders*. So although the basement was only partially finished, it was completely full of stuff. For the insurance claim, I'd been told to keep a list of all we were tossing on a form poignantly titled "Schedule of Loss." Six-foot artificial Christmas tree, obsolete desktop computer, five-foot wooden toboggan, floor polisher, carpet sweeper, vacuum cleaner, circular saw, three suitcases, two ancient TV sets, white wicker loveseat and two matching chairs, coffee table, rollaway bed, dog crate, two floor lamps, several mats and throw rugs. The list grew longer. The pile in the driveway grew higher, wider, deeper.

On Wednesday morning, the full cleanup crew arrived, six men in white haz-mat suits who removed the heavy items, including the ugly plaid water- and sewage-filled sofa bed that was down there when we moved in and that now had to be hacked into pieces with a chainsaw to be removed. They pulled up all the floor coverings and ripped out the drywall that had sucked up the water and was now saturated with sewage. The cats hid under the bed, and I spent most of the day trying to comfort the little dogs, who were quivering and barking and peeing on the floor.

In the midst of the chaos, the insurance adjuster arrived to assess the damage. They would cover the basement but not, she said, the roof and the now cracked and ruined plaster ceilings in three rooms on the main floor. If the storm had ripped shingles off the roof, it would have been covered, but the roof had leaked because the shingles were old, she said, and that was not covered. That was my own damn fault, she seemed to be implying, for having been negligent in the maintenance of my home. The shingles had looked fine to me, no worn or lifted areas, no evidence of crumbling or breaking. How was I to know that twenty-five-year shingles are not what they claim to be? I'd had the roof done in 1992, so those shingles were only nineteen years old. I thought they had a few good years left in them yet. Winmar would patch the roof for now, and I would have to make my own arrangements to have it redone and figure out how to pay for that and the interior ceiling repairs myself.

Shane could not help me in a practical hands-on way, but he proved to be an unflagging source of moral support. In other situations, he had seemed to have a knack for making my life harder than it needed to be, but in this case, except for the one time he suggested maybe I was getting a little too fond of this Frank person, he was indeed making my life easier. He didn't complain about the fact that I was missing visits and phone calls, that I wasn't paying much attention to him, that I was often irritable and impatient. In fact, this was the upside of the whole flood fiasco: yes, he could put himself aside and be there for me. Yes, he could be the person I could lean on. It had been a long time since I'd felt this.

In retrospect, the other upsides of the flood were that my basement had finally been cleaned out, I was completely cured of my pack rat tendencies, and from here on in, I would always know the exact location of my insurance documents.

IT HAD BEEN NEARLY THE END OF JULY before any progress was made on getting our PFVs reinstated. Not surprisingly this was not the simple process we'd been led to believe it would be. For weeks Shane had been trying to get answers, and then he was reprimanded for asking too many questions and bothering his CMT. I had sent a letter to the warden requesting a meeting or a phone call to discuss the issue. I received no reply. A lengthy report had been prepared by his CMT, most of which was a reiteration of many previous reports, with emphasis on the one regarding his 2009 revocation, which still said he had broken into my house and confronted me naked in the bathtub, even though I had corrected this at the hearing, and on the letter he'd sent me from the TD Centre at KP, which was still being described as "threatening and disturbing," even though it had not been. Eventually we were told we could now have four twelve-hour PFVs before being reviewed and considered for longer ones.

The first of these took place ten days after the flood. I had an extra house key made for Frank, so Winmar could continue their work in the basement while I was at Frontenac. The crew would spend the day cleaning the floors and spraying everything with disinfectant. Alex would keep track of the pets.

For those twelve hours in the trailer, Shane pampered me, fussed over me, cooked for me, and patiently held me while I cried. At home alone, I was still resisting the urge to cry, but there in his arms, it felt so good to let it out. In the afternoon, we watched the Vince Vaughn romantic comedy *Couples Retreat*. Curled up there in our own couples retreat—hardly a tropical island resort, but a retreat nonetheless—I realized it had been years since Shane had reminded me of Vince Vaughn.

IT HAD TAKEN MERE HOURS for the flood damage to be done, but I could see it was going to take months for the recovery—both the physical recovery of the house itself and my emotional recovery. My "Schedule of Loss" extended well beyond the two five-ton truckloads of stinking junk that had been hauled out of the driveway. There were also all those unclaimable items that hadn't even made the list. Like my comprehensive collection of empty cardboard boxes of all sizes that I'd kept because you never know when you'll need a box and because in my family, perhaps since my mother worked in a post office, we considered a good sturdy box to be a thing of beauty. Like the wooden sled that was mine as a child, that I'd used to haul baby Alex around the neighbourhood on winter walks, and that the insurance adjuster said was not quite an antique and so could neither be valued nor replaced. Like any pleasure I might have once taken in the sound of rain on the roof. Like my now-shattered sense of my house as my sanctuary, my refuge, my safe haven, the one place in the world where I did not have to be afraid.

Along with all that I'd lost in the flood, both tangible and intangible, I had also gained a ramped-up sense of my own insecurity, an escalation of my lifelong fear and anxiety, an unrelenting awareness of my own vulnerability, of being perpetually at the mercy of forces beyond my control, of waiting, always waiting, for the next terrible thing to hit me, knowing that whatever it turned out to be, there would be no one here to help me. Irrational though I knew it was, I kept thinking that if only I'd been prepared, if only I hadn't foolishly dropped my usual hypervigilance that morning, if only I'd been *paying attention,* somehow the flood would never have happened. In my own skewed version of magical thinking, it was entirely possible that it had all been my own damn fault. I had also added a new fear to my repertoire, this one called *ombrophobia* or *pluviophobia*: the fear of rain.

There are thousands, probably hundreds of thousands, of people in the world who have been through far more severe floods than mine, not to mention hurricanes, tornadoes, tsunamis, earthquakes, wildfires, and volcanic eruptions. Try as I might to put my own small disaster into perspective, still it was mine, and I couldn't seem to get over it and move forward in the aftermath. This was one more project Louise and I would have to tackle together. Where were my inner resources? Consumed perhaps by Shane? Where was my resilience? Lost perhaps in the welter of the prison world? When I told Louise I was praying for strength every night and sometimes half the day too, she laughed and said, "You'd better stop that. Every time you pray for strength, God will give you something else to prove you are already strong."

I WAS SUPPOSED TO BEGIN a three-month tenure as Writer-in-Residence at Queen's University in early September. I didn't see how I could possibly do a good job there with everything at home still in such an uproar after the flood. I was relieved when the English Department saw no problem in postponing my residency until the January term instead. This proved to be a wise decision. Despite the fact that I was now scrupulously *not* praying for strength as Louise had advised, in the following weeks, there was no remission in the relentless cascade of challenges requiring exactly that. Most of these had nothing to do with prison. Most of these were just my life.

In late August, my basement was flooded again by another downpour only slightly less torrential than the first. Fortunately it was only water this time, not sewage, and everything down there that could be destroyed already had been. The day after the second flood, I had to have our old cat Max put to sleep. He'd been diagnosed with chronic peritonitis when he was young, had suffered and recovered from many bouts of it since. But now he was fifteen years old and this time could not recover. The new roof had to be installed, and I had to find four thousand dollars to pay for it. Both the microwave and the TV set died and had to be replaced. There was an electrical fire in my oven, and as I tried to rescue the lovely and expensive roast of lamb inside, I burned my right hand badly, necessitating a trip to Emergency. Then I had to buy a new stove. The car required the fourteen-hundred-dollar replacement of the front control arms and stabilizer links. There was a problem with the bathroom plumbing, again due to the existing pipes not being compatible with anything now available. In the end, I had Bath Fitter install a whole new unit complete with a fancy hand-held showerhead that I chose with Shane in mind.

I was broke and exhausted, well beyond frazzled. For every task, event, or obligation I completed and crossed off my list, there were three or four more to be added the next day. For every crisis dealt with or averted, there was another one waiting in the wings, biding its time, getting ready to blow. I was always clenched—not my teeth or my fists or my jaw, but all of me—bracing for the next thing.

And still there were readings to be given and attended, a story commissioned by CBC Radio to be written and recorded, a short piece to be completed for a national magazine. I was having problems with this piece, and when I complained about it to Shane, he said, "You keep talking about how much you love writing, but you're always just bitching about it. Maybe you should find a new line of work."

If I'd hoped that by now Shane was getting the idea that life out here in the free world was not a piece of pie, so to speak, I was sadly mistaken. It seemed there'd been a time limit on how long he was prepared to be my Rock of Gibraltar. After about two months, his warrant as my sturdy support system had abruptly expired. I had used up all my let-me-lean-on-you credits, and he had reverted back to his former stance as the needy one—aggrieved, benighted, and unwell.

Throughout the fall, he had again been having problems with his esophagus. The follow-up tests he was supposed to have after the esophageal bleed back in 2007, and that were again recommended by Dr. Chapman at the end of 2008, had never been done. Now it was becoming increasingly difficult for him to swallow food of any kind without choking or vomiting or both. After he'd been rushed to both outside hospitals a number of times, finally the follow-up tests were scheduled.

We had now been back together for as long as we'd been together in the first place. Things were not going well. It wasn't that I had stopped loving him. Rightly or wrongly, I did love him. But I could no longer convince myself that this would ever be a healthy relationship. It had been a very long time since we'd had anything to add to our file box of happy memories. But that other box was filled to overflowing. We were back on the *Tough Guys* train without a rainbow in sight. I had to admit that I was unhappy more often than not, that both my hope and my faith were fading—my hope that through the sheer force of my will, I could make this relationship work—my faith that if only I could be strong enough, patient enough, devoted enough, we would live happily ever after, amen.

I had been as strong as I could be for as long as I could be. Now I had been feeling frazzled and anxious for so long that when there did come a quiet peaceful day in which I had no real reason to feel that way, I did anyway. I thought this must be what it was like for Shane: when there did come a time when he had no reason to feel angry, miserable, and filled with hate, he did anyway. If only because he didn't know what else to do, didn't know how else to *be*. His anger and hate, I could see now, were what kept him going. I could also see that my hope, my faith, and my love were no match for that. Things were not getting better. Things were getting worse. I had to admit to myself that I couldn't go on much longer. Perhaps he knew it too.

I finally understood that he had to live in a constant state of chaos and crisis. No matter how often he claimed to want a quiet, simple, peaceful life, every time he got anywhere close to that, he couldn't stand it. He could only go for a few days in a state of relative calm. If a crisis didn't then present itself, he would manufacture one to satisfy his need for drama and destruction. He loved nothing more than an uproar, especially one he'd created himself. That was his comfort zone. I could seldom keep myself from being sucked into the vortex of his twisted misery.

Brenda from the prison group had once given me a fridge magnet made by Tammy's inmate husband. Illustrated with a large wooden cross planted in a bed of pink tulips, it featured the words WAIT, HOPE, TRUST, REJOICE in a rainbow arc across the top, and across the bottom, a quote from the Bible, Romans 8:28: *All things work together for good.* Brenda was a devout Christian. She said the magnet would give me strength. I took it off the fridge where it had been for a year or more and put it in the junk drawer.

SETTLING IN TO EAT MY SUPPER while watching the six o'clock news on a Friday evening in late October, I was startled to recognize a familiar intersection in the video footage of the lead story. There was my Tim Hortons. There was Subway and the sushi place. There was the apartment building where Shane had lived. And yes, there was the call centre—with a cluster of police vehicles in front and many uniformed officers bringing people out of the building.

The call centre had been raided earlier that day. Nine people were arrested in Kingston and another twelve in Belleville at the second branch of the operation of what police were now calling "a major telemarketing scam." By early estimate, thousands of people and businesses in both Canada and the United States had been defrauded of more than three million dollars since 2008. Kingston Police had begun investigating the call centre in late May, the news announcer said, and were joined over the summer by the OPP and the RCMP.

Just minutes after the story ended, the phone rang. Shane had been watching the news too.

Over the next few days, we learned that concerns had been expressed early on about the wisdom of sending inmates to work at the call centre, that the police had advised against it due to the ongoing investigation. I might have pursued this issue with more determination had other events not intervened.

IN EARLY NOVEMBER, after all the medical testing had been completed, Shane had an appointment to see a gastroenterologist at Hotel Dieu Hospital to discuss the results. We were very worried. The last time I'd asked if I could accompany him to a medical appointment, his parole officer, Dennis Walker, had said I was probably planning to take him a gun and help him escape, so this time I didn't even ask.

I paced around the house all morning waiting for the phone to ring. When it finally did, I grabbed it in the middle of the first ring.

I said, "Hello."

Shane said, "Cancer."

THREE WEEKS LATER, we were back in the same upstairs room at Frontenac where the first parole hearing I'd attended had been held just over four years ago. Today's hearing was to address Shane's request for a series of UTAs to an Ottawa halfway house, a preliminary step towards doing day parole there. It had been twice postponed, because the necessary paperwork had not been done.

That morning I met Shane and his lawyer, as well as Stuart and Edward Blake, in the visiting room at eight o'clock. After some time waiting there, we went upstairs and waited some more in the staff lunchroom across the hall from the hearing room. There was some kind of commotion farther down the hallway—a raised voice, a slamming door, hurried footsteps. Perhaps this was what was causing the delay.

Finally we were ushered into the room where two male Board members and the female hearing officer were already seated at one long table. Shane and his lawyer took their places at the second table. Stuart, Edward, and I sat in three chairs close behind them. I was in the middle, staring directly at the bald spot on the back of Shane's head. Last to enter was Dennis Walker, who sat down beside Shane. They did not look at each other. In fact, Dennis didn't look at anyone. He was visibly upset, his face was red and shiny, and although it was a chilly late-November morning, he was sweating so profusely that under the arms of his tight lilac dress shirt, there were dark wet circles almost down to his waist. While the hearing officer went through the usual preliminaries, Dennis was breathing hard and flipping violently through the paperwork on the table in front of him. For a whole year, Shane had been complaining about how strange and unbalanced he seemed. I had never met him nor even spoken to him on the phone, but now I could see that Shane might not have been exaggerating.

Following the usual procedure, Dennis, as the parole officer, was asked to speak first. He sounded blustering and belligerent. He made it abundantly clear, however, that he absolutely did not support either UTAs or day parole for Shane. He'd written to the Ottawa Parole Office about Shane smoking on his work release, because this was indicative of his inability to follow the rules. Consequently the Ottawa Parole Office, he said, had withdrawn their support of him coming to their city.

Again following standard procedure, the lead Board member took Shane back to the beginning of his criminal activity, then followed a circuitous path to the present day in a tone that was consistently stern and humourless. Passing and non-specific reference was made to Shane's current health problems. The second Board member, who looked and sounded like a marine, added only a couple of questions, then concluded that every time Shane had been released or even come close to release, he had screwed it up.

From there they moved on to the current issue—the issue, it was soon obvious, about which Dennis Walker was so upset. Now there was conflicting information. There had been an email just two days ago stating that the Ottawa halfway house was still in support of Shane coming there. Dennis said he hadn't seen this email until that very morning, right before the hearing. The discussion that followed did little to help clear up the confusion.

By the time they were done hashing it out and Shane's lawyer had said a few words on his behalf in closing, we were feeling quite optimistic when we went back to the lunchroom to await the decision. We all agreed that Shane had acquitted himself well.

Beckoned back into the hearing room after not more than ten minutes, we were stunned when the lead Board member said, "Denied."

I WAS PERMITTED TO STAY WITH SHANE in V&C for some time afterwards. They were obviously watching closely to see how he would react to this outcome. I couldn't help but feel they were expecting me to keep him calm. In fact, he *was* calm—filled with purpose and not thinking about cancer now. Being well aware of the rule that states "an offender may appeal any negative decision regarding conditional release that is made by the Parole Board, as well as any grant that is more restrictive than was requested," Shane spent this time gulping down bad coffee from the vending machine and making notes for his appeal.

PART FIVE

December 2011 to July 2012

"What exactly did the doctor say?"

It was the morning after the hearing, and I'd arrived back at Frontenac at eight-thirty with my little blue bag. We had had four twelve-hour PFVs in the interim, and this was to be our first twenty-four since the kite and the cancellation back in June. There were no problems getting in, and by nine-thirty, we'd made the bed, hung up the towels, put away the food, and were in the kitchen making coffee and toast.

This time we were in the trailer closest to the visiting room, the one we'd been in for our first PFV, facing the stone wall and the guard tower of Collins Bay. Usually I preferred to be in one of the other two, with their backs to the prisons, but this time I was glad to be in the closer one. I hadn't told Shane that I was anxious about this PFV. What if he suddenly took ill? What if he started choking and gagging, what if he passed out, what if he started vomiting blood all over the place? I am not, generally speaking, good with sick people, especially if there is vomit involved. Yes, there was an emergency phone in each trailer, but

I knew from experience—once when we had to call because the sheets we'd been given were too small for the bed and another time when the coffeemaker wouldn't work—that they didn't always answer. What would I do if I needed help in the middle of the night? I didn't think it would be a good idea to run out of the trailer and try to climb over the fence to get to the building. I would be directly in the sightline of the armed guards in the Collins Bay tower. No, definitely not a good idea. At least in this trailer, we were close enough that I figured if I stood outside waving my arms and screaming for help, they'd see me and hear me and come on the run.

"What exactly did the doctor say?" I asked as we sat down at the kitchen table. I also hadn't told Shane that I had some questions about the cancer diagnosis. It had been almost a month now, and it seemed that none of the prison staff knew anything about it. Visiting one Saturday since, I'd mentioned it to a member of his CMT who was working that day. She looked at me strangely and said, "He never told me about that." I knew that once a cancer diagnosis was made, the medical team quickly went into high gear to begin treatment. I assumed this would be true even if the patient was a federal inmate. But nothing was happening. I didn't know whether to be suspicious or concerned.

"What exactly did the doctor say?"

Maybe Shane had misunderstood. A year before I met him, I had to have a biopsy on my left breast after a suspicious mammogram. Thankfully it revealed the presence of nothing more than benign calcifications. But early in our relationship, Shane had persisted in referring to this as the time I had cancer. Perhaps I still hadn't made him understand that I never had cancer, that a biopsy doesn't mean you have cancer, but is simply a test to determine if you do or don't.

Now, thanks to the combination of doctor–patient confidentiality and CSC's privacy policies, I had no way of getting more information about his condition.

"Did he say you *have* cancer? Or did he say you have to have a biopsy to see if you *might* have cancer?"

"How the fuck am I supposed to remember what he said?" Shane snarled and went into the bedroom.

Things went downhill from there. We were both exhausted after a stressful month and upset about the negative outcome of yesterday's hearing. I wanted only to spend the day relaxing on the couch reading and watching TV. But he was already in bed, and it was clear what he wanted. I stayed in the living room.

The day passed. We were counted, then we had lunch. We were counted again, then we had supper. We were counted one more time, then we watched TV. By the time we went to bed, I was feeling better. But Shane said he was feeling sick now, he was too tired to have sex now, it was too late—why did I make him wait so long? Shutting the bedroom door behind him, he went back to the living room. I stayed in bed and tried to sleep.

The room as usual was bathed in white stripes by the Collins Bay spotlight. I lay flat on my back and looked down at them falling across my body. I stretched my arms up and wiggled my fingers in the stripes. I imagined I could feel them across my face.

I heard Shane coming back down the hall. He flung open the door, flicked on the ceiling light, and stood there staring at me. I stared back at him and said nothing. He shut the door and went away. Half an hour later, he was back again, coming into the room this time to get his clothes.

I dared to ask, "Where are you going?"

He grunted and said, "Nowhere. As usual." He left the bedroom again.

He came back several more times, dressed now, and stood in the doorway in the stripes of white light.

I pictured the phone on the wall at the other end of the hallway. What would he do if I tried to use it? I pictured the knives in the kitchen drawer. I pictured him in the living room equidistant from the knives on one side and the phone on the other. What if I called them, and they didn't come fast enough? What if I called them, and they didn't come at all? I got up and got dressed.

I went down the hallway to the living room without looking at the phone. He was sitting in the dark scowling at the TV just like he used to at home. When he saw me with my clothes on, he said, "Here we go. Now I suppose you're going to call them."

"No, I just thought since you had your clothes on, I'd put mine on too," I said inanely.

I sat down on the couch beside him. It was still dark. I don't remember what time it was. I don't remember what was on TV. I don't remember if we talked. We sat there until the sun came up. Then I went back to the bedroom and packed my bag, brought it out to the living room. He cleaned up the kitchen, stripped the bed, put the sheets in the basket with the towels. He vacuumed the whole place just like he always did. At eight-thirty they came to let us out.

We followed them into the building, and with Shane standing over me, I filled out the form indicating that all had gone well. Just like I always did. I signed out on the clipboard, date and time. It was December 1: the fifth anniversary of the day I gave him the I-love-you card. We went into the bubble, where we were interviewed by the keeper. Just like we always were. I don't remember which keeper was working that day. What was the point of this post-PFV interview? I wondered. Just like I always did. With Shane sitting right there beside me, I said everything was fine. Just like I always did.

Shane went back to his cell, and I went home. He called shortly after I arrived. Just like he always did. "Are you okay?" he asked.

"Yes, I'm fine," I said. But I was lying. I knew what I had to do.

My term as Writer-in-Residence at Queen's began the second week of January. I was excited and anxious—excited because it had been a long time since I'd had a "real job," not to mention a real paycheque at the end of each month; anxious because I didn't know how Shane was going to handle all the changes to our routine that the job would necessitate. What were the chances he was going to make my life easier rather than harder? Would he be able to "let me" do what I needed to do instead of trying to sabotage me, as he'd often seemed to be doing in the past?

In addition to my office hours three days a week, I would be arranging, hosting, and giving a number of readings at other times in other locations, some in the evening as well. The people who had made appointments to see me at Queen's would be sending me their work ahead of time by email. There would be much reading and critiquing to be done every day. Because my residency contract required that I also do something in the community outside of Queen's, I would be facilitating a writing group at 99 York with interested members of the prison group. We would meet every other Wednesday morning for three hours. Somewhere in there, I was also going to have to find time to do my own work and keep up with the domestic end of things. The bottom line was, I'd have very little time for Shane in the next three months.

I'd already told him that I wouldn't be able to continue our monthly counselling sessions with Edward Blake for the duration and that I'd be visiting on Saturdays only, staying home on Sundays to work. Fortunately he'd been approved to attend Sunday mass at the convent the way he used to. I warned him that I wouldn't have much time during the day or the evening to be talking on the phone. Since Christmas I'd had him "in training" for this. We'd agreed that he wouldn't call until after he'd had his supper, around five o'clock. He was doing quite well with this, although when he did call, I could sometimes hear that he was feeling twisted and resentful and sorry for himself—as if this were some outrageous and peculiar thing I was forcing him to do.

I said, "I love you with all my heart."

He said, "I hope so. Sometimes I wonder."

I didn't see how he could wonder. I felt I'd done everything I possibly could for him, and still it was never enough. I had now been with him longer than any other man I'd been involved with.

I said, "Maybe I'm just not self-sacrificing enough to be in this relationship."

He said, "What's that supposed to mean?"

We were on the phone. Again. Yes, he'd waited until five o'clock before calling. But it was now shortly after nine, and he'd called four times since.

I said it meant I was not willing to give up everything for him—my work, my friends, my independence, my sanity, my self, my life. I was on the edge of sarcasm, because, in truth, I felt I'd already sacrificed more than enough for him.

Expert though he was at slinging around the sarcasm himself, it often went over his head when he was on the receiving end. In this case, he agreed with me. Sincerely. In a tone that made it clear that he thought this was how relationships were supposed to work and that my shortcomings in the self-sacrifice department were another sad failing on my part, just one more thing he had to put up with. What had he ever sacrificed for me? I wondered but did not ask.

He'd said often enough in the early days that we would fall in love and become one. By "one," I knew now, he meant him.

Even Dr. Quinn had once tried to dissuade him of this pop-song notion of love by drawing a Venn diagram on his notepad: two overlapping circles with the intersecting area in the middle coloured in to represent our relationship and the exterior areas of each circle representing our separate selves. Shane had persisted in not understanding this, had drawn instead two separate circles labelled *SHANE* and *DIANE*, and then two more circles, one on top of the other, labelled *LOVE*.

Shane said when two people truly loved each other, they'd stay together no matter what happened, no matter how badly one treated the other, no matter how unhappy one or the other or both of them might be. The more he elaborated on this theory, the clearer it became that when he said both people must abide by this compact, he meant the woman. He said this was unconditional love. Unfortunately he used his own parents' marriage as an example. Dr. Quinn didn't seem to find this nearly as preposterous as I did.

I HAD ALREADY TOLD HIM that I wouldn't be able to have another PFV until late February during Reading Week, when I would have no office hours at Queen's, and that I wouldn't be able to have another one after that until April, when the residency was over. Since the last disastrous PFV, the truth was, I didn't want to have another one at all ever again. If I had been waiting, subconsciously at least, for the last straw, I knew that had been it. I finally understood that I'd been mixed up for a long time about what being strong meant in this circumstance. That being strong did not mean staying. Being strong meant leaving. But I also knew I had to do this residency first, and I intended to do an excellent job of it.

Did I think I could postpone the catastrophes of my love life to accommodate the schedule of my working life? Yes, I did. Did I think

I could put my work first while leaving Shane on the back burner for three months? Yes, I did. Yes, for once I did. First I would deal with the residency and all it required. Then I would deal with Shane.

The night before my residency began, he called late. We'd already talked three times that evening, him in a different mood each time, none of them good. I was already in bed, almost asleep. This time he said he was feeling afraid of what this year would bring. I knew he meant his health. It had been two months now, and he'd had a few more tests, but there had still been no definite treatment program outlined or implemented. I knew he was trying to manipulate me, putting his health issues in the front of my mind. How could I leave him if he had cancer? I knew he wanted me to feel guilty for being preoccupied with other things. How could any of those things be more important than him? I knew he wanted me to make him feel better. But I was annoyed and half asleep. I did not oblige.

Then he asked me if I would nurse him if he was dying.

"No," I said. "No, I will not."

I HAD BEEN WORKING AT HOME ALONE for so many years that I thought it would take some time to adjust to going out to an office instead. But in fact, I recognized almost immediately the appeal of having someplace else to go, of being able to close the door, get in the car, and leave it all behind: the dishes not done, the kitty litter box not changed, the floors not washed, the bathroom not cleaned. And Shane. I knew better than to have the office number added to his phone list, and he, surprisingly, hadn't suggested it. I'd warned him that I wouldn't have my cell phone on while I was in the office. Even better, I discovered once I got there that there wasn't much reception inside those old stone buildings, and it didn't work anyway.

I had often envied other people their ability to compartmentalize their lives, a fine art I'd never been able to master. But now I discovered I could do it after all, and I could do it well. I could do it without even trying. Each time I got in the car and headed to the university, I forgot all about him, all about prison, all about cancer, all about all of it.

Each time I walked down the hallway towards the office with my laptop in one hand and my briefcase in the other, I thought, This is my life.

Each time I went to the washroom at the end of the hall, I looked at myself in the mirror and thought, Hello again, there you are. Long time no see. Sometimes, if the washroom was otherwise empty, I said it out loud.

IN THE MIDDLE OF MARCH, Shane had the first of what would be a lengthy series of procedures on his esophagus. As I understood it, the procedure, which took place under sedation in the operating room, involved the insertion of a dilating balloon that was then slowly inflated in an attempt to increase the circumference of his esophagus gradually so he'd be able to swallow and eat properly.

On the last day of March, my residency was officially over. Except for the prison writing group—they were all enjoying it so much, we'd agreed to keep meeting at 99 York every other Wednesday morning until the end of June. Which was not to say I was now going to take a vacation. I hadn't had much time for my own writing for the past three months and was eager to get back to it. Plus I was now preparing to present my latest work at a national conference to be held at Humber College in Toronto in early May.

I decided not to resume Sunday visiting, would use the day to work instead. Shane was still going to the convent on Sunday mornings, but the rules had changed, and nobody was allowed to meet their partners there anymore. This rule change was said to be due to a couple having been caught in a compromising position in a church bathroom one Sunday—not at the convent, not even at some other church in Kingston, but somewhere in the western provinces. Following the same policy as teachers who punish the whole class when one student has done something wrong, CSC had prohibited the practice nationwide.

Edward Blake and I had agreed that there didn't seem much point in resuming our counselling sessions at Frontenac. He would continue seeing Shane alone, although he said he wasn't sure that was having much positive effect either.

Busy as I'd been throughout the residency, I'd kept every single one of my regular Tuesday appointments with Louise. She was the only person I had been entirely honest with about what had happened during the PFV at the end of November. She and Edward were the only people to whom I had admitted that I was now waiting for Shane to die, that I had resurrected my deathbed fantasy, that I figured this would make a good ending to our story, a clean and tidy ending that would let me off the hook, guilt-free.

On the final Tuesday of March, as we were winding down yet another hour of me going on about the problems with Shane, Louise waited until I stopped to catch my breath and then asked, "Would you be putting up with all this if he wasn't in prison?"

I hadn't thought about it this way before. But I didn't have to think about my answer either.

"No," I said, "I would not."

D<small>URING THE MONTH OF</small> A<small>PRIL</small>, Shane had two more dilation procedures on his esophagus. Between treatments he'd been taken to the
hospital several times because of choking, usually caused by his having
become so hungry that he'd eaten something solid when he was supposed to be on a soft diet. In fact, he was supposed to be having Ensure,
the commonly available liquid nutritional supplement, but Shane said
the prison doctor had refused to order it for him. It took the interven-
tion of a keeper to get him the Ensure.

In mid-April we had what was to be our last twenty-four-hour PFV
before we moved up to forty-eight. Like the previous one in February
during Reading Week, this PFV went well enough. I did what I had to
do to keep the peace. But still when I awoke the next morning, Shane
was already up, sitting in the living room scowling at the TV. I had no
idea what was wrong and no intention of trying to worm it out of him.
They would be coming to get us in an hour. I couldn't help but think
that if this were a forty-eight-hour PFV, I would have another whole
twenty-four hours to get through.

We got ready to leave. Since he was already in a mood, I figured now
was as good a time as any to tell him I didn't want to move up to forty-
eight hours. Moments before Grant and another guard came to let us
out, I told him.

We followed them into the building as usual, towing our stuff in
the wagon behind us like children returning from the playground.
As I filled out the form and signed the clipboard, I saw that John
Logan was the keeper on duty. He was walking down the hallway to
his office. Rather than going into the bubble with Shane to wait for
John to come and interview us, I headed across the visiting room and

down the hallway after him. I didn't look back, and Shane, who had now put on his good-mood face for their benefit, didn't follow me.

I tapped on the glass of John's half-open door and went in. Without preamble and in a voice as lighthearted as I could muster, I told him I'd decided I didn't want to move up to forty-eight-hour PFVs after all. I was well aware that I was doing something mutinous and revolutionary by refusing to take the next step. I did not say I didn't want to be alone with Shane for that long. I said I was so busy with my work that I just wouldn't be able to manage it. And besides, I said, I really couldn't stand not being able to smoke. True. John was looking very surprised.

"Not only that," I went on, "but the truth is, I don't like being locked up." Also true. The novelty of these prison sleepovers had now worn off completely. Of course, I'd never admitted this to Shane. After all, he'd been locked up for more than thirty years—who was I to complain that I could hardly handle it for twenty-four hours, let alone forty-eight? Who was I to complain about missing my son, my pets, my books, my computer, my iPad, my iPhone, my own bed, my own bathroom, my daily trip to Tim Hortons? How could I tell him that when I got home after only twenty-four hours in the trailer, it was with such a sense of joyful relief that you'd think I'd been gone for two weeks?

Now John was laughing. "I've done over thirty years," he said, "and nobody has ever said that to me before."

"Nobody?" I asked incredulously.

"I mean no *visitor*. No visitor has ever said that to me before."

I may have been the only one who ever had the nerve to say it out loud, but I was quite sure I wasn't the only one who'd ever thought it.

ON THE DAY OF THAT PFV, CSC announced it was cutting all funding to the LifeLine program, which would be completely discontinued—this despite the fact that it was an internationally renowned program that had received awards from the International Corrections and Prisons Association, the American Correctional Association, and just six months previously, was the recipient of the Canadian Criminal Justice Association's Achievement Award. Not only would Stuart and the two dozen other lifers employed by LifeLine now be out of a job, but Shane and the thousands of other lifers they worked with would lose yet another essential means of support. The psychology departments had already been so pared down that an inmate might well have to wait months to see someone. The chaplaincies had also been reduced to the point that at Frontenac, there was now only one full-time on-site chaplain who was trying to look after more than two hundred men of all faiths.

A spokesperson for Public Safety Minister Vic Toews told *CBC News* that LifeLine "wasn't producing any results that improved public safety. We will not spend a dollar on Corrections that is not necessary to keep Canadians safe." And yet the LifeLine program had been credited over and over again, even by CSC itself under previous governments, with having played an important role not only in the rehabilitation of lifers still in prison but also in their successful reintegration back into society without ever reoffending.

With the closing of LifeLine, I was struck again by the short-sightedness of the Harper government's Tough on Crime policies. None of the people making these decisions seemed to grasp the basic fact that almost all of the inmates currently serving time in federal institutions across Canada were going to get out one day. They were going to get out of their prisons and come straight into our communities without benefit of sufficient support or counselling either while inside or after their release. This was not going to go well for any of them. This was not going to go well for any of us. There would be more crimes. There would be more victims.

Those who would say this could all be avoided if they just kept those criminals locked up forever should be reminded that, according to the Office of the Correctional Investigator, the annual average cost of keeping a male federal inmate incarcerated is now more than a hundred thousand dollars, and nearly twice that for each female inmate.

Eliminating the LifeLine program was yet another measure that had nothing to do with protecting public safety, yet another egregious decision that put all of us at greater, rather than lesser, risk.

THERE WAS MORE BIG NEWS TO COME. Following the cancellation of LifeLine on Monday, we learned that Vic Toews himself would be holding a news conference on Thursday afternoon to deliver another announcement. For some time, there had been rumours about the possible closing of Kingston Penitentiary. Surely it couldn't be that. Even the guards were saying surely it couldn't be that.

It was that.

With little preamble, Toews announced that Kingston Penitentiary would be closed and decommissioned within two years. The Regional Treatment Centre (RTC), a separate maximum-security psychiatric institution for mentally ill offenders located on the KP grounds, would also be closed, as well as medium-security Leclerc Institution in Laval, Quebec. These closures, Toews said, would save CSC 120 million dollars a year.

Opened in 1835 and designated a National Historic Site in 1990, Kingston Penitentiary was not only the most famous prison in the country, housing Canada's most notorious criminals, but it was also one of the oldest continuously operating prisons in the world. It was a storied, legendary place, not only among the inmates but among the staff as well. One of the guards at Bath, when once asked by another visitor going in ahead of me if he'd ever worked at KP, said yes, he had, for twenty years, and it was like going to Beirut every day.

Vic Toews said an institution built in the nineteenth century was no longer effective or appropriate in the twenty-first century. He did not mention that in recent years, hundreds of millions of dollars had been pumped into KP to address these concerns. The closure of these three institutions would mean moving almost a thousand inmates, six hundred of them from KP and RTC. About the same number of prison employees would be affected. There did not seem to be a clear plan as to how this would be accomplished or where these inmates and staff members would go. He did not offer any suggestion as to how the profoundly mentally ill offenders from RTC could possibly be taken care of properly in an ordinary institution. Toews said no new prisons would be built, but existing institutions would be expanded. Again, there did not seem to be an actual plan in place to accomplish any of this.

Immediately after the press conference, the phone rang.

Shane said, "The mothership has gone down."

If I'd imagined he would be jubilant about this news, I was wrong. In fact, he was stunned. They all were. I could hear the other guys on the phones all around him, calling home in shocked disbelief. Not only was KP was an integral part of the history and identity of the city of Kingston, but also of all the men, like Shane, who had ever been incarcerated there. It was a badge of honour, I think, for him and the other prisoners who could say they'd done time there and survived, had escaped the place, so to speak, with their lives. A part of each of them would be stripped away by this closure.

They were scared too.

"If they can do *this*," Shane said, "they can do anything."

∞

I THOUGHT I HAD PLENTY OF TIME, but then the train was late getting into Toronto, and I hadn't factored in the trouble my taxi would have getting through the construction in front of Union Station. Now I was running around the Lakeshore Campus of Humber College, trying to find first the building in which I'd be staying and then the building in which I'd be delivering my paper in less than an hour. I was clutching a campus map in my teeth, my overnight bag and my briefcase were banging against my legs, and my purse was ringing.

After checking into my dorm room, changing my clothes, organizing my papers, and charging across the campus to the second building, I had just a few minutes to gather my thoughts before my presentation. I sat down on a bench outside and fished around in my purse for my cigarettes and my phone.

During April and early May, Shane had had four more dilation procedures on his esophagus. They appeared to be working. He said it now looked like he didn't have cancer after all. That was good news. He was having another procedure, the sixth, that morning. He'd left a message, and I had to listen to it several times before I could make out the words. His voice was faint and gasping. He said, "I nearly died on the table."

I turned off my phone, dropped it back into my purse, put out my cigarette, and went inside.

I talked for an hour about my new work, an experimental project called *By the Book,* a collection of stories drawn in various ways from old books from the late-nineteenth and early-twentieth centuries. Putting them together had been like doing a jigsaw puzzle and ending up with a picture entirely different from the one on the front of the box. I was illustrating these stories with full-colour collages, which I showed in a PowerPoint on a large screen behind me while I read from the book.

Shane had had a hand in the genesis of this unusual project. When he was working at the recycling plant in Peterborough, he'd rescued a book from certain death by pulp and brought it home to me. Published in New York in 1900, it was a guidebook for Italian citizens immigrating to the United States at the turn of the century. He said he thought I might like it. Indeed I did. It so captured my imagination that it became the source book for the first and title story of this new collection.

Now here I was, four years later, finally bringing the project to an audience, and they were enthusiastic and excited. I was not thinking about Shane or the recycling plant or all that had happened since. I was not thinking about my cell phone silenced in my purse.

THE EVENING KEYNOTE SPEAKER was the American writer Tim O'Brien, one of my longtime favourite authors, especially for his book *The Things They Carried.* Published more than twenty years ago, it is now considered a classic work about the Vietnam War—or any war, for that matter. It is also about the process and power of storytelling itself. On the title page, it calls itself *A Work of Fiction*—but is it? Is it a novel or a book of stories or something else entirely? In the end, it doesn't matter what you call it. In the end, it is a masterpiece about courage and fear, imagination and memory, truth and reality, loyalty and love—a tour de force of reasons to write and reasons to live.

The keynote was a public event being held not at Humber but half an hour away at Harbourfront. We were all talking on our phones in the parking lot while waiting for the bus that would take us there and back. Shane called again, said he was feeling better now; maybe he didn't nearly die on the table, but it sure felt like it. Our bus arrived, a big yellow school bus of the sort I hadn't ridden since Alex was in Grade 2, and I had accompanied his class on a field trip to the Toronto Zoo.

At Harbourfront we all found seats in the crowded room, the lights went down, and a small man in faded jeans and a red baseball cap took the stage. As always seems to be the case with someone I've admired and looked up to but never met, I had thought he would be much taller. He did not give a lecture, a speech, or a conventional reading. He told us a story—a story, he said, that was hard to tell, a story that still made him squirm even now, more than forty years after the fact.

It was the story of what had happened after he received his draft notice in June 1968. He was twenty-one years old, had just graduated from college, was still living with his parents in Worthington, Minnesota, working in a meatpacking plant for the summer. He was against the war. He told us the story of how he took his father's car and drove north that August, north to the Rainy River, which marks the border between Minnesota and Ontario. I know the Rainy River. I've been there. It is about four hundred kilometres west of Thunder Bay.

The entire audience was entranced as he told the story of finding an old fishing lodge in the bush, how the elderly owner let him stay in a cabin for six days, how he kept looking at the Rainy River and across to Canada. He told the story of how on the sixth day, the old man took him out fishing on the river, how he tried to decide what to do, how he cried in the boat. He stayed in the boat, did not swim across to Canada, went back to the lodge with the old man that night, and in the morning, he got back in his father's car and drove home. And then he went to Vietnam. Many people in the audience, myself included, were tearful now.

Then Tim O'Brien said none of this really happened. We gasped. This was just a story, he said. In reality, he was drafted; he did not want to go to the war, but he went. This was not an act of courage, he said, but of cowardice. It had been so long since I'd reread *The Things They Carried* that I hadn't recognized this story as one from the book: "On the Rainy River."

Reality, he said in conclusion, has an important function in the world—of course it does. But it isn't always sufficient. Sometimes it is only a story that can tell the truth, only a story that can save us.

Afterwards the applause went on and on. Then there was a crush of people at the book table. I was too shaken to line up with the others to buy a signed book from Tim O'Brien, to perhaps exchange a few words with him. How ridiculous and crazed would I sound if I shuffled up to the table clutching his book to my chest and told him he had just made me see the truth of my own life? The truth I'd been unable or unwilling to face or accept—the truth I'd been avoiding or disregarding for years.

I made my way through the crowd without speaking to anyone, stood outside, and smoked. Darkness had descended, and the street lights had come on. I got on the empty yellow school bus to wait for the others.

I sat alone on the bus staring out the window at the passing traffic and at the reflection of my own face in the glass. For the first time in years, I could see myself. That night I finally understood that I was in love with the story of my relationship with Shane. That the story—oh, the story—was so beautiful, tender, and romantic. But the reality was not any of those things. The reality was only abusive, destructive, and unbearable. I knew Tim O'Brien was right when he said stories can save us. I am a writer of stories after all. But now I understood that they can strangle us too. That night I understood that for all those years, I'd been in love with the story—not the reality—of my life joined to Shane's. The story of myself as the one who could lead him out of the darkness, the one who could make him whole, healthy, happy. The story of myself as the one who could save him.

∞

Two days after I returned from Humber, I had my regular Tuesday appointment with Louise. I told her about the conference, and then, despite my revelation, I found myself going on and on about the same old stuff with Shane. I was inching ever closer to leaving him. I knew I had to do it, had known it for months, had intended to do it right after my residency at Queen's, but still I'd been dragging my heels, waiting for the right moment—whatever that meant. Trying to break free of any kind of addiction or obsession—be it alcohol, cigarettes, food, heroin, or love—is never a simple or straightforward process. Even when you know you have to. Even when you know your life depends on it.

I was trying to explain to Louise—again—why I hadn't done it yet. A month before, at her request, I'd given her a list of the reasons. Because I didn't want to admit I'd failed at yet another relationship. Because I didn't want to be one more person who'd given up on him. Because I was afraid of falling apart the way I had after we broke up the first time. Because I was afraid of what he might do, not to me but to himself. Because I was afraid that the chaos of leaving him would be even bigger than the chaos of staying. Because I still loved him. Yes, despite everything that had happened, I did.

Suddenly I stopped myself and asked, "Are you getting bored with this?"

Louise smiled wryly and said, "Are you?"

At the end of our hour, she wrote down the name of a book she wanted me to read: *The Betrayal Bond: Breaking Free of Exploitive Relationships* by Patrick Carnes.

That day I went directly from her office to the prison. I didn't usually go on Tuesday evenings anymore, but this time, having not seen Shane for ten days because of the conference, I'd booked a visit. He was unpleasant all evening. He wasn't interested in hearing anything about the conference. When I tried to tell him how encouraging it was, how much they liked my new work, he waved his hand in the direction of my mouth and said, "I thought you would at least whiten your teeth and get rid of your moustache before you went."

I finally understood that the only parts of me and my life that mattered to him were those that existed in relation to him. That he could not bear to see me feeling too good, too confident, too happy—if what had caused me to feel that way was not him. That he wanted to divest me of all pride, self-esteem, and self-respect, to knock me down until I was as miserable as he was. That he was afraid I was going to wake up one morning, take a look at my life, and come to my senses—that I was finally going to realize I would be better off without him, that he really was, as he'd often said, an albatross around my neck.

I said, "Stop it."

He said, "What?"

He said the bottom line was, he needed to know *now* if I was going to stay with him forever. He said he needed to know *for sure* before his next parole hearing, which would be in the summer if his appeal was approved.

I said, "Don't worry. You'll know by then."

He said if I broke up with him, how was he to know that I wouldn't show up at another hearing as a victim, like I did back in 2009?

I said, "Don't worry. If I break up with you this time, you will never see me again."

THE FOLLOWING MORNING, after popping over to Tim Hortons to get my French Vanilla, I came home to find a phone message. "What about that book you're supposed to be writing?" said Shane in a withering voice.

I had an appointment in the early afternoon with a woman named Julie, who'd brought her writing to me at Queen's and had now hired me to continue working with her privately. Shane called again just before I left to meet her. We argued about the earlier message. He demanded to know where I was. I demanded to know why he'd called me during my work time *again*. He said obviously I wasn't working, I was out. I reminded him that I always went to Tim Hortons to get a coffee in the morning, had done so for years; it was just part of my routine, and he knew that. He said he wondered about that. What was I really doing, and who was I doing it with?

Julie had invited me to attend her monthly writing group at an art gallery downtown at five-thirty. Our afternoon meeting ran long, and there seemed no point in going all the way home again before going to her group. Instead I had a sandwich downtown. Shane called, and I told him what I was doing. The writing group wrapped up shortly after nine o'clock. Afterwards, as I got into the car and headed home, my phone began to ring. Of course it did. He seemed to think that because he had a stand-up count at nine o'clock, I did too. I kept driving. The phone kept ringing. When I got home around nine-thirty, I discovered he'd been calling there too—a dozen times in half an hour. He called again. We argued some more.

The next morning, he had the seventh procedure on his esophagus. In the immediate aftermath of these procedures, he found it difficult to talk, but still he called several times that afternoon. Each time the phone rang, I heard Louise's voice in my head: Don't answer it, don't answer it. But usually I did. Usually he was unpleasant. That was Thursday. Friday was more of the same.

I was booked to visit on Saturday as usual. I considered not going. But I went. I wanted to say what I had to say one more time and to his face, calmly and firmly and not over the phone.

Once we got settled at our usual table with our vending machine coffee, I said, "Shane, I love you with all my heart."

His eyes filled with tears.

"And if you keep treating me this way, I will leave you."

I might have been still struggling with Louise's advice not to answer the phone, but finally I had learned her lesson that following the phrase "I love you" with the word "but" cancels out the second part. I finally understood that unconditional love, a concept that had previously made sense to me only in terms of my son, does not mean you have to put up with anything your loved one throws at you. Shane seemed to think unconditional love gave him a licence to do whatever he wanted, and I would stay with him anyway. With Louise's help, I finally understood that it was the "stay with him anyway" clause that wasn't true. That I could, in fact, love him *and* leave him.

Over and over again, I had stood up to him. Over and over again, I had let him pull me back in. I didn't know yet that this would be the last visit.

He said nothing for a long time. Then we went on with our regular Saturday. At home afterwards, I did some yardwork: it was the middle of May, almost time to plant. He called only twice. He was pleasant both times and didn't mention what I'd said at the beginning of the visit. Late in the evening, I put on my pyjamas and curled up on the couch to begin reading *The Betrayal Bond*, which I'd purchased as an e-book on my iPad.

> *Over time I learned that I bonded with people who were very hurtful to me and remained loyal to them despite betrayal and exploitation. . . . Betrayal. You can't explain it away anymore. A pattern exists. You know that now. You can no longer return to the way it was (which was never really as it seemed). That would be unbearable. But to move forward means certain pain. No escape. No in-between. Choices have to be made today, not tomorrow.*

I stayed up very late reading.

> *The worst is a mind-numbing highly addictive attachment to the people who have hurt you. You may even try to explain and help them understand what they are doing—convert them into non-abusers. You may even blame yourself, your defects, your failed efforts. You strive to do better as your life slips away in the swirl of intensity. These attachments cause you to distrust your own judgment, distort your own realities and place yourself at even greater risk. The great irony? You are bracing yourself against further hurt.*
>
> *The result? A guarantee of more pain. These attachments have a name. They are called* betrayal bonds.

On Sunday and Monday, Shane was fine, but by Tuesday, he was starting again, his voice on the phone sliding into sarcasm and nasty innuendo. I worked in the morning, and, by force of habit, I booked my Saturday visit as usual. I had a late lunch with Brenda, Tammy, and Rosemary from the prison group at our usual Chinese place. He called several times while we were eating. I answered the first time, then I turned it off. I went home to take the dogs out before going to see Louise at five. He called again, suggesting I'd had more in my mouth than Chinese food. I spent my hour with Louise going over my notes from *The Betrayal Bond*. I wasn't even halfway through the book, but I had pages and pages of notes.

On Wednesday he was worse. I had a session with the prison writing group in the morning, then I went to a book launch downtown in the evening. I was home shortly after nine, not because I was trying to obey the curfew he'd imposed on me, but because that was when the book launch ended and everybody left. His phone calls that night were almost an exact duplicate of those the previous Wednesday after I got home from Julie's writing group.

Thursday during the day was more of the same. In the morning, I worked, and he had an appointment at the Heart Clinic. It seemed there could be problems with his heart again. In the afternoon, I went to the garden centre. It was the twenty-fourth of May, the traditional spring planting day. I whispered a few encouraging words to the bleeding heart plants that were once again coming up in the driveway. I didn't think about the time Shane and I had done the planting together. I didn't know whether to be pleased or bothered by the fact that I was now able to carry on around his unpleasant phone calls without even feeling upset.

He called again in the early evening. He began by saying he knew he wasn't like all the uptown writers I knew. He went on about being sick and how I said I wouldn't nurse him. He said I thought he wasn't good enough for me. He said I thought he wasn't worthy. He said I thought I was better than him. Again he accused me of being with someone else—a healthy wealthy writer perhaps.

I warned him. "Remember what I said on Saturday."

He said, "How am I supposed to remember what the fuck you said on Saturday? You're always saying things. You're always just talking and talking and talking all the fucking time."

Then he started going on about everything I'd taken away. The Tuesday evening visits. The Sunday visits. The counselling with Edward Blake. The forty-eight-hour PFVs. Then he said, "What else are you going to take away?"

Although I hadn't planned that today would be the day, I said, "I am going to take it all away."

He was so deeply involved in his own twisted misery that he just kept talking. I had to say it twice more before he heard me.

"I'm going to take it all away. Right now. It's over. I'm done. Just to be clear: the bottom line is, you no longer have a girlfriend." Then I hung up and turned off all the phones.

HE CALLED AGAIN TWICE THAT EVENING and left messages. In the first, he was tearful and contrite. Sorry sorry, so sorry. He wasn't feeling well. He had a bad day. His blood pressure was up. His leg hurt, his esophagus too. There was blood on his pillow. Now there was his heart. Sorry sorry, so sorry. These weepy apologies had always worked before.

In the second message, he was calm and practical. What about his CPP cheques, and what about his stuff? Since turning sixty, he'd been collecting just over a hundred dollars a month from the Canada Pension Plan. Through his lawyer, I'd acquired Power of Attorney, so his cheques could be delivered to me, thus avoiding the usual CSC deduction for room and board. Each month I took him a money order for a hundred dollars, which was then deposited into his inmate account to cover the phone calls and some canteen items. As for his stuff, shortly after we got back together, I'd made a trip to Kenworth to pick up several boxes of his belongings that had been stored in Roy and Darlene's garage.

Early the next morning, he called again. Miraculously I had no problem not answering the phone. He didn't leave a message. I sent Louise an email to tell her the news. She sent me a note of congratulation and a reminder to feel what I was feeling, to give myself time to adjust, to be good to myself. She said, "If you need me, I'll be here."

He didn't call again. I didn't call anyone. I knew how happy Dorothy and my other friends would be—but I wasn't yet ready to hear their hoorays. The only person I told was Alex. He, as usual, didn't say much, but I could tell he was pleased. I spent the morning reading *The Betrayal Bond* and replaying last night's phone call word for word in my head a hundred times.

I had a long nap in the afternoon. He still didn't call. I treated myself to lamb chops for dinner. They came in a package of six. I ate them all and wished for more. He didn't call in the evening either. This was so strange that by bedtime, my imagination was running wild in several directions at once. What the hell was happening? There was no end of possibilities to feed my growing anxiety: stroke, heart attack, esophagus, suicide, escape. Maybe he'd acted up and been shipped out. His uncharacteristic silence kept me on the line, still embroiled in his drama, still bracing for whatever he was going to do next.

I recognized this feeling from when we broke up the first time. Fortunately I'd learned enough by now from all my hours with Louise and from reading *The Betrayal Bond* to know that this was part of it— part of the trauma bond that had held me so tightly to him before, that had made getting back together seem like a reasonable thing to do, that had kept me believing everything would be okay eventually if only I could hang on long enough to get to the good part.

He didn't call on Saturday. Now I felt relieved. Someone must have made him realize it would be better for *him* if he didn't harass me by phone. I was sure they were keeping close tabs on him. I was booked for a visit that day, and I wasn't there. I was sure I'd be hearing from them any day now. They'd want to know what happened; they'd want to hear my side of the story. In the afternoon, I packed up some of his things. I felt neither elated nor upset, and I was not talking to him in my head while I did it. I put the beautiful jacket and the WAIT, TRUST, HOPE, REJOICE fridge magnet in a bag to be donated to Vinnie's. For once in my life, I felt neutral and detached.

He didn't call on Sunday.

He didn't call on Monday.

He didn't call on Tuesday.

I was now feeling more surprised that I still hadn't heard from "them" than I was by not hearing from him.

The next morning, his familiar handwriting appeared in my mailbox, and some of my questions were answered. This letter was two neatly typewritten pages, with his full signature at the end, his name and inmate number typewritten above it, and a note requesting that a copy be attached to his file and another sent to Psychology. Please and thank you. Even I could see this letter was more for their benefit than mine.

It had been written on Saturday. He said he'd cancelled our next scheduled PFV and taken me off his visiting and phone lists, so no one could accuse him of calling too much. I felt he had done me a favour there, sparing me having to take myself off his lists, but I also knew he'd done it to make himself look good in their eyes. And perhaps, I realized later, to avoid giving me an opportunity to speak to them myself. He sounded calm and reasonable, just like he always did in letters. He wished me the best in all my endeavours, which, he said, were sure to bring me money, prestige, and happiness. He noted that although the word *controlling* had often been directed at him, in fact *I* was the one who'd been controlling and that people have to give and take, not just dictate. He referred to his ill health a few times, asked again what we were going to do about his CPP cheques, noting that these were all he had, and no one else was stepping up to help him. He said he'd talked to his CMT, Psychology, and Stuart, and he was now ready to get on with his life. Even I could see this letter was mostly a matter of emotional manipulation, to which I did not succumb.

The next morning, the phone rang early. In the call display, it said "Government of Canada." When Shane called, it always said "Bell Pay Phone." Finally, I thought, finally they were calling to find out from me what had happened. But no, it wasn't them. It was him. A member of his CMT had given him permission to call me from her office about the CPP cheques. It was a two-minute conversation. Then he said he would always love me, started to cry, and hung up. I felt nothing.

OVER THE NEXT FEW WEEKS, I stopped expecting CSC to contact me. Clearly they had no desire to hear my side of the story. Considering that in all these years, they had never replied to a single one of my letters or phone calls, I didn't think there was any point in attempting to contact them.

I received a handful of letters from Shane and one more phone call. Early on a Sunday morning near the middle of June, the phone rang, and the call display said, "Sisters of Providence." So I knew it was from the convent, and I knew he'd likely be there for mass right then. But I didn't seriously think it could be him on the line. Maybe the nuns were calling me for some reason. What? To tell me he was dead? In retrospect I realize this didn't make much sense, but I answered the phone. There he was. He said his escort said he could call me. I knew this was definitely not allowed. He was crying and wanted to know if this was really the end. He asked if I broke up with him because there was somebody else. Clearly he wanted to believe this was the case. Then he could feel like a victim: Oh, poor Shane, that nasty bitch left him for another man. How could she?

By now I knew he was never going to accept or understand the truth. I replied in a calm clear voice. I didn't use any of the words that always sent him into a rage.

Controlling.

Manipulative.

Narcissist.

Bully.

Abuse.

I said, "No, Shane, I broke up with you for one reason and one reason only. Because you treated me badly, and I deserve better."

IN THE LETTERS, he was rapidly cycling from one mood to another, the salutations flipping wildly from an indignantly formal *Ms. Schoemperlen* to a simple *Diane*, and finally, to *Hello again Pixie*.

He said the staff had been rallying around him—even the ones he didn't get along with before, even the ones who'd liked me better than him—and commending him for how well he was handling the breakup. He said he could feel personal growth taking effect, that he'd become such a gentleman now, but only if he received respect too. As if I was going to believe he'd become a whole new person in less than a month. If a total transformation was that easy, why didn't he do it when we were still together?

THIS IS NOT MY LIFE

He said the CPP representative had been to Frontenac again and told him I was eligible to receive his survivor's pension after his death. Would I please accept this as a gift from his heart to mine? Several times he said he wanted to be friends, that we'd be better friends than lovers. He said he knew it couldn't be as friendly as I was with some of my other former lovers, but still he'd like to have a letter and a phone call once in a while. He said he missed me.

Over and over again, I could feel him trying to pull me back in. With Louise's help, I resisted. Each time I received another letter, we parsed it together line by line, her helping me see how these missives cast him as both the victim and the hero in this sorry little narrative and me as the villain, how afterwards he'd be able to claim that he was the reasonable one who just wanted to be friends, and I was the nasty vengeful bitch who refused.

He said his appeal had been successful, and his next hearing was scheduled for mid-July. Would I be attending? No, I told him, I would not.

In my replies, I stuck to practical matters. I declined his offer to make me the recipient of his survivor's pension. Despite his protests to the contrary, I knew this was a trap. I said several times that I would no longer be the person in charge of his end-of-life care and his death. I reminded him to tear up the Living Will. He persisted in acting as if he did not understand what I was saying, kept asking the same things over and over. As he requested, I sent him a list of all his belongings, now packed safely in three Rubbermaid tubs. Roy and Darlene came and picked them up, a brief exchange involving less than five awkward minutes in the driveway. I mailed the necessary documents to resign as his Power of Attorney. I closed the bank account in his name and had his CPP cheques sent directly to Frontenac.

Each of his letters caused me some degree of upset, as did writing my replies. I'd thought I could follow what in *The Betrayal Bond* was called

"The Path of Limited Contact." But now I realized I had to choose the other path: "The Path of No Contact."

I closed my next and final letter by saying, *Once we've finished sorting out the practical matters, I do not want to have continued contact with you by letter or phone in the future.* He did not reply.

TRUE TO MY WORD, I did not attend the summer parole hearing at which Shane was again requesting a series of UTAs to the Ottawa halfway house. Because I was still signed on with the Parole Board Registry of Decisions, I received a copy of the paperwork a week later. Seven legal-size pages, typewritten, single-spaced, written in the second person, as these decisions always were, addressing the offender directly in a personal and conversational tone.

His request had been granted. I skimmed the first three pages, the usual recap of his earlier crimes, convictions, and incarceration. On the fourth page was their commentary on recent events. Here it stated that Shane had told them at the hearing that he had ended our relationship in late May because he felt I was pulling away, and he was not prepared to go through the agony of another separation. They noted that although it was evident this had been a painful situation for him, he had handled it with maturity and wisdom.

Parole hearings don't include swearing on the Bible, but I had always considered them to be like courtroom proceedings, where everyone, especially the offender, is required to tell the truth, the whole truth, and nothing but the truth. Of course, I wasn't entirely surprised that

Shane had lied at the hearing. Maybe the lie shouldn't have mattered as much as it did. Maybe part of my outrage was just me wanting to set the record straight, wanting to have the last word. But I was surprised that the Board members had apparently believed him. I was also still surprised that no one from CSC or the Parole Board had ever contacted me to get my side of the story. Would knowing the truth have changed their decision?

I felt some obligation to enlighten them. For two weeks I pondered how best to do this. I was reluctant to do it directly, because I didn't want to become enmeshed in the whole mess again, nor did I want to further enrage Shane for fear of possible retaliation. In the end, I wrote him a letter telling him that I'd received the decision paperwork and knew he'd lied at the hearing. I reminded him that I had ended our relationship in no uncertain terms on the phone on the evening of May 24. I concluded by once again stating that I wished to have no further contact with him, *now or in the future, by telephone, letter, in person, or by any other means.*

Much as I wanted him to know that I knew he'd lied, mostly I was doing what he'd done: writing this letter for *their* benefit. I hoped the officer who checked his mail would read it and feel compelled to do something. They always had the right to monitor our phone calls. I hoped maybe they'd heard and recorded that one on May 24. But nothing happened.

A month later, my letter was returned to me inside a larger CSC envelope addressed in someone else's handwriting. Across the original envelope, Shane had written PLEASE RETURN. NO CONTACT. My letter itself had obviously been carried in a pocket, passed from hand to hand, read and reread, folded and refolded many times.

I never heard from or saw him again.

FINALLY ALL OF MY QUESTIONS HAD BEEN ANSWERED. Finally I understood that I could not fix him or heal him or make him happy. I could not make the world a better place for him. I could not lead him out of the darkness. Finally I understood that no matter how much I loved him, I did not have the power to make up for or undo the damage—neither the damage he'd suffered nor the damage he'd done. Finally I had stepped out of the story and surrendered to reality.

Now I knew I could not save him. I could only save myself.

EPILOGUE

Narrative begs an ending. The desire to wrap up loose ends, to make meaning, is human, and ancient. But things do not end.

—ALISON PICK, *BETWEEN GODS*

According to statistics released by Public Safety Canada, as of December 2013, there were just under 1,500 convicted killers—166 first-degree and 1,332 second-degree—out on full parole in Canada. Shane was not one of them. But he was not in prison anymore either.

A year after our relationship ended, he was again granted day parole and moved to the Ottawa halfway house he'd been aiming for. This time the copy of the decision I received was heavily redacted. Names and details of people, cities, institutions, organizations, and his criminal history had all been blacked out, as had his security classification and his inmate number. As if, now that I was no longer part of the story, I also no longer knew him or all that had come before. Our entire relationship was covered in one brief paragraph—six years of my life reduced to two sentences out of five legal-size pages, typewritten, single-spaced.

If only it were that simple.

∽

THIS TIME I GOT OFF the *Tough Guys* train and stayed there. This time I did not fall apart. This time I went forward instead of back. But not every day was a good day.

Immediately after the breakup, I was elated and energized with the sense of my own freedom, as if I were the one who had finally been granted full parole.

Then I was angry. One day Brenda from the prison group said, "Don't be mad at God. You shouldn't be mad at God."

"I'm not mad at God!" I snapped. "I'm mad at Shane."

I was mad at myself too. Of course I was.

There was the matter now of confronting the price I'd paid for being in love with the story at the expense of reality—a price that was not only emotional and psychological but financial as well.

I began to compile and consider my "Schedule of Loss." Each Tuesday I packed up my pain, my anger, my grief, and carried it all to Louise. Together we sifted through it, shard by shard, picking apart the story until all that remained was reality. Each week I cast off another piece of the story and took another step back into my life. Each week I went home afterwards with my heart in my hands, bleeding.

I was no longer having a bad relationship with Shane—now I was having a bad relationship with hope. Now it was hard to believe that good things were ever going to happen again. I stopped hoping that my life would ever get easier, happier, *better,* and found myself hoping instead that I would have the strength to deal with whatever hard things lay ahead. For those first two months, I was functioning, but my heart wasn't in it. Mostly I was just going through the motions. It was never far from my mind that things could always get worse. My default position during this period was dread. While my chronic anxiety rose up like stalagmites from this baseline, its devoted companion, depression, dredged out the downward troughs into which I frequently sank.

It may or may not be true that time heals all wounds, but soon enough I was, if not healing, then certainly fed up with feeling bad. Little by little, with Louise's wise weekly guidance, I began to feel stronger. Using the insurance settlement I'd received following the flood the previous summer, I hired a contractor to address the drainage issues around my house and to install all new basement windows and eavestroughs. While they dug, drilled, hammered, and sawed all summer long on the outside, I flew into a frenzy of cleaning, sorting, and organizing on the inside, both upstairs and down. Even at the time, I could appreciate the analogical aptness of this. By the end of the summer, the whole house was vastly improved and so was I.

By the beginning of September, I was back to work, not only on the book I had presented at the conference at Humber in the spring, but also on a number of other projects. Motivated and energized by the desperate financial situation I was now in, throughout the fall I was also editing, writing reviews, and giving readings and workshops both in Kingston and away. By November I had finished my collage book that should have been finished years ago and sent it out into the world to find a publisher. By December I was making notes for a book about my prison years.

In the early months of 2013, I was spending more and more time with Dorothy and Lily. I was no longer hiding parts of myself from them, and our friendships were stronger than they'd ever been. I was making new friends too, with people around whom I did not feel anxious, inferior, envious, or judged. Still interested in prison issues, I continued to be repeatedly outraged by the further Tough on Crime measures being taken by the Harper government, but I had drifted away from the prison group. I was no longer an "insider" and could not figure out how I fit with them now.

Sometimes still I caught myself wanting to tell Shane things. I wanted to tell him that the collage book had found a publisher. That I was renovating the back room and had repaired the damaged ceiling and installed the new flooring all by myself. That I was still afraid of rain. That Alex's girlfriend had broken up with him, and he was devastated. That my dear Nelly had suddenly become very ill, and I'd had to have her put to sleep. She was eleven years old and had never had a bad day in her life, until the last four. I wanted to tell him that for weeks afterwards, Maggie would pull all the toys out of the wicker basket one by one and spread them around on the living room rug, then sit there in the middle of them with her sad little chin resting on her crossed paws, waiting for Nelly to come and play with her.

I wanted him to comfort me when things were going badly and to share my happiness when things were going well. With Louise's help, I understood that this was me slipping back into the story, that beautiful story in which he would have done both those things—whereas in reality, he had seldom been able to do either of them.

That summer it took me some time to adjust to the news that he was out of prison and living at the halfway house in Ottawa. Since the breakup, I'd always known where he was—right there at Frontenac, not ten minutes from my house. When he was moved to Ottawa, two hundred kilometres away, I had to relocate him on my internal map. I also had to wonder if he might show up at my door one day. I kept reminding myself that he was smarter than that, and besides, he wasn't allowed to leave the city of Ottawa without permission. He didn't.

That summer one of the dozen bleeding heart plants that grew through the cracks in my driveway heaved up a chunk of asphalt two inches thick, four inches wide, and eight inches long. I measured it. I took this as a sign, a very good sign. I would give up on rainbows and put my faith in the power of bleeding hearts instead.

"WHY THE HELL WOULD ANYBODY want to do *that*?" Dorothy asked.

Laughing, I said, "I'll take that as a rhetorical question."

We'd resumed our old habit of long leisurely phone conversations once or twice a week. That day it had been announced that after Kingston Penitentiary was entirely emptied of inmates and formally decommissioned on September 30, it would be opened for public tours for a three-week period as a fundraiser for United Way.

"Tell me you're not," she said.

"I am." I could hear her rolling her eyes.

"It's only going to upset you."

"It might," I conceded.

"Why torture yourself?"

"Another rhetorical question, I presume," I said and changed the subject.

Three days later, the tickets went on sale, online only, twenty dollars each for a ninety-minute tour. Apparently I was not the only one who wanted to do *that*. More than nine thousand tickets were sold out within minutes. I considered myself lucky to get one for an early after-noon tour in mid-October.

WHEN I PULLED INTO THE PARKING LOT beside the looming east wall, the sailboats in the adjacent marina were bobbing gently, and the water of Lake Ontario was sparkling in the sun. The lot was already crowded with vehicles. We would be going through in groups of two dozen, each group led by a CSC employee. By force of habit, I locked my purse in the trunk and put my driver's licence in my pocket. Before leaving home, I had managed to resist the reflex to do my usual clean-ing routine, but I still found it hard to believe that, as stated in the tour information, there would be no security measures in place. Equally strange to me was the fact that tour participants were encouraged rather than forbidden to bring their cameras.

I was anxious about going in. Maybe Dorothy was right—maybe I was just torturing myself. I had been doing well—so well, in fact, that I'd now graduated to seeing Louise only once a month instead of every week. Maybe I was just setting myself up for more misery and a major setback in my recovery. This was why I wanted to make the tour by myself, so I could, as Louise always advised, feel what I was feeling and not have to keep reassuring someone else that I was okay if I wasn't. Shane and I had now been apart for sixteen months. I was still in the habit of counting this out on my fingers, not now as a register of anx-iety or dread but as a victorious tally of getting on with my life.

Anxiety aside, I was also curious. I had spent thousands of hours at both Frontenac and Bath, but I had never really been "inside," had never been in deeper than the visiting room and the trailers. Nor had I ever been into a maximum-security institution. Whether curiosity killed the cat or not, this was my chance.

It was a short walk from the parking lot to the entrance, and with each step I could feel my body changing as I assumed my old prison stance—head up, spine straight, shoulders back, arms a peculiar combination of relaxed and ready. I took long steady strides up the sidewalk, my cowboy boots resounding firmly on the concrete. By the time I reached the gatehouse, I had put on my prison face—a complex layering of cordiality, gravitas, innocence, experience, compliance, courtesy, and confidence—topped off with a tiny dollop of defiance.

Still astonished that all I had to do was sign my name and hand over my ticket—no ion scanner, no metal detector, no drug dog—I followed the rest of my group down a twisting hallway through a series of doors that I knew would otherwise have been locked but that were now propped wide open. We were ushered into the visiting room to meet our group leader, a middle-aged man who introduced himself as someone who had taught in the prisons, including this one, for more than twenty years. I didn't recognize him or any of the other tour participants, two dozen strangers of all ages with their cameras in hand who seemed to be collectively excited and eager to be amazed, astounded, and horrified.

We stepped out on the other side of the gatehouse into a labyrinth of iron gates and razor-wire-topped fences, paved exercise yards, concrete walkways, manicured lawns, looming guard towers, and two-, three-, and four-storey limestone buildings with metal roofs, massive arched doors, and dozens of tall barred windows. I was stunned by the sheer size of it, ten acres at least, all completely invisible from the outside. From behind the walls, the outside was invisible too, except for the tops of a few trees just beginning to change colour beneath the arching bright blue October sky.

I hung back from the group, trailing along behind them, while the leader pointed out various attractions around the grounds. I wanted to take it all in as privately as possible. I still did not know if or how much this was going to upset me.

We made our way to the actual cellblocks. This was what I most wanted to see: the inside of the inside.

The hallways were narrow, dingy, and unclean, the concrete walls marked with peeling paint and graffiti: WHEN IS ENOUGH ENOUGH!? EMBRACE SUFFERING! PLEASE FUCK OFF. Above a burned-out electrical outlet in black felt marker it said: DON'T PLUG TOASTER AND MICROWAVE IN THIS! It was not hard to imagine the sound of rats' claws scritching down these hallways at night, a sound Shane said had haunted him for years.

Set in two levels down one side of each range, there were eighteen or twenty cells per level, classic prison cells with bars, locks, and no windows. Many were decorated with drawings, posters, writings, and photos cut from magazines: hockey team emblems, racing cars, buxom women in bikinis, two loons on a lake, three horses in a field, a snow-covered mountain beneath a full moon.

Several cells were open and still furnished, as if the prisoner would be back in a minute. Had these men abandoned everything when they were moved out, or had these cells been staged for our benefit? We were allowed to go right inside and have a good look around. No more than five feet wide and nine feet long, these were all single cells—no room for double-bunking here. The narrow bed sprouted out of one side wall, taking up half the width of the room. Below it was a desk area and below that a small storage space. At the back of each cell was a built-in set of four shelves and beside that a mirror above a shiny metal combination sink and toilet with no lid.

I was not amazed, astounded, or horrified. It was all exactly as Shane had described it. I took pictures along with everyone else. I was moved but not upset. I could not see him there. He was gone.

As I drove home afterwards I knew it was finished. I knew I was free.

TIME HAS PASSED. THINGS HAVE HAPPENED. More time will pass. More things will happen. I have become myself again, but I am not the same. Perhaps I never will be. Perhaps that is a good thing. If this were a novel, I would know how to end it. But this is not a novel. This is my life, and I'm going to live it. I know there will never come a day when I can once again drive past the prisons and think they have nothing to do with me. But there *will* come a day when I do not think of them or him, not even once. There will come a day when I can shine my light into the darkness and not see his face.

ACKNOWLEDGMENTS

So many people have helped me in so many ways during the years of writing this book. Some of them must remain nameless: you know who you are!

As for the rest, thank you to Lauren and Ron Davis, Stacey Hannem, Madelyn Iler, Philomene Kocher, Shannon Moroney, Audrey Ogilvie and Norman Peterson, Joanne and Steve Page, Kathy Page, Barbara Sibbald, Carolyn Smart, Karen Smythe, Susan Barbara Townsend, Carol Whitehead, and Deborah Windsor. As always, but especially in this case, thank you to my dear son Alex, ever the light of my life.

Thank you to my agents, Bella Pomer and Samantha Haywood, and her assistant, Stephanie Sinclair, for taking such good care of me and my book. Thank you to my wonderful editor, Jennifer Lambert, for her sensitivity, her sense of humour, and for gently pushing and pulling me through the long and sometimes difficult writing process.

For financial assistance, I am grateful to the Ontario Arts Council Writers' Reserve Program and the Woodcock Fund of the Writers' Trust of Canada.

I am especially thankful for the fact that on October 19, 2015, the Harper government, after almost ten years in power, was soundly defeated by the Liberals, and Justin Trudeau was elected the twenty-third prime minister of Canada with a solid majority. During the campaign, the Liberals made a commitment to reopening the prison farms. Newly elected Liberal MP for Kingston and the Islands and former mayor of the city, Mark Gerretsen has said he will make this issue a priority. There is great hope that by implementing this and other changes to reverse the Harper government's Tough on Crime policies, the Liberals will bring Canada back to a more humane and effective criminal justice system based on research, evidence, the respect of human rights, and the true protection of public safety.